Carnegie Learning Coordinate Algebra

Student Edition
Volume 2

Carnegie Learning >

Carnegie Learning >

437 Grant St., Suite 918
Pittsburgh, PA 15219
Phone 412.690.2442
Customer Service Phone 877.401.2527
Fax 412.690.2444

www.carnegielearning.com

ISBN: 978-1-60972-165-7
Student Edition, Volume 2

Printed in the United States of America
1-05/2012 B&B

Dear Student,

You are about to begin an exciting endeavor using mathematics! To be successful, you will need the right tools. This book is one of the most important tools you will use this year. Throughout this book there is space for note-taking, sketching, and calculating. You will be given opportunities to think and reason about various mathematical concepts and use tools such as tables, graphs, and graphing calculators.

This year you will face many new challenges both in and outside of the classroom. While some challenges may seem difficult, it is important to remember that effort matters. You must realize that it may take hard work and perseverance to succeed—and your hard work will pay off!

Connections in mathematics are important. Throughout this text, you will build new knowledge based upon your prior knowledge. It is our goal that you see mathematics as relevant because it provides a common and useful language for discussing and solving real-world problems.

I bet the folks at home would like to know what we're going to do this year!

Don't worry—you will not be working alone. Working with others is a skill that you will need throughout your life. When you begin your career, you will most likely work with all sorts of people, from shy to outgoing, from leaders to supporters, from innovators to problem solvers—and many more types of people! Throughout this book, you will have many opportunities to work with your classmates. You will be able to discuss your ideas and predictions to different problem situations; present your calculations and solutions to questions; and analyze, critique and suggest, or support your classmates' answers to problem situations.

Today's workplace demands teamwork and self-confidence. At Carnegie Learning, our goal is to provide you with opportunities to be successful in your math course. Enjoy the year and have fun Learning by Doing(TM)!

—The Carnegie Learning Curriculum Development Team

Acknowledgments

Carnegie Learning Authoring Team

- **Sandy Bartle**
  Senior Academic Officer
- **Joshua Fisher**
  Math Editor
- **David "Augie" Rivera**
  Math Editor
- **David Dengler**
  Director, Curriculum Development
- **Jen Dilla**
  Editorial Assistant
- **Lezlee Ross**
  Curriculum Developer

Contributing Authors

- Jaclyn Snyder
- Dr. Mary Lou Metz

Vendors

- Cenveo Publisher Services
- Mathematical Expressions
- Hess Print Solutions
- Bradford & Bigelow
- Mind Over Media
- Lapiz
- eInstruction

Special Thanks

- Carnegie Learning Managers of School Partnerships for their review of design and content.
- Teacher reviewers and students for their input and review of lesson content.
- Carnegie Learning Software Development Team for their contributions to research and content.
- William S. Hadley for being a mentor to the development team, his leadership, and his pedagogical pioneering in mathematics education.
- Amy Jones Lewis for her review of content.

Table of Contents

8 **Analyzing Data Sets for One Variable**   **453**

9 **Correlation and Residuals**   **521**

Table of Contents

© 2012 Carnegie Learning

12 Geometry on the Coordinate Plane

649

13 Congruence Through Transformations

719

Table of Contents

Perimeter and Area of Geometric Figures on the Coordinate Plane 793

Connecting Algebra and Geometry with Polygons 853

Table of Contents

16 Logic 899

Table of Contents

The Crew

The Crew is here to help you throughout this text. Sometimes they will remind you about things you have already learned. Sometimes they will ask you questions to help you think about different strategies. Sometimes they will share fun facts. They are members of your group—someone you can rely on!

Teacher aides will guide you along your way. They will help you make connections and remind you to think about the details.

Mathematical Representations

Introduction

During this course, you will solve problems and work with many different representations of mathematical concepts, ideas, and processes to better understand the world. Each lesson will provide you with opportunities to discuss your ideas, work within groups, and share your solutions and methods with your class. These process icons are placed throughout the text.

Discuss to Understand

- Read the problem carefully.

- What is the context of the problem? Do we understand it?

- What is the question that we are being asked? Does it make sense?

- Is this problem similar to some other problem we know?

Think for Yourself

- Do I need any additional information to answer the question?

- Is this problem similar to some other problem that I know?

- How can I represent the problem using a picture, a diagram, symbols, or some other representation?

Work with Your Partner

- How did you do the problem?

- Show me your representation.

- This is the way I thought about the problem—how did you think about it?

- What else do we need to solve the problem?

- Does our reasoning and our answer make sense to each other?

- How will we explain our solution to the class?

Share with the Class

- Here is our solution and the methods we used.

- Are we communicating our strategies clearly?

- We could only get this far with our solution. How can we finish?

- Could we have used a different strategy to solve the problem?

Representations

Academic Glossary

Key Terms of the Course

There are important terms you will encounter throughout this book. It is important that you have an understanding of these words as you get started through the mathematical concepts. Knowing what is meant by these terms and using these terms will help you think, reason, and communicate your ideas. The Graphic Organizers shown display a definition for a key term, related words, sample questions, and examples.

You will create graphic organizers like these as your own references of key mathematical ideas.

My folks are always trying to get me to be organized!

Definition

To study or look closely for patterns.

Analyzing can involve examining or breaking a concept down into smaller parts to gain a better understanding of it.

Related Words

- examine
- evaluate
- determine
- observe
- consider
- investigate
- what do you notice?
- what do you think?
- sort and match
- identify

Ask Yourself

- Do I see any patterns?
- Have I seen something like this before?
- What happens if the shape, representation, or numbers change?
- What is the question asking me to accomplish?
- What is the context?
- What does the solution mean in terms of this problem situation?

Analyze

Example

 Alan's camping troop hikes down from their campsite at an elevation of 4800 feet to the bottom of the mountain. They hike down at a rate of 20 feet per minute.

1. Write a function, $h(m)$, to show the troop's elevation as a function of time in minutes.

$h(m) = -20m + 4800$

2. Analyze the function.

   a. Identify the independent and dependent quantities and their units.

   The independent quantity is the number of minutes hiked, and the dependent quantity is the elevation in feet.

   b. Identify the rate of change and explain what it means in terms of this problem situation.

   The rate of change is -20. This represents a decrease of 20 feet every minute.

   c. Identify the y-intercept and explain what it means in terms of this problem situation.

   The y-intercept is 4800. This shows that the troop started their hike at an elevation of 4800 feet.

   d. What is the x-intercept and explain what it means in terms of this problem situation?

   $$0 = -20m + 4800$$
   $$-4800 = -20m$$
   $$\frac{-4800}{-20} = \frac{-20m}{-20}$$
   $$240 = m$$

   The x-intercept is (240, 0). The hikers will be at the bottom of the mountain in 240 minutes, or 4 hours.

Definition

To give details or describe how to determine an answer or solution.

Explaining your reasoning helps justify conclusions.

Related Words

- show your work
- explain your calculation
- justify
- why or why not?

Ask Yourself

- How should I organize my thoughts?
- Is my explanation logical?
- Does my reasoning make sense?
- How can I justify my answer to others?
- Did I use complete sentences in my answer?

Don't forget to check your answers!

Explain Your Reasoning

Example

 A 747 airliner has an initial climb rate of 1800 feet per minute until it reaches a height of 10,000 feet.

1. Identify the independent and dependent quantities in this problem situation. Explain your reasoning.

   The height of the airplane depends on the time, so height is the dependent quantity and time is the independent quantity.

2. Describe the units of measure for:

   a. the independent quantity (the input values).

      The independent quantity of time is measured in minutes.

   b. the dependent quantity (the output values).

      The dependent quantity of height is measured in feet.

 3. Which function family do you think best represents this situation? Explain your reasoning.

   Answers will vary.

   The situation shows a linear function because the rate the plane ascends is constant. So, this situation belongs to the linear function family.

Definition

To display information in various ways.

Representing mathematics can be done using words, tables, graphs, or symbols.

Related Words

- show
- sketch
- draw
- create
- plot
- graph
- write an equation
- complete the table

Ask Yourself

- How should I organize my thoughts?
- How do I use this model to show a concept or idea?
- What does this representation tell me?
- Is my representation accurate?
- What units or labels should I include?
- Are there other ways to model this concept?

Represent

Example

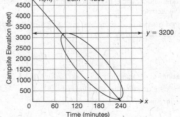

3. Label the function on the coordinate plane.

$h(m) = -20m + 4800$

y = 3200

Campsite Elevation (feet) / Time (minutes)

4. Use the graph to determine how many minutes passed if the troop is below 3200 feet. Draw an oval on the graph to represent this part of the function and write the corresponding inequality statement.

More than 80 minutes has passed if the troop is below 3200 feet.
$m > 80$

5. Write and solve an inequality to verify the solution set you interpreted from the graph.

$$-20m + 4800 < 3200$$
$$-20m + 4800 - 4800 < 3200 - 4800$$
$$-20m < -1600$$
$$\frac{-20m}{-20} < \frac{-1600m}{-20m}$$
$$m > 80$$

Definition

To make an educated guess based on the analysis of given data.

Estimating first helps inform reasoning.

Related Words

- predict
- approximate
- expect
- about how much?

Ask Yourself

- Does my reasoning make sense?
- Is my solution close to my estimation?
- What do I know about this problem situation?
- What predictions can I make from this problem situation?

Estimating gets you in the neighborhood, calculating gets you the address.

Estimate

Example

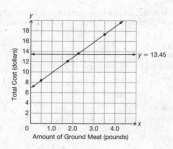

3. Use the data from the table to create a graph of the problem situation on the coordinate plane.

$y = 13.45$

Total Cost (dollars)

Amount of Ground Meat (pounds)

4. Consider a total bill of $13.45.

a. Estimate the amount of ground beef purchased.

The graph of $y = 13.45$ crosses the original graph at about 2, so I predict that 2 pounds of ground meat were purchased.

b. Determine the exact amount of ground meat purchased.

Using the intersection function on my graphing calculator, I determined the exact amount to be 2.2 pounds of ground meat.

Definition

To represent or give an account of in words. Describing communicates mathematical ideas to others.

Related Words

- demonstrate
- label
- display
- compare
- define
- determine
- what are the advantages?
- what are the disadvantages?
- what is similar?
- what is different?

Ask Yourself

- How should I organize my thoughts?
- Is my explanation logical?
- Did I consider the context of the situation?
- Does my reasoning make sense?
- Did I use complete sentences in my answer?
- Did I include appropriate units and labels?
- Will my classmates understand my reasoning?

Describe

Example

 You just worked with different representations of a linear function.

1. Describe how a linear function is represented:

   a. in a table.

   When the input values in a table are in successive order and the first differences of the output values are constant, the table represents a linear function.

   b. in a graph.

   A linear function is represented in a graph by a straight line.

   c. in an equation.

   A linear function is represented by a function in the form $f(x) = ax + b$.

2. Name some advantages and disadvantages of the graphing method and the algebraic method when determining solutions for linear functions.

   Answers will vary.

   Graphs provide visual representations of functions, and they can provide a wide range of values, depending on the intervals. A disadvantage is that I have to estimate values if points do not fall exactly on grid line intersections. The algebraic method provides an exact solution for every input, but I may be unable to solve more difficult equations correctly.

Problem Types You Will See

Worked Example

WHEN YOU SEE A WORKED EXAMPLE

- Take your time to read through it,
- Question your own understanding, and
- Think about the connections between steps.

ASK YOURSELF

- What is the main idea?
- How would this work if I changed the numbers?
- Have I used these strategies before?

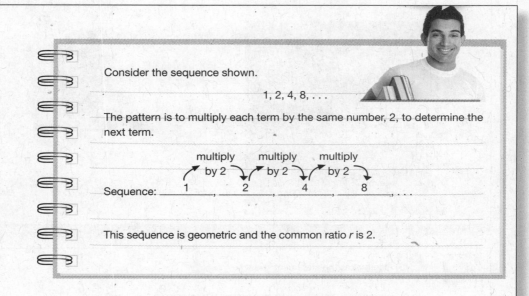

Consider the sequence shown.

$$1, 2, 4, 8, \ldots$$

The pattern is to multiply each term by the same number, 2, to determine the next term.

Sequence: 1, 2, 4, 8, ...
(multiply by 2, multiply by 2, multiply by 2)

This sequence is geometric and the common ratio r is 2.

3. Suppose a sequence has the same starting number as the sequence in the worked example, but its common ratio is 3.

   a. How would the pattern change?

   The sequence would still increase, but the terms would be different. The sequence would increase more rapidly.

   b. Is the sequence still geometric? Explain your reasoning.

   Yes. The sequence is still geometric because the ratio between any two consecutive terms is constant.

   c. If possible, write the first 5 terms for the new sequence.

   1, 3, 9, 27, 81

Thumbs Down

WHEN YOU SEE A THUMBS DOWN ICON

- Take your time to read through the *incorrect* solution.
- Think about what error was made.

ASK YOURSELF

- Where is the error?
- Why is it an error?
- How can I correct it?

5. Analyze the solution set of the system of linear inequalities shown.

$$\begin{cases} x + y > 1 \\ -x + y \le 3 \end{cases}$$

a. Graph the system of linear inequalities.

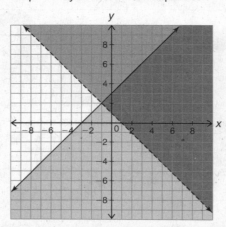

Notice the inequality symbols. How do you think this will affect your graph?

 c. Alan makes the statement shown.

> 👎 **Alan**
>
> The intersection point is always an algebraic solution to a system of inequalities because that is where the two lines meet.

Explain why Alan's statement is incorrect. Use the intersection point of this system to explain your reasoning.

$(-1, 2)$

$-1 + 2 > 1 \qquad -(-1) + 2 \le 3$

$\qquad 1 > 1 \qquad\qquad\qquad 3 \le 3$

Alan is incorrect because the intersection point is not always a solution to the system of linear inequalities. The intersection point for this system only works for one of the inequalities, not both which means it is not a solution. If the inequality symbols are not both "or equal to" then the intersection point is not a solution.

Problem Types

Thumbs Up

WHEN YOU SEE A THUMBS UP ICON

- Take your time to read through the *correct* solution.
- Think about the connections between steps.

ASK YOURSELF

- Why is this method correct?
- Have I used this method before?

8. Pat and George each wrote a function to represent the number of rice grains for any square number using different methods.

 Pat

I compared the exponents of the power to the square number in the table. Each exponent is 1 less than the square number.

$f(s) = 2^{s-1}$

 George

I know this is an exponential function with a common base of 2. If I extend the pattern back on the graph I get the y-intercept of $(0, \frac{1}{2})$, so $a = \frac{1}{2}$.

$f(s) = \frac{1}{2}(2)^s$

Use properties of exponents to verify that 2^{s-1} and $\frac{1}{2}(2)^s$ are equivalent.

$$2^{s-1} = (2^s)(2^{-1})$$
$$= (2^s)\left(\frac{1}{2}\right)$$
$$= \left(\frac{1}{2}\right)(2^s)$$

$$\frac{1}{2}(2)^s = (2)^{-1}(2)^s$$
$$= 2^{-1+s}$$
$$= 2^{s-1}$$

Problem Types

Who's Correct?

WHEN YOU SEE A WHO'S CORRECT? ICON

- Take your time to read through the situation.
- Question the strategy or reason given.
- Determine which solution is correct and which is not correct.

ASK YOURSELF

- Does the reasoning make sense?
- If the reasoning makes sense, what is the justification?
- If the reasoning does not make sense, what error was made?

8. Carlos and Mikala do not like working with fractions. They rewrite their equation so that it does not have fractions. Their work is shown.

Carlos

$$F = \frac{9}{5}c + 32$$
$$(5)F = 5\left(\frac{9}{5}c + 32\right)$$
$$5F = 9c + 160$$
$$5F - 9c = 160$$

Mikala

$$C = \frac{5}{9}(F - 32)$$
$$(9)C = (9)\frac{5}{9}(F - 32)$$
$$9C = 5(F - 32)$$
$$9C = 5F - 160$$
$$9C - 5F = -160$$

Carlos and Mikala got two different equations. Who is correct?

Both Carlos and Mikala are correct. If they divide either equation by −1 they will get the other equation.

The Standards for Mathematical Practice

Effective communication and collaboration are essential skills of a successful learner. With practice, you can develop the habits of mind of a productive mathematical thinker.

Make sense of problems and persevere in solving them.

I can:

- explain what a problem "means" in my own words.
- analyze and organize information.
- keep track of my plan and change it if necessary
- always ask myself, "does this make sense?"

Attend to precision.

I can:

- calculate accurately and efficiently.
- use clear definitions when I talk with my classmates, my teacher, and others.
- specify units of measure and label diagrams and other figures appropriately to clarify the meaning of different representations.

Reasoning and Explaining

Reason abstractly and quantitatively.

I can:

- create an understandable representation of a problem situation.
- consider the units of measure involved in a problem.
- understand and use properties of operations.

Construct viable arguments and critique the reasoning of others.

I can:

- use definitions and previously established results in constructing arguments.
- communicate and defend my own mathematical reasoning using examples, drawings, or diagrams.
- distinguish correct reasoning from reasoning that is flawed.
- listen to or read the conclusions of others and decide whether they make sense.
- ask useful questions in an attempt to understand other ideas and conclusions.

Habits of Mind

Modeling and Using Tools

Model with mathematics.

I can:

- identify important relationships in a problem situation and represent them using tools such as, diagrams, tables, graphs, and formulas.
- apply mathematics to solve problems that occur in everyday life.
- interpret mathematical results in the contexts of a variety of problem situations.
- reflect on whether my results make sense, improving the model I used if it is not appropriate for the situation.

Use appropriate tools strategically.

I can:

- use a variety of different tools that I have to solve problems.
- use a graphing calculator to explore mathematical concepts.
- recognize when a tool that I have to solve problems might be helpful and also when it has limitations.

Seeing Structure and Generalizing

Look for and make use of structure.

I can:

- look closely to see a pattern or a structure in a mathematical argument.
- can see complicated things as single objects or as being composed of several objects.
- can step back for an overview and can shift my perspective.

Look for and express regularity in repeated reasoning.

I can:

- notice if calculations are repeated.
- look for general methods and more efficient methods to solve problems.
- evaluate the reasonableness of intermediate results.
- make generalizations based on results.

© 2012 Carnegie Learning

Habits of Mind

Each lesson provides opportunities for you to think, reason, and communicate mathematical understanding. Here are a few examples of how you will develop expertise using the Standards for Mathematical Practice throughout this text.

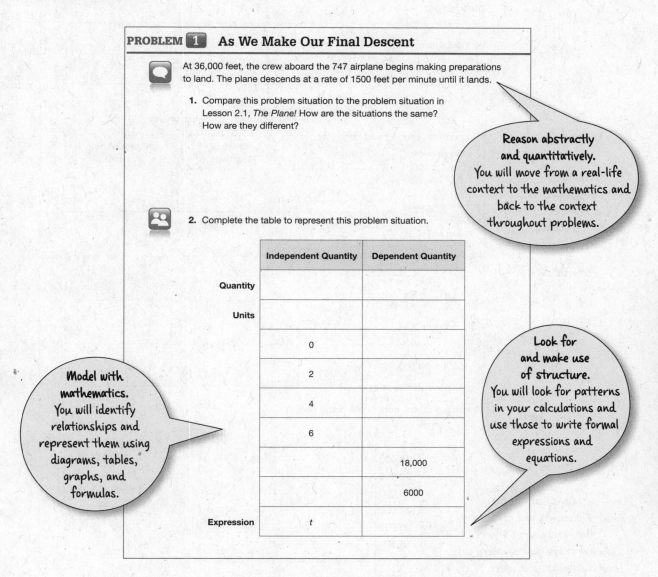

PROBLEM 1   As We Make Our Final Descent

At 36,000 feet, the crew aboard the 747 airplane begins making preparations to land. The plane descends at a rate of 1500 feet per minute until it lands.

1. Compare this problem situation to the problem situation in Lesson 2.1, *The Plane!* How are the situations the same? How are they different?

2. Complete the table to represent this problem situation.

	Independent Quantity	Dependent Quantity
Quantity		
Units		
	0	
	2	
	4	
	6	
		18,000
		6000
Expression	*t*	

Reason abstractly and quantitatively.
You will move from a real-life context to the mathematics and back to the context throughout problems.

Model with mathematics.
You will identify relationships and represent them using diagrams, tables, graphs, and formulas.

Look for and make use of structure.
You will look for patterns in your calculations and use those to write formal expressions and equations.

Habits of Mind

4. Complete the table shown. First, determine the unit of measure for each expression. Then, describe the contextual meaning of each part of the function. Finally, choose a term from the word box to describe the mathematical meaning of each part of the function.

input value	output value	rate of change
	y-intercept	x-intercept

		Description	
Expression	**Units**	**Contextual Meaning**	**Mathematical Meaning**
t			
-1500			
$-1500t$			
$36,000$			
$-1500t + 36,000$			

> **Attend to precision.**
> You will specify units of measure to clarify meaning.

5. Graph $g(t)$ on the coordinate plane shown.

> **Construct viable arguments and critique the reasoning of others.**
> You will share your answers with your classmates and listen to their responses to decide whether they make sense.

> **Use appropriate tools strategically.**
> You will use multiple representations throughout the text.

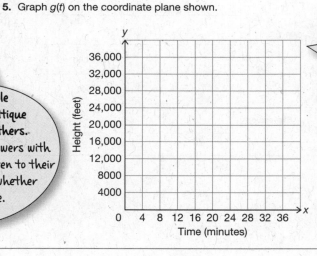

Height (feet) — y-axis: 4000, 8000, 12,000, 16,000, 20,000, 24,000, 28,000, 32,000, 36,000
Time (minutes) — x-axis: 0, 4, 8, 12, 16, 20, 24, 28, 32, 36

Analyzing Data Sets for One Variable

8

People didn't fret over sugar amounts, carbohydrates, nor calories in the late 1800s. However, that didn't stop two famous brothers from offering a healthy alternative to the "most important meal of the day."

Start Your Day the Right Way

Graphically Representing Data

LEARNING GOALS

In this lesson, you will:

- Represent and interpret data displayed on dot plots.
- Represent and interpret data displayed on histograms.
- Represent and interpret data displayed on box-and-whisker plots.

KEY TERMS

- dot plot
- discrete data
- data distribution
- symmetric distribution
- skewed right distribution
- skewed left distribution
- box-and-whisker plot
- five number summary
- histogram
- bin
- frequency
- continuous data

Many nutritional experts call breakfast the most important meal of the day, and many people start their day with a bowl of cereal. However, cereal was not always an option. In the late 1800s, most people's diets consisted mainly of meat products, including breakfasts of pork and beef. However, John Harvey Kellogg and his brother William Keith Kellogg, both of whom worked at a health spa, began creating vegetarian-based breakfast options for their guests using grains. It was actually by mistake that they created some of the first flakes of wheat cereal. This mistake was an immediate success! Just a few years later, the Kellogg Company was selling more than one million cases of cereal a year.

Some of today's cereals still contain the healthy whole grains that the Kelloggs used in their original recipe. However, there are many other cereals that contain other ingredients that are not quite as healthy. What are some healthy cereal options in the stores today? What are some cereals that might not be considered as healthy? What is the difference between these two types of cereal?

455

PROBLEM 1 **How Much Sugar Is Too Much?**

Ms. Romano is a health coach and nutritionist. Recently, she encouraged Matthew to eat a healthier breakfast and recommended a cereal with less sugar. There are many different cereals and it seems like the amount of sugar in each type varies widely. Matthew took a trip to the grocery store and recorded the sugar amount that each cereal has in one serving.

Cereal Name	Sugar Amount in One Serving (grams)
Cocoa Rounds	13
Flakes of Corn	4
Frosty Flakes	11
Grape Nuggets	7
Golden Nuggets	10
Honey Nut Squares	10
Raisin Branola	7
Healthy Living Flakes	7
Wheatleys	8
Healthy Living Crunch	6
Multi-Grain Squares	7
All Branola	5
Munch Crunch	12
Branola Flakes	5
Complete Flakes	4
Corn Crisps	3
Rice Crisps	4
Shredded Wheatleys	1
Puffs	22
Fruit Circles	11

1. Analyze the data collected. What conclusions can you draw about the sugar amount in different types of cereal?

It may be difficult to properly analyze data in a table. One way to better organize the data is to create a graph. A **dot plot** is a graph that shows how *discrete data* are distributed using a number line. **Discrete data** are data that has only a finite number of values or data that can be "counted." Dot plots are best used to organize and display the number of occurences of a small number of data points.

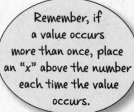

Remember, if a value occurs more than once, place an "x" above the number each time the value occurs.

2. Construct a dot plot to represent the sugar amount in one serving of each breakfast cereal. Label the number line using intervals that will include all the data values. Place an "x" above the number that represents each data value. Make sure you name your dot plot.

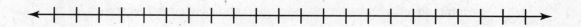

3. Analyze the dot plot. What conclusions can you draw about the sugar amounts in one serving of breakfast cereal from the dot plot?

4. Jordan states that those numbers on the number line that do not contain any data values should be eliminated. Toni disagrees and says that all the numbers on the number line must be included even if there are no data values for that particular number. Who is correct? Explain your reasoning.

When you analyze a graphical display, you can look at several characteristics of the graph to draw conclusions. For example, you can ask yourself:

- What is the overall shape of the graph? Does it have any interesting patterns?

- Where is the approximate middle, or center, of the graph?

- How spread out are the data values on the graph?

The overall shape of a graph is called the *data distribution.* The **data distribution** is the way in which the data is spread out or clustered together. The shape of the distribution can reveal a lot of information about the data. There are many different distributions, but the most common are *symmetric*, *skewed right*, and *skewed left* as shown.

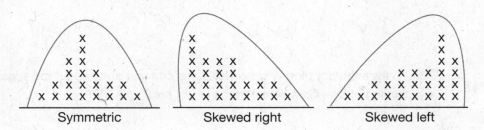

5. Describe the properties of a data distribution that is:

  a. symmetric.

  b. skewed right.

  c. skewed left.

In a **symmetric distribution** of data, the left and right halves of the graph are nearly mirror images of each other. There is often a "peak" in the middle of the graph.

In a **skewed right distribution** of data, the peak of the data is to the left side of the graph. There are only a few data points to the right side of the graph.

In a **skewed left distribution** of data, the peak of the data is to the right side of the graph. There are only a few data points to the left side of the graph.

6. Describe the distribution of the sugar amount in one serving of breakfast cereal. Explain what this means in terms of the problem situation.

7. Do you think the conclusion you came to in Question 6 is true of all breakfast cereals? Why or why not?

PROBLEM 2 Boxing It Up

Another graphical representation that displays the distribution of quantitative data is a *box-and-whisker plot*. A **box-and-whisker plot** displays the data distribution based on a *five number summary*. The **five number summary** consists of the minimum value, the first quartile (Q1), the median, the third quartile (Q3), and the maximum value.

Quantitative data is just another term for numerical data.

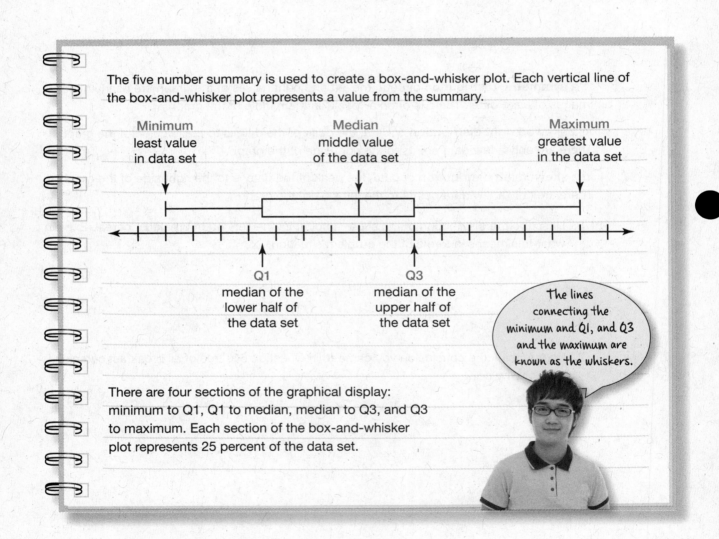

The five number summary is used to create a box-and-whisker plot. Each vertical line of the box-and-whisker plot represents a value from the summary.

Minimum
least value
in data set

Median
middle value
of the data set

Maximum
greatest value
in the data set

Q1
median of the
lower half of
the data set

Q3
median of the
upper half of
the data set

The lines connecting the minimum and Q1, and Q3 and the maximum are known as the whiskers.

There are four sections of the graphical display: minimum to Q1, Q1 to median, median to Q3, and Q3 to maximum. Each section of the box-and-whisker plot represents 25 percent of the data set.

1. Determine each percent of data values for the given sections of the box-and-whisker plot shown in the worked example. Explain your reasoning for each.

   a. Less than Q1

      Greater than Q1

   b. Less than Q3

      Greater than Q3

   c. Less than the median

      Greater than the median

   d. Between Q1 and Q3

2. Construct a box-and-whisker plot of the sugar amount in one serving of each breakfast cereal from Problem 1, *How Much Sugar Is Too Much?*

Before you start constructing, list the data values in order.

<---+++++++++++++++++++++++++++++++++--->

3. Analyze the five number summary and box-and-whisker plot. What conclusions can you draw about the sugar amount in one serving of breakfast cereal from these representations?

Interpret the data in terms of percents.

4. Describe the data distribution shown in the box-and-whisker plot. Interpret the meaning of the distribution in terms of this problem situation.

5. Damon states that more breakfast cereals have over 10 grams of sugar per serving than have under 5 grams of sugar per serving because the whisker connecting the maximum and Q3 is longer than the whisker connecting the minimum and Q1. Is Damon correct? Explain why or why not.

PROBLEM 3 Weekend Gamers

Another way to display quantitative data is to create a *histogram*. A **histogram** is a graphical way to display quantitative data using vertical bars. The width of a bar in a histogram represents an interval of data and is often referred to as a **bin**. A bin is represented by intervals of data instead of showing individual data values. The value shown on the left side of the bin is the least data value in the interval.

The height of each bar indicates the **frequency**, which is the number of data values included in any given bin.

Histograms are effective in displaying large amounts of *continuous data*. **Continuous data** is data which can take any numerical value within a range.

The histogram shown represents the data distribution for the number of hours students spend playing video games on the weekends. The data is gathered to the nearest half-hour.

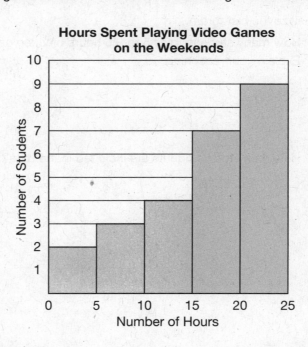

1. What conclusions can you draw from the histogram about the number of hours students spend playing video games on weekends?

2. Jonae and Tyler must identify the greatest value represented in the bin beginning with 15. Their responses are shown.

 Jonae

The bin that begins with the interval 15 includes all data values from 15 to 20.

👍 **Tyler**

The bin that begins with the interval 15 includes all data values from 15 thru, but not including 20.

   a. Explain why Tyler's answer is correct and why Jonae's answer is incorrect.

   b. Represent the bin that contains 15 as an inequality.

3. Analyze the histogram.
   a. How many students play 5 to 9.5 hours of video games on weekends? Explain your reasoning.

   b. How many total students are included in the data? Explain your reasoning.

c. Marcel states that between 0 and 5 students spend 2 hours playing video games on weekends. Is Marcel's statement correct? Explain why or why not.

d. How many students play 22 hours of video games on the weekends? Explain your reasoning.

e. What percent of the students play 10 or more hours of video games on the weekends? Explain your reasoning.

4. Describe the data distribution displayed by the histogram. Interpret its meaning in terms of this problem situation.

Talk the Talk

Analyze each data representation to answer the questions. Justify your reasoning using the characteristics of each representation.

1.

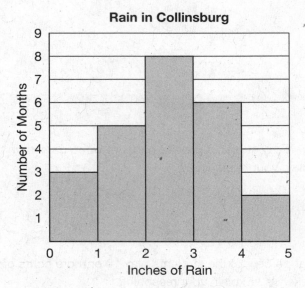

Rain in Collinsburg

a. Describe the information represented in the histogram.

b. How many months are represented on the histogram? Describe how you determined your answer.

c. Identify the intervals represented by each bin.

d. How many months had 4 or more inches of rain?

e. Describe the data distribution and interpret its meaning in terms of this problem situation.

2.

Participants Who Won Gold Medals at the Special Olympics

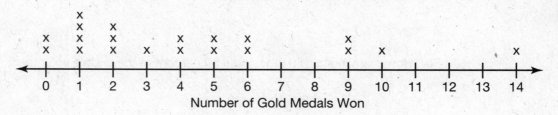

Number of Gold Medals Won

a. Describe the information represented in the dot plot.

b. How many participants are represented in the dot plot?

c. How many participants won 10 or more medals?

d. Describe the data distribution and interpret its meaning in terms of this problem situation.

3.

Volunteers Hours at the Local Animal Shelter

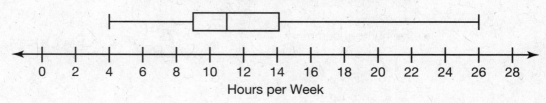

Hours per Week

a. Describe the information represented in the box-and-whisker plot.

b. How many people are represented on the box-and-whisker plot?

c. What percent of the people volunteered 14 or more hours?

d. What percent of people volunteered less than 11 hours?

e. How many hours did the middle 50 percent of the people volunteer?

f. Describe the data distribution and interpret its meaning in terms of this problem situation.

4. Analyze each visual display shown. Describe what information each display provides. Be sure to include advantages and limitations and any specific characteristics for each visual display.
   - table

   - dot plot

   - five number summary

   - box-and-whisker plot

   - histogram

 Be prepared to share your solutions and methods.

Which Measure Is Better?

Determining the Best Measure of Center for a Data Set

LEARNING GOALS

In this lesson, you will:

- Calculate and interpret the mean of a data set.
- Calculate and interpret the median of a data set.
- Estimate the mean and median of a data set from its data distribution.
- Determine which measure of central tendency (mean or median) is best to use for a data set.

KEY TERMS

- statistic
- measure of central tendency

You have probably been able to recite your ABCs since you started school. Now you may even be learning a new language that might use new letters. Some languages have different alphabets, where each letter represents sounds that are unique to that language even if the letters are the same as English. There are also some alphabets, such as the Russian alphabet or the Chinese alphabet, which use different letter symbols altogether.

Today, you will get the opportunity to learn new letters from another alphabet. The letters of the Greek alphabet are often used in mathematics to represent different mathematical ideas. You should already know the letter pi (π), which represents the ratio of the circumference of a circle to its diameter. By the time you finish this chapter you will know at least two more Greek letters! Keep an eye out for them as you work through the lessons.

PROBLEM 1 How Sweet It Is

Previously you analyzed a data set by creating a graphical representation of the data. However, you can also analyze a data set by describing numerical characteristics, or **statistics**, of the data. A statistic that describes the "center" of a data set is called a *measure of central tendency*. A **measure of central tendency** is the numerical values used to describe the overall clustering of data in a set. Two measures of central tendency that are typically used to describe a set of data are the mean and the median.

The arithmetic mean, or mean, represents the sum of the data values divided by the number of values. A common notation for the mean is $\bar{x}$, which is read "x bar."

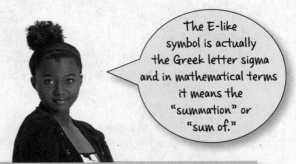

The E-like symbol is actually the Greek letter sigma and in mathematical terms it means the "summation" or "sum of."

The formula shown represents the mean of a data set.

$$\text{mean} \longrightarrow \bar{x} = \frac{\sum x}{n}$$

the sum of the data values

the number of data values

The mean of the data set 5, 10, 9, 7, 5 can be written using this formula.

$$\bar{x} = \frac{5 + 10 + 9 + 7 + 5}{5}$$

$$\bar{x} = 7.2$$

The mean of this data set is 7.2.

Why don't I write the sigma when writing the data values in the formula?

© 2012 Carnegie Learning

Recall that Lesson 8.1 *How Much Sugar Is Too Much?*, Matthew collected data on the sugar amount in one serving of various breakfast cereals. The data collected is shown.

Cereal Name	Sugar Amount in One Serving (grams)	Cereal Name	Sugar Amount in One Serving (grams)
Cocoa Rounds	13	Multi-Grain Squares	7
Flakes of Corn	4	All Branola	5
Frosty Flakes	11	Munch Crunch	12
Grape Nuggets	7	Branola Flakes	5
Golden Nuggets	10	Complete Flakes	4
Honey Nut Squares	10	Corn Crisps	3
Raisin Branola	7	Rice Crisps	4
Healthy Living Flakes	7	Shredded Wheatleys	1
Wheatleys	8	Puffs	22
Healthy Living Crunch	6	Fruit Circles	11

1. Represent the sugar amount in different cereals using the formula for the mean. Then determine the mean of the data set.

You can use your graphing calculator to determine the mean of a data set.

Step 1: Press **STAT** then press **ENTER** to select **1:Edit.**

Step 2: Enter the data values for the data set in List 1.

Step 3: Press **STAT** and scroll over to highlight **CALC.** Press **ENTER** to select **1:1-Var Stats.** Press **ENTER** again.

Step 4: The calculator should now show many values relating to the data set. You can scroll down for more values including the five number summary.

Be sure to check that your lists are clear of old data. Delete any data that might be in your lists before entering new data.

Do the values need to be entered in order?

2. Enter the data set for the sugar amount in various breakfast cereals into a graphing calculator. Then for each given symbol, state what it represents and its calculated value.

   a. $\bar{x}$

   b. Σx

   c. n

3. Compare your answers in Question 2 with the answers you wrote using the formula for determining the mean in Question 1. What do you notice?

4. Determine the median sugar amount in grams in one serving of cereal. Interpret the meaning in terms of this problem situation.

Does the order of the data matter when determining the median?

5. The box-and-whisker plot you constructed in the previous lesson is shown. Locate and label the mean and median values on the dot plot.

Sugar in Breakfast Cereals

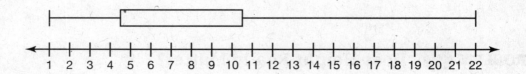

6. Compare the mean and median. Which measure best represents the data set?

Constructing a box-and-whisker plot can take some time when using paper and pencil. Technology can make constructing a box-and-whisker plot more efficient.

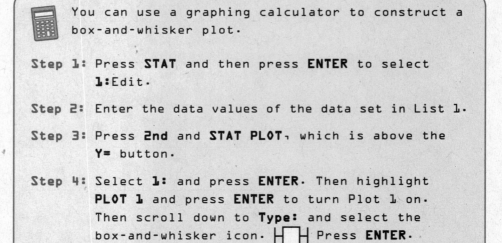

You can use a graphing calculator to construct a box-and-whisker plot.

Step 1: Press **STAT** and then press **ENTER** to select **1:Edit.**

Step 2: Enter the data values of the data set in List 1.

Step 3: Press **2nd** and **STAT PLOT**, which is above the **Y=** button.

Step 4: Select **1:** and press **ENTER**. Then highlight **PLOT 1** and press **ENTER** to turn Plot 1 on. Then scroll down to **Type:** and select the box-and-whisker icon. ⊢⊔⊣ Press **ENTER**.

Step 5: Make sure the **XList** is using the correct list. Then press **GRAPH**.

7. Let's consider the data set without the value of 22.

a. Remove the value of 22 from the data set. Use your graphing calculator to create a box-and-whisker plot for the new data set.

b. Plot above the given box-and-whisker plot your new box-and-whisker plot on the same graph in Question 5.

c. How does the removal of the value 22 affect the distribution of the data set?

d. Did the mean and median change with the removal of the value 22? Does your choice for the best measure of center from Question 6 still hold true?

PROBLEM 2   Does Height Really Matter?

The Mountain View High School basketball team has its first game of the season on their home court. Coach Maynard doesn't know much about the visiting team, but he does have a list of the heights of their top ten players. Coach Maynard wants to compare the heights of his top ten players to those on the visiting team.

Home Team Heights (inches)	Visiting Team Heights (inches)
69	68
70	68
67	68
68	69
66	69
65	67
70	72
70	71
71	66
71	67

© 2012 Carnegie Learning

1. Represent the data for each team on a dot plot.

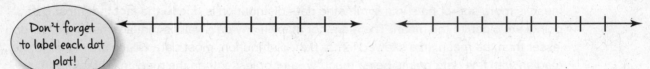

Don't forget to label each dot plot!

2. Analyze each dot plot you created.

   a. Describe the data distribution of each graph and explain what it means in terms of the players' heights on each team.

   b. Based on the dot plots, predict whether the mean or median will be greater for each data set. Explain your reasoning.

   c. Verify your prediction by calculating the mean and median heights for each team. Was your prediction correct?

   d. Which measure of central tendency best describes each data set? Explain your reasoning.

3. Describe the relationship that seems to exist between the data distribution and the values of the mean and median.

When the distribution of data is approximately symmetric, the mean is generally the more appropriate measure of center to use. When the distribution of data is skewed left or skewed right, the median is the more appropriate measure of center to use. The reason why the mean is more appropriate in a symmetric data distribution is due to the fact that most data points are close to the mean. There are not many if any data values that are much greater or lesser than the mean. In a skewed left or right distribution, most data values are closer to the median with few data points being much greater or lesser than the median. Therefore, the median is not affected by these values.

4. The histogram from Lesson 8.1 *Weekend Gamers* is shown.

Hours Spent Playing Video Games on the Weekends

a. Predict whether the mean or median number of hours spent playing video games will be greater. Explain your reasoning.

Remember to use characteristics of the graph to explain your reasoning.

b. Suppose the two measures of central tendency for the given histogram are 16.1 hours and 17.5 hours. Which value is the mean and which value is the median? Explain your reasoning.

Talk the Talk

1. Identify which measure of central tendency would be most appropriate to describe the for each given graph. Then determine the mean and median if possible. If it is not possible, explain why not.

a.

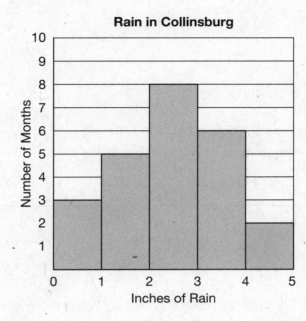

b.

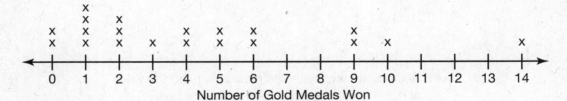

c.   **Volunteer Hours at the Local Animal Shelter**

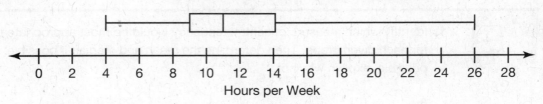

Hours per Week

2. Consider the data set 0, 10, 10, 12, 14.

   a. Construct and label a dot plot of the data.

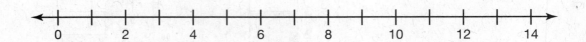

   b. Calculate the mean and median. Which measure do you think best represents the data set?

Why do you think the value 0 was selected to be removed from the data set?

   c. Remove the value of 0 from the data set. How does this affect the distribution of the data set?

   d. Recalculate the mean and median without the value of 0. Does your choice in part (b) for the best measure of central tendency still hold true? Explain why or why not.

 Be prepared to share your solutions and methods.

You Are Too Far Away!
Calculating IQR and Identifying Outliers

© 2012 Carnegie Learning

LEARNING GOALS

In this lesson, you will:

- Calculate and interpret the interquartile range (IQR) of a data set.
- Determine if a data set contains outliers.

KEY TERMS

- interquartile range (IQR)
- outlier
- lower fence
- upper fence

Everywhere in our world there are boundaries that show where something begins and ends. The walls to your classroom are boundaries. The lanes on the road are boundaries. There are boundaries on sports fields and boundaries for each state and country. But what about the universe? Is there a boundary to show where the universe begins and ends?

That is a question that astronomers and physicists have debated for quite some time. For example, in the early 1900s, astronomer Harlow Shapely claimed that the entire universe was located within the Milky Way galaxy (the same galaxy where the Earth is located). He determined the galaxy was 300,000 light-years in diameter and in his opinion, could be thought of as the boundary of the universe. It was not until 1925, when Edwin Hubble showed that there are stars located much farther than 300,000 light years away. At this point, most scientists agreed that the universe must be larger than the Milky Way galaxy.

So we know the universe is larger than the Milky Way galaxy, but will we ever know just how large it is? Scientists have studied the idea that the universe is actually expanding for quite some time. What does this mean in terms of boundaries? Do you think we will ever know the size of the universe?

PROBLEM 1 Touchdown!

Coach Petersen's Middletown 9th grade football team is having a tough season. The team is struggling to win games. He is trying to determine why his team has only won a few times this year. The table shows the points scored in games in 2011 and 2012.

Points Scored (2011)	10	13	17	20	22	24	24	27	28	29	35
Points Scored (2012)	0	7	17	17	18	24	24	24	25	27	45

1. Analyze the data sets in the table.

   a. In which year do you think the football team performed better? Explain your reasoning.

   b. Calculate the five number summary for each year.

   c. Construct box-and-whisker plots of each year's scores using the same number line for each.

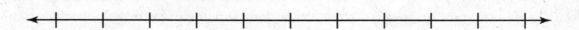

© 2012 Carnegie Learning

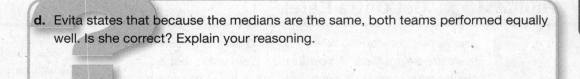

d. Evita states that because the medians are the same, both teams performed equally well. Is she correct? Explain your reasoning.

e. What conclusions can you draw about the points scored each year?

Another measure of data distribution Coach Petersen can use to compare the teams is the *interquartile range* or *IQR*. The **interquartile range, IQR,** measures how far the data is spread out from the median. The IQR gives a realistic representation of the data without being affected by very high or very low data values. The IQR often helps show consistency within a data set. The IQR is the range of the middle 50 percent of the data. It is calculated by subtracting Q3 − Q1.

2. Calculate the IQR for the points scored each year. Then interpret the IQR for each year.

PROBLEM 2 **Get Outta Here!**

Another useful statistic when analyzing data is to determine if there are any *outliers*. An **outlier** is a data value that is significantly greater or lesser than other data values in a data set. It is important to identify outliers because outliers can often affect the other statistics of the data set such as the mean.

An outlier is typically calculated by multiplying the IQR by 1.5 and then determining if any data values are greater or lesser than that calculated distance away from Q1 or Q3. By calculating Q1 − (IQR · 1.5) and Q3 + (IQR · 1.5), you are determining a lower and upper limit for the data. Any value outside of these limits is an outlier. The value of Q1 − (IQR · 1.5) is known as the **lower fence** and the value of Q3 + (IQR · 1.5) is known as the **upper fence**.

Remember in the last lesson, How Sweet It Is, you were asked to remove the data value of 22 and then redraw the box-and-whisker. The value 22 was an outlier. Do you remember the affect?

Let's analyze the data set given to see how outliers can be represented on a box-and-whisker plot.

2, 5, 6, 6, 7, 9, 10, 11, 12, 12, 14, 28, 30

Minimum = 2, Q1 = 6, Median = 10, Q3 = 13, Maximum = 30

IQR = 7

Using the five number summary and IQR, calculate the upper and lower fence to determine if there are any outliers in the data set.

Lower Fence:	Upper Fence:
= Q1 − (IQR · 1.5)	= Q3 + (IQR · 1.5)
= 6 − (7 · 1.5)	= 13 + (7 · 1.5)
= −4.5	= 23.5
There are no values less than −4.5.	Both 28 and 30 are greater than 23.5.

If there are outliers, the whisker will end at the lowest or highest value that is not an outlier.

Since 28 and 30 are both outliers, 14 is the greatest data value that is not an outlier.

© 2012 Carnegie Learning

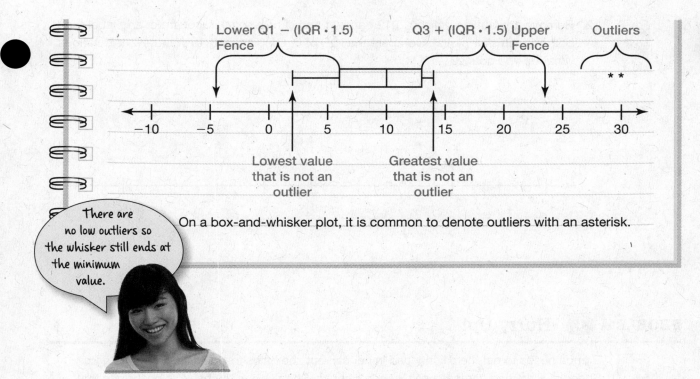

 Recall the data sets from Problem 1, *Touchdown!* The five number summary and IQR for each data set is shown.

2011:

Minimum = 10
Q1 = 17
Median = 24
Q3 = 28
Maximum = 45
IQR = 11

2012:

Minimum = 0
Q1 = 17
Median = 24
Q3 = 25
Maximum = 45
IQR = 8

1. Use the formulas to determine if there are any outliers in either data set.

   a. Determine the upper and lower fence for each year's data set.

   b. Identify any outliers in either set of data. Explain your reasoning.

2. Remove any outliers for the 2012 data set and, if necessary, reconstruct and label the box-and-whisker plot(s). Compare the IQR of the original data to your new calculations. What do you notice?

PROBLEM 3 Hurry Up!

Brenda needs to get the oil changed in her car, but she hates to wait! Quick Change and Speedy Oil are two garages near Brenda's house. She decides to check an online site that allows customers to comment on the service at different local businesses and record their wait times. Brenda chooses 12 customers at random for each garage. The wait times for each garage are shown.

Wait Times (minutes)								
Quick Change					**Speedy Oil**			
10	60	22	15		5	60	45	24
12	24	20	18		40	26	55	30
16	23	22	15		32	85	45	30

Don't forget to label each dot plot!

1. Create a box-and-whisker plot of each data set.

2. Calculate and interpret the IQR for each data set.

3. Describe each data distribution and explain its meaning in terms of this problem situation.

4. Identify the measure of central tendency that best represents each data set. Explain your reasoning.

5. Identify any outliers in the data sets.

© 2012 Carnegie Learning

6. Remove any outliers in each data set and, if necessary, reconstruct the box-and-whisker plot. Compare the IQR of the original data to your new calculations. What do you notice?

7. Does your choice for the best measure of center from Question 4 still hold true?

8. Based on the data gathered, which garage should Brenda choose if she is in a hurry?

Talk the Talk

1. Why is the IQR not affected by extremely high or low data values in a data set? Explain your reasoning.

2. Use the two box-and-whisker plots shown to answer each question.

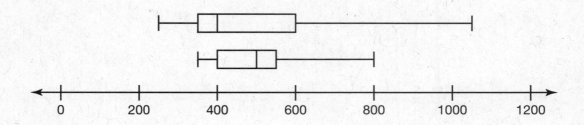

   a. Estimate the five number summary for each box plot to the nearest 50.

   b. Based on your estimates, calculate the IQR of both box-and-whisker plots.

c. Determine if there are any outliers in either data set shown in the box-and-whisker plots.

d. Lydia was told to assume that each data set has one outlier and that there are data values at the upper and lower fences. Lydia recreated the two box plots from Question 2 to represent the outliers. Her box plots are shown.

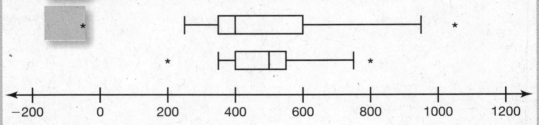

Are Lydia's box plots correct? Explain why or why not.

 Be prepared to share your solutions and methods.

Whose Scores Are Better?

Calculating and Interpreting Standard Deviation

LEARNING GOALS

In this lesson, you will:

- Calculate and interpret the standard deviation of a data set.
- Compare the standard deviation of data sets.

KEY TERMS

- standard deviation
- normal distribution

How many times this year have you asked about your grade in a class? Most students who are serious about their learning and the future are interested in their progress in classes. Some students may even keep track of their own grades throughout the semester. But did you know that every country in the world has its own grading system?

Most likely your school uses letter grades from A to E or F which represent a percent of the points you earned in a class. However, if you went to school in Tunisia, your grades would range from 0 (worst) to 20 (best) and any score below a 10 is a fail. In Denmark, a 7-step-scale is used which ranges from 12 (excellent) to −3 (unacceptable). The grading in Denmark is also very strict with very few students receiving a 12 grade. In some schools in Italy, grades vary from 2 to 8 and each teacher can apply his or her own grading customs. The grades between 5 and 6 could range from $5+, 5++, 5\frac{1}{2}, 5/6, 6--, 6-$. The symbols on these grades have no real mathematical meaning so calculating grades is somewhat arbitrary. Lately though there has been some push to try to get these schools to use a more uniform system like 1 through 10.

Are you familiar with any other grading scales or techniques teachers use in the classroom? Do you think some grading scales are easier or harder than others? Do you think anything else other than earned points can be used to determine a grade?

PROBLEM 1 Spelling S U C C E S S

Ms. Webb is determining which student she should add to the spelling bee roster that will represent Tyler High School. The chart shows the 10 most recent scores for three students.

Jack	Aleah	Tymar
33	20	5
32	42	10
30	45	12
50	51	40
49	49	45
50	47	55
35	58	88
73	53	60
71	55	90
77	80	95

1. Determine the mean and median for each student's spelling bee scores.

2. What conclusions can you draw about the data from the mean and median scores?

3. Construct box-and-whisker plots of each student's spelling bee scores using the same number line.

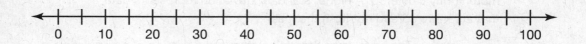

4. Interpret the test scores of each student.
- Jack

- Aleah

- Tymer

5. Do you think these three students performed about the same on all the tests? Why or why not?

You have learned about the spread of data values from the IQR, which is based on the median. However, is there a way to measure the spread of data from another measure of central tendency? **Standard deviation** is a measure of how spread out the data is from the mean. A formula can be used to determine the standard deviation of a data set. A lower standard deviation represents data that are more tightly clustered. A higher standard deviation represents data that are more spread out from the mean.

> So, if the IQR is the measure of how spread out data is from the median, and standard deviation is the measure of how spread out data is from the mean, I wonder which will be affected by outliers?

The formula to determine standard deviation of a population is represented as:

$$\sigma = \sqrt{\dfrac{\sum\limits_{i=1}^{n}(x_i - \bar{x})^2}{n}}$$

where σ is the standard deviation, x_i represents each individual data value, $\bar{x}$ represents the mean of the data set, and n is the number of data points.

> The symbol to the left of the equals sign is a lower case sigma. This represents the standard deviation.

Let's look at each part of the standard deviation formula separately.

Follow the steps to determine the standard deviation. Let's use the data set 6, 4, 10, 8 where $\bar{x} = 7$.

First, think of each data value as its own term labeled as x_1, x_2, and so on.

$x_1 = 6$

$x_2 = 4$

$x_3 = 10$

$x_4 = 8$

The first part of the formula identifies the terms to be added. Since n represents the total number of values and $i = 1$, add all the values that result from substituting in the first term to the fourth term.

$$\sum\limits_{i=1}^{n}$$

> This part of the formula just gives you information. You will not sum anything until after the next step.

Next, evaluate the expressions to be added. Take each term and subtract it from $\bar{x}$ and then square each difference.

$(x_i - \bar{x})^2$

$(6 - 7)^2 = 1$

$(4 - 7)^2 = 9$

$(10 - 7)^2 = 9$

$(8 - 7)^2 = 1$

Now determine the sum of the squared values and divide the sum by the number of data values.

$$\frac{1 + 9 + 9 + 1}{4} = \frac{20}{4} = 5$$

Finally, calculate the square root of the quotient.

$\sigma = \sqrt{5}$.

$\sigma \approx 2.24$

The standard deviation is approximately 2.24.

So the standard deviation for the given data set is approximately 2.24. It is important to note that if the data values have a unit of measure, the standard deviation of the data set also uses the same unit of measure.

1. Do you think the standard deviation for each student's spelling bee scores will be the same? If yes, explain your reasoning. If no, predict who will have a higher or lower standard deviation.

2. Now, let's use the standard deviation formula to determine the standard deviation of Jack's spelling bee scores.

   a. Identify the data values you will use to determine the standard deviation. Explain your reasoning.

   b. Determine the $\bar{x}$ value.

   c. Complete the table to represent each part of the formula. The data values have been put in ascending order.

x_i	$(x_i - \bar{x})^2$
30	$(30 - 50)^2 = 400$
32	
33	
35	
49	
50	
50	
71	
73	
77	
$\dfrac{\sum\limits_{i=1}^{n}(x_i - \bar{x})^2}{n}$	
$\sigma = \sqrt{\dfrac{\sum\limits_{i=1}^{n}(x_i - \bar{x})^2}{n}}$	

3. Determine the standard deviation for Jack's spelling bee scores and interpret the meaning.

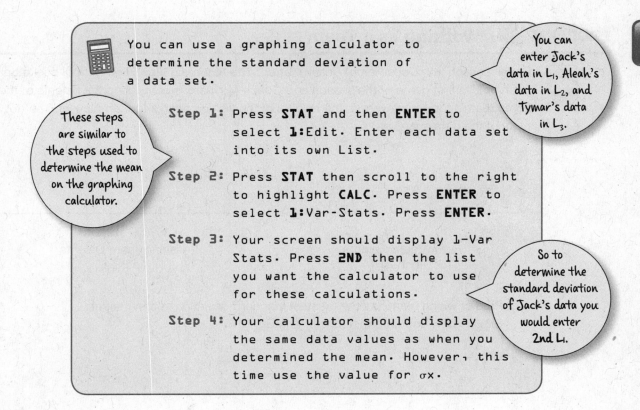

You can use a graphing calculator to determine the standard deviation of a data set.

These steps are similar to the steps used to determine the mean on the graphing calculator.

You can enter Jack's data in L_1, Aleah's data in L_2, and Tymar's data in L_3.

Step 1: Press **STAT** and then **ENTER** to select **1:Edit**. Enter each data set into its own List.

Step 2: Press **STAT** then scroll to the right to highlight **CALC**. Press **ENTER** to select **1:Var-Stats**. Press **ENTER**.

Step 3: Your screen should display 1-Var Stats. Press **2ND** then the list you want the calculator to use for these calculations.

So to determine the standard deviation of Jack's data you would enter 2nd L_1.

Step 4: Your calculator should display the same data values as when you determined the mean. However, this time use the value for σx.

4. Use a graphing calculator to determine the standard deviation of Aleah's and Tymar's spelling bee scores.

5. Was the prediction you made in Question 1 correct? What do the standard deviations tell you about each student's spelling bee scores?

6. Which student do you think Ms. Webb should add to the spelling bee roster? Use the standard deviation for the student you recommend to add to the roster to justify your answer.

PROBLEM 3   **Working as a Team**

 Recall Lesson 8.2, *Does Height Really Matter?* The Mountain View High School basketball team has its first game of the season and Coach Maynard is comparing the heights of the home team's top ten players to the heights of the visiting team's top ten players. The dot plots of the data are given.

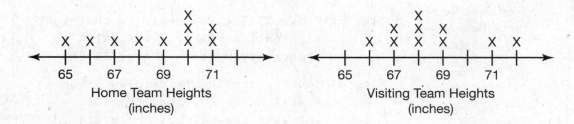

1. Predict which team has the greatest standard deviation in their heights. Explain how you determined your answer.

2. Determine the standard deviation of the heights of each team. Describe what this means in terms of this problem situation. How does this information help Coach Maynard?

PROBLEM 4 68–95–99: The Combination to Standard Deviation

So far, you have determined the standard deviation for different data sets. You have also interpreted the standard deviations to make decisions given a problem situation. Standard deviation can also be represented graphically by graphing a data set.

Recall that Ms. Webb is the spelling bee coach in Problem 1, *Spelling S U C C E S S*. Her class is preparing for their first spelling bee scrimmage. Ms. Webb needs to determine which student should be the spelling bee captain. Ms. Webb believes the captain should have the greatest mean score of the team. The two top spelling bee students' scores are shown.

Maria	Heidi
81	81
73	68
94	60
86	109
70	82
68	88
97	60
93	102
81	78
67	69
85	84
77	103
79	92
103	60
90	108

1. Analyze each student's spelling bee scores.

   a. Determine the mean spelling bee score for each student.

Ms. Webb wants to also use the standard deviation to help her determine which student is a more consistent speller.

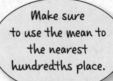

b. Determine the standard deviation of Maria's scores. Then determine the value of the spelling bee scores that are 1 standard deviation from the mean. Explain how you determined her spelling bee point values.

Make sure to use the mean to the nearest hundredths place.

c. Determine the standard deviation of Heidi's scores. Then determine the value of the spelling bee scores that are 1 standard deviation from the mean. Explain how you determine her spelling bee point values.

You have calculated 1 standard deviation for the data sets in previous problem situations. However, you can also determine different numbers of standard deviations. For example, 2 standard deviations or greater are calculated by multiplying the standard deviation by the number of standard deviations you are determining. Therefore, if a data set has a standard deviation of 15, then 2 standard deviations would be 30, and 3 standard deviations would be 45.

When you determine the standard deviation of a data set, you can represent it graphically. You can also determine the general percent of data values that are within 1 standard deviation, and the percent of data values that lie within 2 standard deviations in *normal distributions*. A **normal distribution** is a collection of many data points that form a bell-shaped curve.

The mean of Maria's spelling bee scores is 82.93 points and 1 standard deviation is 10.61 points.

To graph the normal distribution of Maria's spelling bee scores, first graph the mean on a number line as: $x = 82.93$.

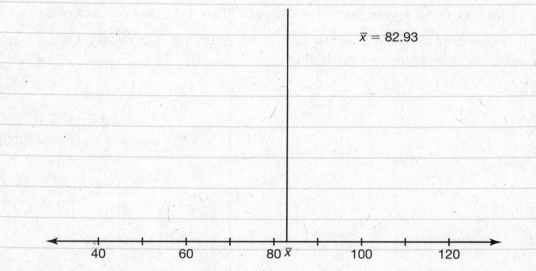

$\bar{x} = 82.93$

Next, graph 1 standard deviation from the mean. For Maria's spelling bee scores, the standard deviation is 10.61. Therefore, the values of the standard deviation from the mean are 72.32 and 93.54.

Use a dotted lines as $x = 72.32$ and $x = 93.54$.

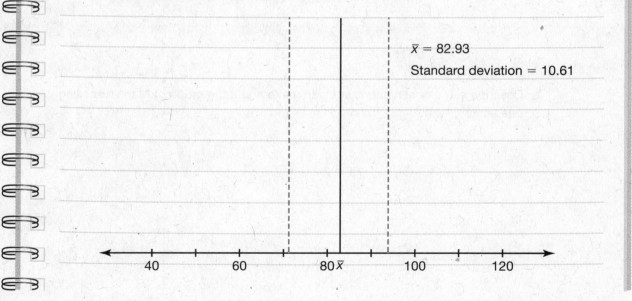

$\bar{x} = 82.93$

Standard deviation = 10.61

Then graph 2 standard deviations and 3 standard deviations from the mean. To determine 2 standard deviations, multiply the standard deviation by 2. To determine 3 standard deviations, multiply the standard deviation by 3.

For Maria's scores, 2 standard deviations would be 21.22 and 3 standard deviations would be 31.83.

Mark an "x" for the two points as 61.71 and 104.15 represent a standard deviation of 2. Mark an "o" for the two points 114.76 and 51.10 for a standard deviation of 3.

Finally draw a smooth curve starting from the far left minimum value. The smooth curve should resemble a bell-shaped curve.

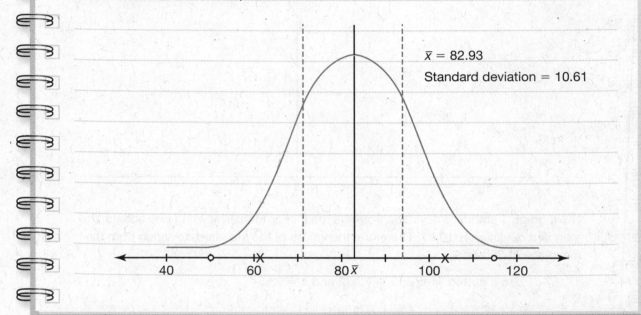

$\bar{x} = 82.93$

Standard deviation = 10.61

2. Describe some observations you can make about the graph of Maria's spelling bee scores.

3. Plot each of Maria's scores on the graph of the worked example. Mark an "x" for the approximate location on the number line for each score.

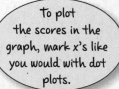

To plot the scores in the graph, mark x's like you would with dot plots.

   a. Determine how many spelling bee scores are within 1 standard deviation of the mean for Maria's spelling bee scores.

   b. Determine how many spelling bee scores are within 2 standard deviations of the mean for Maria's spelling bee scores.

   c. Determine how many spelling bee scores are within 3 standard deviations of the mean for Maria's spelling bee scores.

Within the graph of a normal distribution, you can predict the percent of data points that are within one, two, or three standard deviations from the mean. Generally, 68% of the data points of a data set will fall within one standard deviation of the mean; while 95% of the data points of a data set will fall within two standard deviations of the mean; and 99% of the data points of a data set will fall within three standard deviations of the mean.

4. Analyze the number of data points you determined lie within 1, 2, or 3 standard deviations.

   a. What percent of data points from Maria's spelling bee scores fall within 1 standard deviation of the mean? Explain how you determined your answer.

   b. What percent of data points from Maria's spelling bee scores fall within 2 standard deviations from the mean? Explain how you determined your answer.

c. What percent of data points from Maria's spelling bee scores fall within 3 standard deviations from the mean? Explain how you determined your answer.

d. Did the prediction about the percent of data points that fall within 1, 2, or 3 standard deviations match Maria's data set? Why do you think it did or did not?

It is important to note that the guideline regarding 68%, 95% and 99% is simply a guideline. In fact, there may be some data sets in which all of the data points lie within two standard deviations of the mean while other data sets may actually need four or greater standard deviations to encapsulate the entire data set. It is also important to know that because standard deviation is based on the mean of a data set, outliers may affect the standard deviation of the data set.

5. Graph 1, 2, and 3 standard deviations on the number line shown for Heidi's scores using a bell-shaped curve.

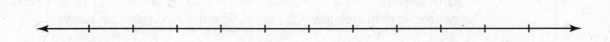

6. What similarities and differences do you notice between Maria's spelling score graph and Heidi's spelling score graph?

© 2012 Carnegie Learning

7. Advise Ms. Webb whom she should choose to captain the spelling bee team given the information about each student's standard deviation.

Talk the Talk

Mean and median are both measures of central tendency.

1. Identify which is more resistant to outliers, and which is more sensitive to outliers. Explain your reasoning.

The interquartile range and the standard deviation both measure the spread of data.

2. Identify which is more resistant to outliers, and which is more sensitive to outliers. Explain your reasoning.

Be prepared to share your solutions and methods.

© 2012 Carnegie Learning

Putting the Pieces Together
Analyzing and Interpreting Data

© 2012 Carnegie Learning

LEARNING GOALS

In this lesson, you will:

- Analyze and interpret data graphically and numerically.
- Determine which measure of central tendency and spread is most appropriate to describe a data set.

KEY TERMS

- stem-and-leaf plot
- side-by-side stem-and-leaf plot

Taking a trip on an airplane is always exciting. However, the process of flying can sometimes be frustrating. One of the most challenging tasks is boarding the plane before take-off. The most common method used to board passengers is boarding people by zone or row so that passengers in the back of the plane board first. This seems like it should be the most efficient way to board because people in the front won't be blocking the way. However, this is not necessarily the case. An astrophysicist used a computer simulation to try and determine the best method for loading passengers. After many simulations he found that passengers in even-numbered window seats near the back should board first, followed by even-numbered window seats in the middle, and even-numbered window seats in the front. This trend then continues through even-numbered middle seats, and even-numbered aisle seats. The whole process is then repeated with odd numbered seats.

So why does this work? It seems that allowing passengers a row between each other gives them more space to load their luggage and allows them to move if a passenger needs to get past them. This is not the only method that works, but it is the simplest for passengers to understand. Do you think airlines should try to change their methods for loading to this one? How much time do you really think it would save?

PROBLEM 1 Go For the Gold

When a participant takes part in the Special Olympics, each person receives a number. The chart shown represents the first twenty people labeled by their participation number and the number of gold medals each participant won.

Participation Number	Gold Medals Won
001	6
002	14
003	1
004	6
005	0
006	0
007	9
008	1
009	1
010	9
011	5
012	10
013	1
014	2
015	2
016	5
017	4
018	3
019	4
020	2

1. Analyze the data. Calculate the mean and standard deviation, and then interpret the meaning of each in terms of this problem situation.

2. Construct a box-and-whisker plot of the data and include any outliers.

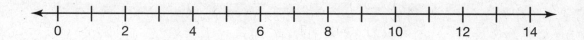

3. Interpret the IQR.

4. Which measure of central tendency and spread should you use to describe this data? Explain your reasoning.

5. What conclusions can you draw about the number of gold medals participants won?

6. Shelly states the median and standard deviation should be used to describe the data because the standard deviation is less than the IQR. Is Shelly correct? Explain why or why not.

PROBLEM 2 Flying High

Data were collected from two rival airlines measuring the difference in the stated departure times, and the times the flights *actually* departed. The average departure time differences were recorded for each month for one year. The results are shown in the *side-by-side stem-and-leaf plot* given.

Difference in Departure Times (minutes)							
My Air Airlines				**Fly High Airlines**			
	5	0	0	7	8		
9	5	1	1	4	5	6	
6	0	0	2	4	7	9	
4	3	3	3	0	2		
		0	4	5	9		

2|4 = 24 minutes

A **stem-and-leaf plot** is a graphical method used to represent ordered numerical data. Once the data is ordered, the stem and leaves are determined. Typically, the stem is all the digits in a number except the right most digit, which is the leaf. A **side-by-side stem-and-leaf plot** allows a comparison of two data sets. The two data sets share the same stem, but have leaves to the left and right of the stem.

Oh I remember stem-and-leaf plots! There should be a key somewhere which represents the value of each data point.

1. Describe the distribution of each data set.

© 2012 Carnegie Learning

2. Based on the shape of the data, calculate an appropriate measure of central tendency and spread for each data set.

3. What conclusions can you draw from the measure of central tendency and spread you calculated?

4. You are scheduling a flight for an important meeting and you must be there on time. Which airline would you schedule with? Explain your reasoning.

Talk the Talk

When analyzing data it is important to use both graphs and numbers to describe the data.

- The mean describes the average data point.

- The median describes the middle data point.

- Standard deviation describes the spread of the data from the mean.

- The interquartile range (IQR) describes the spread of the data from the median.

- For data that is symmetric, the mean is the most appropriate measure of central tendency and the standard deviation is the most appropriate measure of spread.

- For data that is skewed, the median is the most appropriate measure of central tendency and the IQR is the most appropriate measure of spread.

1. Analyze the box-and-whisker plot shown.

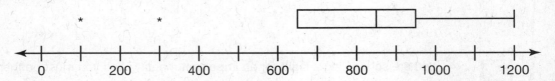

   a. Amina's teacher wants her students to create a list of data values that could result in the box plot shown. Amina states that she can just use the data values graphed as her list. She lists 100, 300, 700, 850, 950, and 1200 as her list. Is Amina's thinking correct? If yes, will this work for all box-and-whisker plots. If no, explain why not.

   b. Create a list of values that when graphed would result in the given box-and-whisker plot shown.

   c. Describe the data using an appropriate measure of central tendency and spread.

2. A data set ranges from 10 to 20. A value of 50 is added to the data set.

    a. Explain how the mean and median are affected by this new value.

    b. Which measure of central tendency and spread would you used to describe the original data set before the new value is added? Explain your reasoning.

    c. Which measure of central tendency and spread would you use to describe the data set after the new value is added? Explain your reasoning.

 Be prepared to share your solutions and methods.

Chapter 8 Summary

- dot plot (8.1)
- discrete data (8.1)
- data distribution (8.1)
- symmetric distribution (8.1)
- skewed right distribution (8.1)
- skewed left distribution (8.1)
- box-and-whisker plot (8.1)
- five number summary (8.1)

- histogram (8.1)
- bin (8.1)
- frequency (8.1)
- continuous data (8.1)
- statistic (8.2)
- measure of central tendency (8.2)
- interquartile range (IQR) (8.3)

- outlier (8.3)
- lower fence (8.3)
- upper fence (8.3)
- standard deviation (8.4)
- normal distribution (8.4)
- stem-and-leaf plot (8.5)
- side-by-side stem-and-leaf plot (8.5)

8.1 Representing and Interpreting Data Displayed on Dot Plots

A dot plot is a graph that shows how discrete data are graphed using a number line. Discrete data are data that have only a finite number of values. Dot plots are best used to organize and display a small number of data points. The overall shape of the graph is called the distribution of the data, which is the way in which the data are spread out or clustered together. The most common distributions are symmetric, skewed right, and skewed left.

Example

A random sample of 30 college students was asked how much time he or she spent on homework during the previous week. The following times (in hours) were obtained:

16, 24, 18, 21, 18, 16, 18, 17, 15, 21, 19, 17, 17, 16, 19, 18, 15, 15, 20, 17, 15, 17, 24, 19, 16, 20, 16, 19, 18, 17

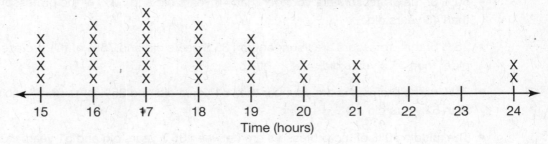

Time Spent on Homework in College

Time (hours)

The data are skewed right.

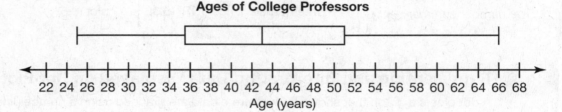

8.1 Representing and Interpreting Data Displayed on Box-and-Whisker Plots

A box-and-whisker plot displays the distribution of data based on a five number summary. The five number summary consists of the minimum value, the first quartile (Q1), the median, the third quartile (Q3), and the maximum value.

Example

The ages of 40 randomly selected college professors are given:

63, 48, 42, 42, 38, 59, 41, 44, 45, 28, 54, 62, 51, 44, 63, 66, 59, 46, 51, 28, 37, 66, 42, 40, 30, 31, 48, 32, 29, 42, 63, 37, 36, 47, 25, 34, 49, 30, 35, 50

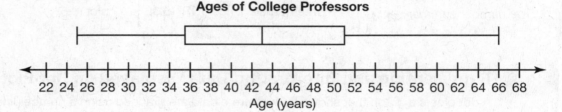

Ages of College Professors

Age (years)

Five-Number Summary:

- Lower bound: 25

- First quartile (Q1): 35.5

- Median: 43

- Third quartile (Q3): 51

- Upper bound: 66

The following information can be determined from the box-and-whisker plot and five number summary:

- 50% of the professors are younger than 43 years old and 50% of the professors are older than 43 years old

- 25% of the professors are younger than 35.5 years old and 75% of the professors are older than 35.5 years old

- 75% of the professors are younger than 51 years old and 25% of the professors are older than 51 years old

- The middle 50% of the professors are between 35.5 years old and 51 years old.

Representing and Interpreting Data Displayed on Histograms

A histogram is a graphical way to display quantitative data using vertical bars. The width of a bar represents an interval of data, and the height of the bar indicates the frequency. Histograms are effective in displaying large amounts of continuous data, which are data that can take any numerical value within a range.

Example

The histogram shows the starting salaries for college graduates based on a random sample of graduates.

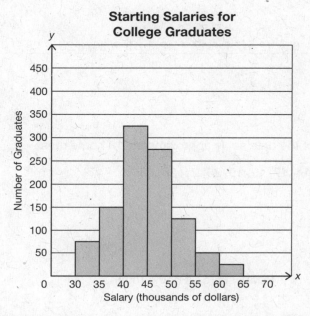

Starting Salaries for College Graduates

The histogram shows that 325 graduates earned at least $40,000 but less than $45,000, 75 graduates earned at least $30,000 but less than $35,000, and only 25 graduates earned at least $60,000 but less than $65,000.

8.2 Calculating the Mean and Median of a Data Set

The measures of central tendency describe the "center" of the data set. Two measures of central tendency that are typically used to describe a set of data are the mean and the median. The arithmetic mean, or mean, represents the sum of the data values divided by the number of values. The median is the middle value of the data values.

Example

The number of home runs hit by each of the 12 batters for the York High School varsity baseball team is 0, 4, 8, 12, 14, 17, 19, 19, 23, 25, 28, and 48.

$$\bar{x} = \frac{\Sigma x}{n}$$

$$\bar{x} = \frac{0 + 4 + 8 + 12 + 14 + 17 + 19 + 19 + 23 + 25 + 28 + 48}{12}$$

$$\bar{x} = \frac{217}{12}$$

$$\bar{x} \approx 18.08\overline{3}$$

The mean of the data set is approximately 18 home runs.

0, 4, 8, 12, 14, 17, 19, 19, 23, 25, 28, 48

$$\text{median} = \frac{17 + 19}{2}$$

$$= \frac{36}{2}$$

$$= 18$$

The median of the data set is 18 home runs.

8.2 Determining the Measure of Center which Best Represents a Data Set

The mean and median are two measures of central tendency which can be used to describe data. The distribution of the data set can be used to determine which measure is more appropriate. If the data is symmetric, the mean is more appropriate. If the data is skewed, the median is more appropriate because it is closer to most of the data points.

Example

The number of home runs hit by each of the 12 batters for the York High School varsity baseball team is represented on the box-and-whisker plot.

Home Runs for York High School Varsity Baseball

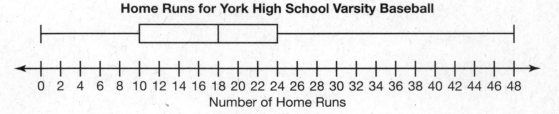

Number of Home Runs

The data are skewed right, so the median would be the most appropriate measure of central tendency to describe the data.

© 2012 Carnegie Learning

Using the Interquartile Range to Determine if a Data Set Contains Outliers

The interquartile range, IQR, measures how far the data are spread out from the median. The IQR gives a realistic representation of the data without being affected by very high or very low data. The IQR is the range of the middle 50 percent of the data and is calculated by subtracting Q3 − Q1. An outlier is a data value that is significantly greater or lesser than the other data values. An outlier is typically calculated by multiplying the IQR by 1.5 and then determining if any data values are more than that distance away from Q1 or Q3.

Example

The data set represents the calorie count of 9 commercial breakfast sandwiches.

212, 361, 201, 203, 227, 224, 188, 192, 198

The five-number summary is:

- Minimum = 188
- First quartile = 195
- Median = 203
- Third quartile = 225.5
- Maximum = 361

IQR = 224 − 195

IQR = 29

The upper and lower fence are:

Lower Fence = Q1 − (IQR · 1.5)   Upper Fence = Q3 + (IQR · 1.5)

= 195 − (29 · 1.5)   = 225.5 + (29 · 1.5)

= 151.5   = 269

There are no values less than 151.5. One value, 361, is greater than 269. Therefore, 361 is an outlier.

8.4 Calculating and Interpreting the Standard Deviation of a Data Set

Standard deviation is a measure of how spread out the data are from the mean. A smaller standard deviation represents data that are more tightly clustered. A larger standard deviation represents data that are more spread out from the mean. The formula to determine standard deviation of a population is represented as:

$$\sigma = \sqrt{\frac{\sum_{i=1}^{n}(x_i - \bar{x})^2}{n}}.$$

A graphing calculator can also be used to determine the standard deviation.

Example

The data sets give the ages of 6 recent U.S. Presidents and the ages of the first 6 U.S. Presidents at their inauguration.

Recent Presidents	
President	Age
Carter	52
Reagan	69
G. H. W. Bush	64
Clinton	46
G. W. Bush	54
Obama	47

First Presidents	
President	Age
Washington	57
J. Adams	61
Jefferson	57
Madison	57
Monroe	58
J. Q. Adams	57

$\sigma \approx 8.48$ $\sigma \approx 1.46$

The ages of the 6 recent U.S. Presidents are more spread out than the ages of the first 6 Presidents because that data set has a higher standard deviation.

8.4 Graphing Standard Deviation for a Normal Distribution of Data

When you determine the standard deviation of a data set, you can represent it graphically in most normal distributions. A normal distribution is a function of a data distribution of many data points that form a bell-shaped curve.

By graphing the standard deviation, you can quickly determine which data set has a greater or lesser standard deviation. If a data set has a greater standard deviation, the data are more spread out from the mean in most normal distributions. If a data set has a lesser standard deviation, the data will be more clustered about the mean.

Example

The graph representing the ages of the 6 most recent U.S Presidents is more spread out from the mean. The graph representing the ages of the first 6 U.S. presidents is clustered about the mean.

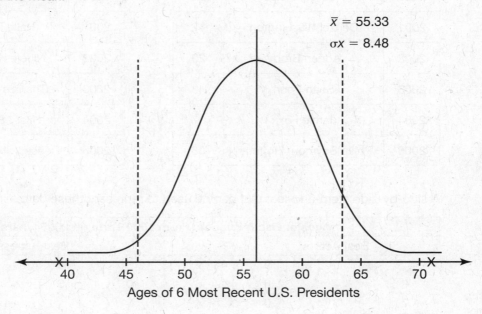

$\bar{x} = 55.33$

$\sigma x = 8.48$

Ages of 6 Most Recent U.S. Presidents

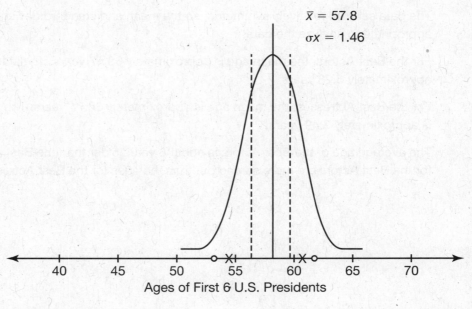

$\bar{x} = 57.8$

$\sigma x = 1.46$

Ages of First 6 U.S. Presidents

8.5 **Determining which Measure of Center and Spread is Most Appropriate to Describe a Data Set**

A stem-and-leaf plot is a graphical method used to represent ordered numerical data. A side-by-side stem-and-leaf plot allows a comparison of two data sets.

Example

The data sets give the ages of Oscar winners from 1999 through 2005 at the time of the award.

Year	Best Actor	Age
1999	Kevin Spacey	40
2000	Russell Crowe	36
2001	Denzel Washington	47
2002	Adrien Brody	29
2003	Sean Penn	43
2004	Jamie Foxx	37
2005	Philip Seymour Hoffman	38

Year	Best Actress	Age
1999	Hilary Swank	25
2000	Julia Roberts	33
2001	Halle Berry	35
2002	Nicole Kidman	35
2003	Charlize Theron	28
2004	Hilary Swank	30
2005	Reese Witherspoon	29

A side-by-side stem-and-leaf plot can be used to represent these data sets.

Ages of Oscar Winners From 1999 Through 2005 (years)							
Best Actors				Best Actresses			
		9	2	5	8	9	
8	7	6	3	0	3	5	5
7	3	0	4				

The data sets are relatively symmetric, so the mean and standard deviation are more appropriate to analyze the data.

For the Best Actors, the mean age is approximately 38.57 years. The standard deviation is approximately 5.26 years.

For the Best Actresses, the mean age is approximately 30.71 years. The standard deviation is approximately 3.49 years.

The average age of the Best Actors is about 8 years older than the Best Actresses. The ages for the Best Actors are more spread out than the ages for the Best Actresses.

Correlation and Residuals

9

Having pets is not only fun, but it can be good for your health, too. Studies show that there is a correlation between pet ownership and blood pressure, mood, and the ability of your immune system to fight off disease!

Like a Glove
Least Squares Regression

LEARNING GOALS

In this lesson, you will:

- Determine and interpret the least squares regression equation for a data set using a formula.
- Use interpolation to make predictions about data.
- Use extrapolation to make predictions about data.

KEY TERMS

- interpolation
- extrapolation
- least squares regression line

How do the nerve cells in your brain communicate with each other? Signals have to be sent all across the brain—from your eyes to your occipital lobe in the back of your brain, from your ears to your temporal lobe, and so on. How does this happen?

In a sense, your nerve cells actually communicate using shapes. When a nerve cell is activated, it releases chemical messengers called neurotransmitters. These messengers have specific shapes, and they fit like keys into the locks on the next cell receiving the message. This message tells the next cell what to do.

And this process happens trillions of times per day!

The table shows the percent of all recorded music sales that came from music stores for the years 1998 through 2004.

Year	1998	1999	2000	2001	2002	2003	2004
Percent of Total Sales from Music Stores	50.8	44.5	42.4	39.7	36.8	33.2	32.5

1. Represent the data as ordered pairs with the percent of total sales that came from music stores as a function of time. Let x represent the number of years since 1998.

If 1998 is the first year, do I represent it as 1 or 0?

2. Use your calculator to construct a scatter plot of the data. Sketch the scatter plot on the coordinate plane. Label the axes.

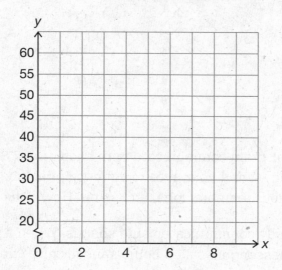

3. Describe any patterns you see in the data.

4. Use a graphing calculator to calculate the linear regression equation for the data. Round the values to the nearest hundredth.

5. Interpret the equation of the line in terms of the problem situation.

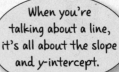

When you're talking about a line, it's all about the slope and y-intercept.

If there is a linear association between the independent and dependent variables of a data set, you can use a linear regression to make predictions within the data set. Using a linear regression to make predictions within the data set is called **interpolation**.

6. Use your equation to predict the percent of total music sales that came from music stores in the year 2000.

7. Compare the predicted percent in 2000 to the actual percent in 2000.

8. Use your equation to predict the percent of total music sales that came from music stores in 2003.

9. Compare the predicted percent in 2003 to the actual percent in 2003.

10. Do you think a prediction made using interpolation will always be close to the actual value? Explain your reasoning.

To make predictions for values of *x* that are outside of the data set is called **extrapolation**.

11. Use the equation to predict the percent of total music sales that would come from music stores in:

  a. 2010.

  b. 2020.

  c. 1900.

12. Are these predictions reasonable based on the problem situation?

PROBLEM 2 Best vs. Good

1. Suppose a data set is composed of the points (1, 3), (−3, −7), and (5, 7) on a coordinate plane.

Collinear points are points that are located on the same line.

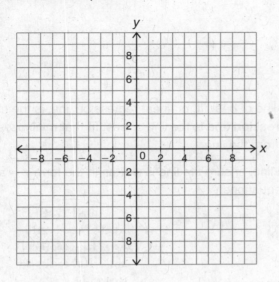

2. Are these points collinear? How can you tell?

3. Determine the equation of a line passing through the points at (1, 3) and (5, 7). Graph this line on the coordinate plane.

4. Determine and graph the equation of a line passing through the points at:

   a. (−3, −7) and (5, 7).

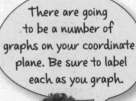

There are going to be a number of graphs on your coordinate plane. Be sure to label each as you graph.

   b. (−3, −7) and (1, 3).

5. Would you consider any of the three lines you just graphed to be a line that "best fits" the three points? If yes, explain your reasoning. If no, describe where the line of best fit should be drawn.

One method to determine the line of best fit, or linear regression line, is the method of least squares. A **least squares regression line** is the line of best fit that minimizes the squares of the distances of the points from the line.

For a least squares regression line, ensure the line is written in the form $y = ax + b$. To calculate a and b, use the equations:

$$a = \frac{n\Sigma xy - (\Sigma x)(\Sigma y)}{n\Sigma x^2 - (\Sigma x)^2}$$

$$b = \frac{(\Sigma y)(\Sigma x^2) - (\Sigma x)(\Sigma xy)}{n\Sigma x^2 - (\Sigma x)^2}$$

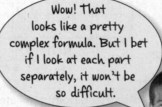

Wow! That looks like a pretty complex formula. But I bet if I look at each part separately, it won't be so difficult.

where x represents all x-values from the data set,
y represents all y-values from the data set, and
n represents the number of coordinate pairs in the data set.

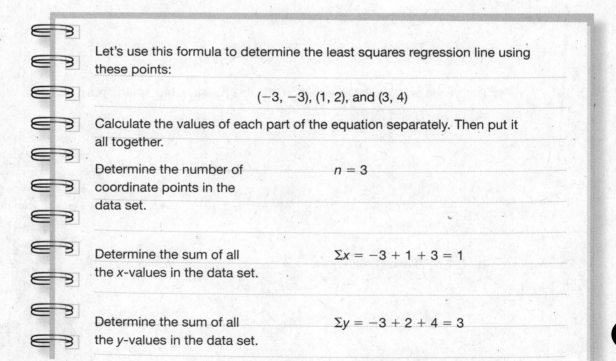

Let's use this formula to determine the least squares regression line using these points:

$$(-3, -3), (1, 2), \text{ and } (3, 4)$$

Calculate the values of each part of the equation separately. Then put it all together.

Determine the number of coordinate points in the data set.

$$n = 3$$

Determine the sum of all the x-values in the data set.

$$\Sigma x = -3 + 1 + 3 = 1$$

Determine the sum of all the y-values in the data set.

$$\Sigma y = -3 + 2 + 4 = 3$$

Determine the sum of the squares of the *x*-values.	$\Sigma x^2 = (-3)^2 + 1^2 + 3^2 = 19$
Determine the sum of the products of each coordinate pair.	$\Sigma xy = (-3 \cdot -3) + (1 \cdot 2) + (3 \cdot 4)$ $= 23$
Determine the square of the sum of the *x*-values.	$(\Sigma x)^2 = 1^2 = 1$
Insert each part into the formulas to solve for the values of *a* and *b*.	$a = \dfrac{n\Sigma xy - (\Sigma x)(\Sigma y)}{n\Sigma x^2 - (\Sigma x)^2}$ $= \dfrac{(3)(23) - (1)(3)}{(3)(19) - 1} = \dfrac{66}{56}$ $a \approx 1.18$ $b = \dfrac{(\Sigma y)(\Sigma x^2) - (\Sigma x)(\Sigma xy)}{n\Sigma x^2 - (\Sigma x)^2}$ $= \dfrac{(3)(19) - (1)(23)}{(3)(19) - 1} = \dfrac{34}{56}$ $b \approx 0.61$

6. What is the equation of the line of best fit for the points given in the worked example?

7. Margie calculated the least squares linear regression for the worked example.

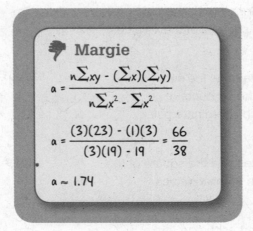

Margie

$$a = \frac{n\sum xy - (\sum x)(\sum y)}{n\sum x^2 - \sum x^2}$$

$$a = \frac{(3)(23) - (1)(3)}{(3)(19) - 19} = \frac{66}{38}$$

$$a \approx 1.74$$

Explain to Margie why her solution is incorrect.

8. Calculate the least squares linear regression using the points from Question 1.

    a. Calculate the sums and values for each part of the equation.

    b. Calculate the values of a and b.

    c. Write the equation of the line of best fit.

    d. Graph the line on the coordinate plane in Question 1. Does this line "fit" the data better than the others? Explain your reasoning.

PROBLEM 3 One More Time

 The table shown displays the median weekly earnings for U.S. workers according to the number of years of schooling they received.

Years of Schooling	Median Weekly Earnings (dollars)
11	444
12	626
13	712
14	767
16	1038
18	1272
22	1510

1. Calculate the equation of the least squares regression line. Define your variables.

2. Interpret the least squares regression equation in terms of this problem situation.

3. Predict the weekly earnings of a worker with 12 years of schooling using the least squares regression equation. How does this compare to the actual earnings?

 4. Predict the weekly earnings of a doctor with 25 years of schooling using the least squares regression equation. How does this compare to the actual earnings?

Talk the Talk

 1. Why are predictions made by extrapolation more likely to be inaccurate than predictions made by interpolation?

 Be prepared to share your solutions and methods.

Gotta Keep It Correlatin'
Correlation

LEARNING GOALS

In this lesson, you will:

- Determine the correlation coefficient using a formula.
- Interpret the correlation coefficient for a set of data.

"New Study Links Dark Chocolate to Heart Health." "Video Games Shown to Boost I.Q." "College Graduates Live Longer, New Study Finds."

You have probably seen or heard headlines similar to these in magazines, on TV, and online. Each one of these headlines is the result of a correlational study. In a correlational study, researchers compare two variables to see how they are associated. They do this through the use of surveys or even by researching documents such as medical records.

What methods do you think researchers could have used to produce the results mentioned in the headlines above?

PROBLEM 1 Associate, Formulate, Correlate!

 Recall that data comparing two variables can show a positive association, a negative association, or no association.

1. Describe the type of association between the independent and dependent variables shown on each scatterplot. Then, draw a line of best fit for each, if possible.

a.

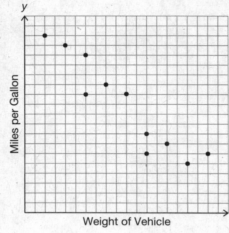

b.

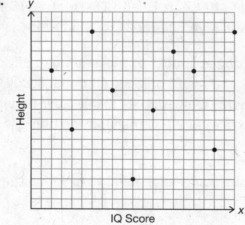

c.

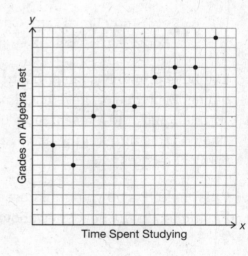

A measure of how well a linear regression line fits a set of data is called correlation. The correlation coefficient is a value between −1 and 1 which indicates how close the data are to forming a straight line. The closer the correlation coefficient is to 1 or −1, the stronger the linear relationship is between the two variables. The variable r is used to represent the correlation coefficient.

I remember that the correlation coefficient either falls between −1 and 0 if the data show a negative association, or between 0 and 1 if the data show a positive association.

2. Determine whether the points in each scatter plot have a positive correlation, a negative correlation, or no correlation. Four possible r-values are given. Circle the r-value you think is most appropriate. Explain your reasoning for each.

a.

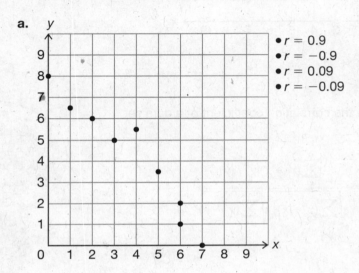

- $r = 0.9$
- $r = -0.9$
- $r = 0.09$
- $r = -0.09$

The closer the r-value gets to 0, the less of a linear relationship there is in the data!

b.

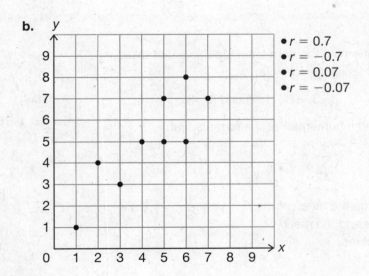

- $r = 0.7$
- $r = -0.7$
- $r = 0.07$
- $r = -0.07$

c.

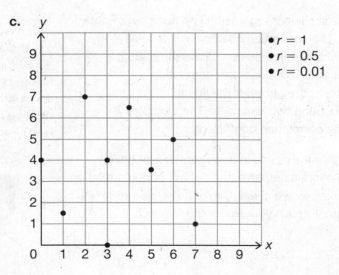

- $r = 1$
- $r = 0.5$
- $r = 0.01$

You can calculate the correlation coefficient of a data set using this formula:

$$r = \frac{\sum_{i=1}^{n}(x_i - \bar{x})(y_i - \bar{y})}{\sqrt{\sum_{i=1}^{n}(x_i - \bar{x})^2}\sqrt{\sum_{i=1}^{n}(y_i - \bar{y})^2}}$$

Most of the pieces of this formula look familiar. I think we used them in the formula for standard deviation!

Let's determine the correlation coefficient of this data set using the formula.

$$(-3, -3), (1, 2) \text{ and } (3, 4)$$

Look at the numerator of the formula first.

$$\sum_{i=1}^{n}(x_i - \bar{x})(y_i - \bar{y})$$

Determine the mean of the x-values and the mean of the y-values.

$$\bar{x} = \frac{1}{3} \qquad \bar{y} = 1$$

Keep in mind that the notation $\sum_{i=1}^{n}$ just tells you that you will be determining the sum of all the data values.

© 2012 Carnegie Learning

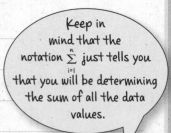

© 2012 Carnegie Learning

Notice these differences are used throughout the formula.

Determine the difference between each data value and the mean for both the x-coordinates and the y-coordinates.

$(x_i - \bar{x})$

$\left(-3 - \dfrac{1}{3}\right) = -\dfrac{10}{3}$

$\left(1 - \dfrac{1}{3}\right) = \dfrac{2}{3}$

$\left(3 - \dfrac{1}{3}\right) = \dfrac{8}{3}$

$(y_i - \bar{y})$

$(-3 - 1) = -4$

$(2 - 1) = 1$

$(4 - 1) = 3$

Determine the product of the differences in each pair. Then, determine the sum of those products. This is your numerator.

$$\sum_{i=1}^{n}(x_i - \bar{x})(y_i - \bar{y})$$

$\left. \begin{array}{l} \left(-\dfrac{10}{3} \cdot -4\right) = \dfrac{40}{3} \\[2mm] \left(\dfrac{2}{3} \cdot 1\right) = \dfrac{2}{3} \\[2mm] \left(\dfrac{8}{3} \cdot 3\right) = 8 \end{array} \right\}$ $\dfrac{40}{3} + \dfrac{2}{3} + 8 = 22$

Now let's analyze the denominator of the formula.

$$\sqrt{\sum_{i=1}^{n}(x_i - \bar{x})^2}\ \sqrt{\sum_{i=1}^{n}(y_i - \bar{y})^2}$$

Determine the sum of the squares of the differences between each value and its mean.

$(x_i - \bar{x})^2$

$\left. \begin{array}{l} \left(-\dfrac{10}{3}\right)^2 = \dfrac{100}{9} \\[2mm] \left(\dfrac{2}{3}\right)^2 = \dfrac{4}{9} \\[2mm] \left(\dfrac{8}{3}\right)^2 = \dfrac{64}{9} \end{array} \right\} = \dfrac{56}{3}$

$(y_i - \bar{y})^2$

$\left. \begin{array}{l} (-4)^2 = 16 \\ (1)^2 = 1 \\ (3)^2 = 9 \end{array} \right\} = 26$

Determine the square root of each sum.

$$\sqrt{\sum_{i=1}^{n}(x_i - \bar{x})^2} \qquad \sqrt{\sum_{i=1}^{n}(y_i - \bar{y})^2}$$

$\sqrt{\dfrac{56}{3}} \approx 4.32$ $\qquad$ $\sqrt{26} \approx 5.099$

Determine the product of these two values. This is your denominator.

$$\sqrt{\sum_{i=1}^{n}(x_i - \bar{x})^2}\ \sqrt{\sum_{i=1}^{n}(y_i - \bar{y})^2}$$

$(4.32)(5.099) = 22.02768$

3. Put the pieces together. Determine the correlation coefficient of the data set.

 4. Interpret the correlation coefficient of the data set.

PROBLEM 2 The Doctor Will See You Now

 The Center for Disease Control collected data on the percent of children, aged 12 to 19, that were considered obese between the years 1971 and 2007. The data are given in the table.

Year	Percent of Obese Children
1971	6.4
1976	5.0
1988	10.5
1999	14.8
2001	16.7
2003	17.4
2005	17.8
2007	18.1

What do you notice as you read through the data?

1. Identify the independent and dependent quantities in this problem situation.

2. Construct a scatter plot of the data using your graphing calculator.

   a. Sketch the scatter plot. Label the axes.

   b. Do you think a linear regression equation would best describe this situation? Explain your reasoning.

3. Use a graphing calculator to determine whether a line of best fit is appropriate for these data.

   a. Determine and interpret the linear regression equation.

Wait! There's an r and an r^2 value on my calculator. Which one do I use?

   b. Determine the correlation coefficient.

   c. Would a line of best fit be appropriate for this data set? Explain your reasoning.

4. The amount of antibiotic that remains in your body over a period of time varies from one drug to the next. The table given shows the amount of Antibiotic X that remains in your body over a period of two days.

Time (hours)	0	6	12	18	24	30	36	42	48
Amount of Antibiotic X in Body (mg)	60	36	22	13	7.8	4.7	2.8	1.7	1

a. Determine and interpret a linear regression equation for this data set.

b. Determine and interpret the correlation coefficient of this data set.

c. Does it seem appropriate to use a line of best fit? If no, explain your reasoning. If yes, determine and interpret the least squares regression equation.

d. Sketch a scatter plot of the data.

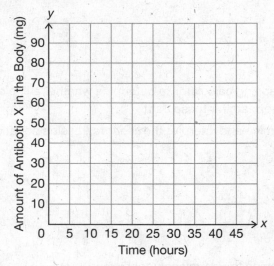

e. Look at the graph of the data. Do you still agree with your answer to part (c)? Explain your reasoning.

  Be prepared to share your solutions and methods.

The Residual Effect
Creating Residual Plots

LEARNING GOALS

In this lesson, you will:

- Create residual plots.
- Analyze the shapes of residual plots.

KEY TERMS

- residual
- residual plot

Maybe you once made a lot of spelling mistakes in an essay that you wrote. The next time you wrote an essay, you made sure to do a spell check (or use a dictionary). Maybe you noticed that you missed a lot of free throws in basketball games. You decided to practice your free throw shooting to improve. Maybe you told a joke that hurt your friend's feelings. You remembered to be more sensitive around him or her in the future.

We all learn from our mistakes. In mathematics, too, you can learn a lot about data by looking at error. That's what this lesson is all about!

PROBLEM 1 Hit the Brakes!

You have used the shape of data in a scatter plot and the correlation coefficient to help you determine whether a linear model is an appropriate model for a data set. For some data sets, these measures may not provide enough information to determine if a linear model is most appropriate.

In order to be a safe driver, there are a lot of things to consider. For example, you have to leave enough distance between your car and the car in front of you in case you need to stop suddenly. The table shows the braking distance for a particular car when traveling at different speeds.

Speed (mph)	Braking Distance (feet)
30	48
40	80
50	120
60	180
70	240
80	320

1. Construct a scatter plot of the data.

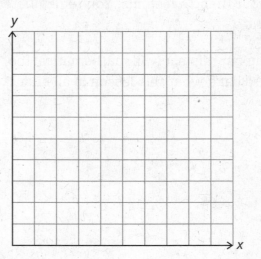

2. Based on the shape of the scatter plot, do you think a linear model is appropriate? Explain your reasoning.

3. Calculate the line of best fit for the data. Write a function $d(s)$ to represent the line of best fit.

4. Interpret the function in terms of the problem situation.

 5. Determine and interpret the correlation coefficient.

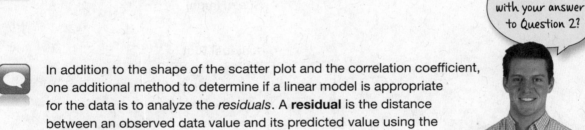

Do you still agree with your answer to Question 2?

In addition to the shape of the scatter plot and the correlation coefficient, one additional method to determine if a linear model is appropriate for the data is to analyze the *residuals*. A **residual** is the distance between an observed data value and its predicted value using the regression equation.

 6. Complete the table to determine the residuals for the braking distance data.

Speed (mph)	Observed Braking Distance (feet)	Predicted Braking Distance (feet)	Residual Value Observed Value – Predicted
30	48		
40	80		
50	120		
60	180		
70	240		
80	320		

Now, let's analyze the relationship between the observed braking distances and the predicted braking distances using graphs. The graph of the line of best fit for the observed braking distances is shown.

Use the graph to answer Questions 7–9 and then construct a residual plot.

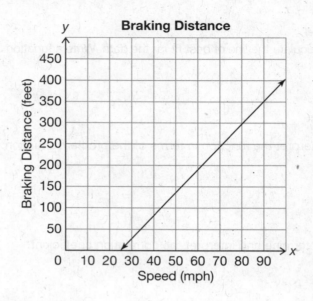

Braking Distance

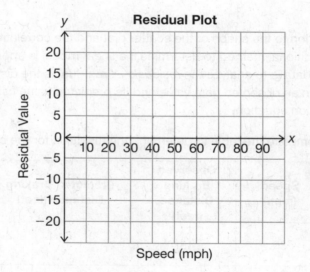

Residual Plot

7. For each data point, there is a residual equal to the difference between the observed measured braking distance and the value predicted by the line of best fit.

   a. Plot each observed value on the Braking Distance graph.

   b. Connect each observed value to its predicted value using a vertical line.

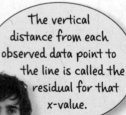

The vertical distance from each observed data point to the line is called the residual for that x-value.

8. Examine the scatter plot and the residual values.

    a. When does a residual have a positive value?

    b. When does a residual have a negative value?

The residual data can now be used to create a *residual plot*. A **residual plot** is a scatter plot of the independent variable on the *x*-axis and the residuals on the *y*-axis.

The residual plot displays the residual values you calculated in the table.

    9. Construct a residual plot of the speed and braking distance data.

10. Interpret each residual in the context of the problem situation.

- At 30 mph, the braking distance is 20 feet greater than predicted.

- At 40 mph, the braking distance is _____.

- At 50 mph, the braking distance is _____.

- At 60 mph, the braking distance is _____.

- At 70 mph, the braking distance is _____.

- At 80 mph, the braking distance is _____.

11. What pattern, if any, do you notice in the residuals?

The shape of the residual plot can be useful to determine whether there may be a more appropriate model other than a linear model for a data set.

If a residual plot results in no identifiable pattern or a flat pattern, then the data may be linearly related. If there is a pattern in the residual plot, the data may not be linearly related. Even if the data are not linearly related, the data may still have some other type of non-linear relationship.

A residual plot can't tell you whether a linear model is appropriate. It can only tell you that there may be a model other than linear that is more appropriate.

Residual Plots Indicating a Possible Linear Relationship

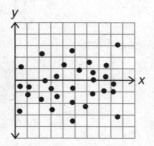

There is no pattern in the residual plot. The data may be linearly related.

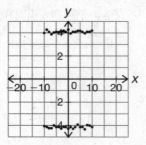

There is a flat pattern in the residual plot. The data may be linearly related.

Residual Plots Indicating a Non-Linear Relationship

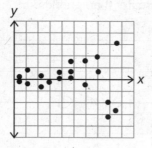

There is a pattern in the residual plot. As the x-value increases, the residuals become more spread out. The data may not be linearly related.

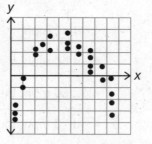

There is a pattern in the residual plot. The residuals form a curved pattern. The data may not be linearly related.

12. Interpret the residual plot for the braking distance data.

13. Anita thinks the residual plot looks like it forms a curve. She says that this means the data must be more quadratic than linear. Is Anita correct? Why or why not?

Keep in mind that this only represents a portion of the entire data set.

14. Is the least squares regression line you determined in Question 3 a good fit for this data set? Explain your reasoning.

PROBLEM 2   Attendance Matters

Over the last semester, Mr. Finch kept track of the number of student absences. Now that the semester is over, he wants to see if there is a linear relationship between the number of absences and a student's grade for the semester. The data he collected are given in the table.

Student	Number of Absences	Grade (percent)
James	0	95
Tiona	5	73
Mikala	3	84
Paul	1	92
Danasia	2	92
Erik	3	80
Rachael	10	65
Cheyanne	0	90
Chen	6	70
Javier	1	88

1. Construct a scatter plot of the data.

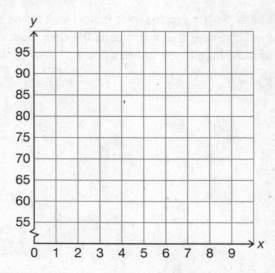

2. Describe the association shown in the scatter plot.

3. Determine the equation of the least squares regression line. Interpret the equation for this problem situation.

4. Determine and interpret the correlation coefficient.

5. Determine the residuals for the data. Interpret each residual.

Student	Number of Absences	Algebra Grade (percent)	Predicted Value	Residual	Interpretation
James	0	95	92.6	2.4	For 0 absences the actual grade is 2.4% greater than predicted.
Tiona	5	73			
Mikala	3	84			
Paul	1	92			
Danasia	2	92			
Erik	3	80			
Rachael	10	65			
Cheyanne	0	90			
Chen	6	70			
Javier	1	88			

6. Construct and interpret a residual plot of the data.

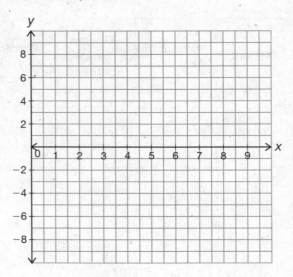

Talk the Talk

1. Explain what you can conclude from each residual plot about whether a linear model is appropriate.

a.

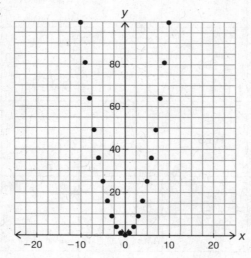

b.

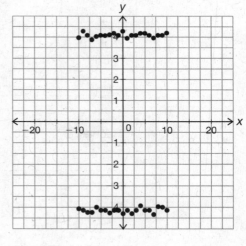

c.

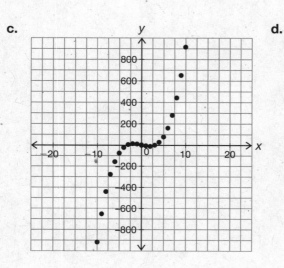

d.

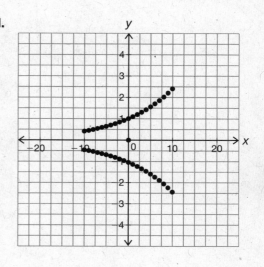

2. How would you describe the difference between "line of best fit" and "most appropriate model"?

Be prepared to share your solutions and methods.

To Fit or Not To Fit?
That Is The Question!
Using Residual Plots

LEARNING GOALS

In this lesson, you will:

- Use scatter plots and correlation coefficients to determine whether a linear regression is a good fit for data.
- Use residual plots to help determine whether a linear regression is the best fit for data.

Have you ever had to make a big decision? One characteristic of a "big" decision is that you often need to use many different sources of information to tackle it.

What kind of car should you drive? To make this decision, you have to think about finances, safety, how you will use the car, gas mileage, and so on. What college should I attend? For this big decision, you might think about the reputation of the school, its distance from home, cost, and so on.

In this lesson, you will learn that even in mathematics we often need multiple sources of information to help us make the best decisions.

The table shows the number of franchised car dealerships in the United States since 1990. Sandy wants to know if the relationship between the time since 1990 and the number of car dealerships can be best modeled with a linear function.

Time Since 1990	Number of Franchised New Car Dealerships
0	24,825
10	22,250
13	21,650
14	21,640
15	21,495
16	21,200
17	20,770
18	20,010
19	18,460
20	17,700

What does this table tell you?

1. Construct a scatter plot of the data on the coordinate plane shown.

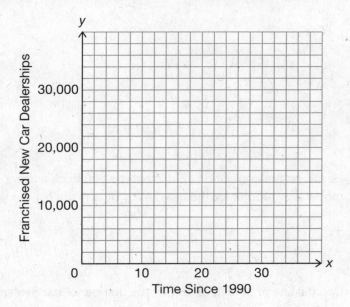

2. Based on the shape of the scatter plot, do you think a linear model is a good fit for the data? Why or why not?

3. Calculate the line of best fit for the data. Write a function $c(t)$ to represent the line of best fit. Interpret the line of best fit in terms of this problem situation. Then, graph the line of best fit on the same coordinate plane as the scatter plot.

Don't always trust what you see. A little more analysis is in order!

4. Determine and interpret the correlation coefficient.

Does the correlation coefficient change your opinion on whether a linear model is good?

5. Based on the correlation coefficient, do you think a linear model is a good fit for the data? Why or why not?

6. Use the line of best fit to predict the number of car dealerships in each year.

a. 1995

b. 2015

c. 2025

7. Calculate and interpret the residuals for the data.

Time Since 1990	Number of Franchised New Car Dealerships	Predicted Value	Residual	Interpretation
0	24,825			
10	22,250			
13	21,650			
14	21,640			
15	21,495			
16	21,200			
17	20,770			
18	20,010			
19	18,460			
20	17,700			

You can use a graphing calculator to plot residuals.

 You can use a graphing calculator to show how the actual values of a data set differ from the values predicted by a linear regression.

Step 1: Enter the data values, press **STAT**, select **CALC**, and then select **4:LinReg(ax+b)**. Scroll down to **Store RegEQ:** Press **VARS**, select **Y-VARS** at the top, and then press **1** two times. Then select **Calculate**.

Step 2: Press **STAT** and then **1**. Then press the right arrow key until you get to **L6**. Press the up arrow key and then the right arrow key.

Step 3: If the list of residuals is not already displayed, press **2ND** and then **LIST**. Select **7↓RESID**. Press **ENTER**.

Step 4: Press **2ND**, **STAT PLOT**, **1** to turn on the plot and choose the type of display for the graph. Press **ZOOM** and then **9** to show the data and the line of best fit.

You can also use a graphing calculator to graph a residual plot.

Step 5: Press **STAT** and then **1**. Copy the data from the residuals list to L6. You can round the data values if you wish.

Step 6: Press **2ND**, **STAT PLOT**, and then **1**. Make sure L1 is entered next to **Xlist** and L6 is entered next to **Ylist**.

Step 7: Press **STAT**, select **CALC**, and then select **2:2-Var Stats**. Make sure L1 is entered next to **Xlist** and L6 is entered next to **Ylist**. Select **Calculate** and then press **ZOOM**, **9** to see the residual plot.

© 2012 Carnegie Learning

8. Create a residual plot of the data using a graphing calculator on the coordinate plane shown.

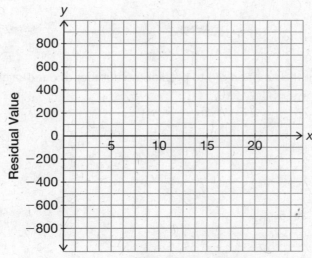

Time Since 1990

9. Based on the residual plot, do you think a linear model is a good fit for the data? Why or why not?

Remember that a residual plot can't tell you whether a linear model is appropriate. It can only tell you that there may be something better.

You used the shape of the scatter plot, the correlation coefficient, and the residual plot to determine whether a linear model was a good fit for the data. Let's consider a different function family.

10. Graph the function $q(t) = -15.657t^2 - 1.2709t + 24{,}650$ on the same coordinate plane as the scatter plot.

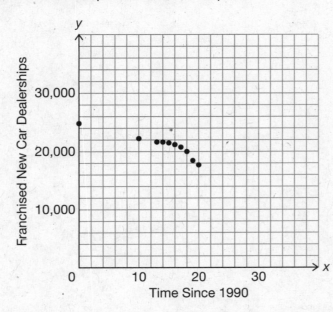

Time Since 1990

11. Do you think the function $q(t)$ is a better fit for the data than the line of best fit? Explain your reasoning.

12. Use the function $q(t)$ to predict the number of car dealerships in each year.

    a. 1995

    b. 2015

    c. 2025

13. Compare the predictions using the line of best fit $c(t)$ and the predictions using the function $q(t)$. What do you notice?

Talk the Talk

1. Explain how you can use each to help determine if a linear model is an appropriate fit for a data set.

   a. Shape of scatter plot

   b. Correlation coefficient

   c. Residual plot

2. Why is it important to use more than one measure to determine if a linear model is a good fit for a data set?

3. Do you think determining the best fit for a data set is more important for interpolation or extrapolation? Explain your reasoning.

 Be prepared to share your solutions and methods.

Who Are You? Who? Who?
Causation vs. Correlation

LEARNING GOALS

In this lesson, you will:

- Understand the difference between correlation and causation.
- Understand necessary conditions.
- Understand sufficient conditions.

KEY TERMS

- causation
- necessary condition
- sufficient condition
- common response
- confounding variable

Contrary to what you might see on TV, forensic scientists don't always catch the criminals. It is a complex science, and often a forensic team is not able to gather enough evidence to prove to a court that a criminal should be charged with a crime. In many cases, the criminal or criminals aren't found at all.

Some investigations get shelved for long periods of time until new evidence or information arrives. These are often referred to as "cold cases." DNA evidence has made it possible to solve many cold cases that were shelved before DNA testing was used. In 2011, DNA evidence was used to convict a man for a crime he committed 43 years earlier!

PROBLEM 1 Experiments and Conclusions

Students in an Atlanta classroom were asked to design an experiment, gather data, determine the correlation between the quantities, and draw conclusions about their results. For each experiment, decide whether the students' conclusions are supported by their results or are in error. Explain your reasoning.

1. One group of students found that the number of people that carried umbrellas is highly correlated to the days that it rained. Their conclusion was that people carrying umbrellas caused it to rain.

2. Another group found that the number of snow cones sold by a sidewalk vendor is highly correlated to the temperature. They concluded that the number of snow cones sold causes higher temperatures.

3. A third group found that high rates of school absenteeism are correlated to lower grades. They concluded that high rates of school absenteeism caused students to have lower grades.

© 2012 Carnegie Learning

PROBLEM 2 Proving Causation

The experiments in Problem 1, *Experiments and Conclusions,* showed us that even though two quantities are correlated, this does not mean that one quantity caused the other. This is one of the most misunderstood and misapplied uses of statistics.

Causation is when one event causes a second event. A correlation is a **necessary condition** for causation, but a correlation is not a **sufficient condition** for causation. While determining a correlation is straightforward, using statistics to establish causation is very difficult.

1. Many medical studies have tried to prove that smoking causes lung cancer.

   a. Is smoking a necessary condition for lung cancer? Why or why not?

   b. Is smoking a sufficient condition for lung cancer? Why or why not?

   c. Is there a correlation between people who smoke and people who get lung cancer? Explain your reasoning.

   d. Is it true that smoking causes lung cancer? If so, how was it proven?

2. It is often said that teenage drivers cause automobile accidents.

   a. Is being a teenage driver a necessary condition to have an automobile accident? Why or why not?

   b. Is being a teenage driver a sufficient condition to have an automobile accident? Why or why not?

   c. Is there a correlation between teenage drivers and automobile accidents? Explain your reasoning.

   d. Is it true that teenage drivers cause automobile accidents? Explain your reasoning.

3. Let's revisit the example of school absenteeism causing poor performance in school. A correlation between the independent variable of days absent to the dependent variable of grades makes sense. However, this alone does not prove causation. In order to prove that the number of days that a student is absent causes the student to get poor grades, we would need to conduct more controlled experiments.

  a. List several ways that you could design additional experiments to attempt to prove this assertion.

  b. Will any of these experiments prove the assertion? Explain your reasoning.

4. There are two relationships that are often mistaken for causation. A **common response** is when some other reason may cause the same result. A **confounding variable** is when there are other variables that are unknown or unobserved.

  a. In North Carolina, the number of shark attacks increases when the temperature increases. Therefore, a temperature increase appears to cause sharks to attack. List two or more common responses that could also cause this result.

  b. A company claims that their weight loss pill caused people to lose 20 pounds when following the accompanying exercise program. List two or more confounding variables that could have had an effect on this claim.

5. For each, decide whether the correlation implies causation. List reasons why or why not.

   a. The number of cavities in the teeth of elementary school children is highly negatively correlated to the students' reading vocabulary.

   b. The number of homeless people who sleep in shelters is negatively correlated to the number of ice cream cones sold.

Talk the Talk

1. Look in magazines or online for stories that report on correlational studies. Identify the variables being compared, the type of association, and the method used (if mentioned) to gather the data.

2. For each of your stories, identify possible confounding variables or common responses.

Be prepared to share your solutions and methods.

Chapter 9 Summary

- interpolation (9.1)
- extrapolation (9.1)
- least squares regression line (9.1)
- residual (9.3)
- residual plot (9.3)
- causation (9.5)
- necessary condition (9.5)
- sufficient condition (9.5)
- common response (9.5)
- confounding variable (9.5)

9

9.1 Interpreting a Linear Regression Equation

If there is a linear association between the independent and dependent variables, a linear regression can be used to make predictions within the data set. Using a linear regression to make predictions within the data set is called interpolation. To make predictions outside the data set is called extrapolation.

Example

Nina makes keychain charms that she sells to her classmates. She tracked the sales of her charms over the months since she began selling them.

Month	1	2	3	4	5	6
Charms Sold	3	7	8	12	17	24

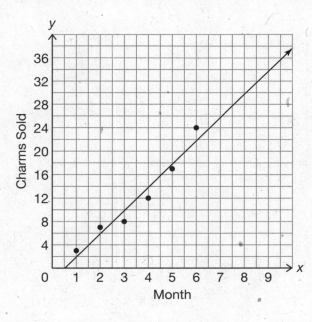

The linear regression equation is:

$y = 3.97x - 2.07$.

Using the equation to interpolate, Nina should sell about 14 charms in the fourth month.

$$y = 3.97x - 2.07$$
$$= 3.97(4) - 2.07$$
$$= 13.81$$

Using the equation to extrapolate, Nina should sell about 30 charms in the eighth month.

$$y = 3.97x - 2.07$$
$$= 3.97(8) - 2.07$$
$$= 29.69$$

9.1 Determining a Least Squares Regression Equation

A least squares regression line is the line of best fit that minimizes the squares of the distances of the points from the line. A least squares regression line is written in the form $y = ax + b$. To calculate a and b, use these formulas:

$$a = \frac{n\Sigma xy - (\Sigma x)(\Sigma y)}{n\Sigma x^2 - (\Sigma x)^2} \qquad b = \frac{(\Sigma y)(\Sigma x^2) - (\Sigma x)(\Sigma xy)}{n\Sigma x^2 - (\Sigma x)^2}$$

where x represents all x-values from the data set, y represents all y-values from the data set, and n represents the number of coordinate pairs in the data set. A graphing calculator can also be used to determine a least squares regression equation.

Example

Data set: $(-4, -3)$, $(1, 2)$, $(5, 4)$, $(8, 8)$

The equation of the line of best fit is $y = 0.87x + 0.57$.

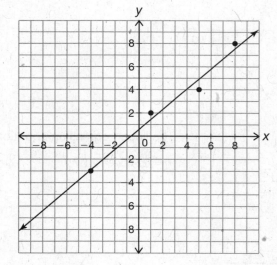

Analyzing Correlation Using the Correlation Coefficient

A measure of how well a linear regression line fits a set of data is called correlation. When dealing with regression equations, the variable r is used to represent a value called the correlation coefficient. The correlation coefficient indicates how close the data are to forming a straight line. The correlation coefficient either falls between -1 and 0 if the data show a negative association or between 0 and 1 if the data show a positive association. The closer the r-value gets to 0, the less of a linear relationship there is in the data.

Example

Possible choices for r:

- $r = -0.88$

- $r = -0.11$

- $r = 0.88$

- $r = 0.11$

The data has a positive correlation. Because of this the value of r must be positive. Also, the data are fairly close to forming a straight line so of the choices, $r = 0.88$ would be the most accurate.

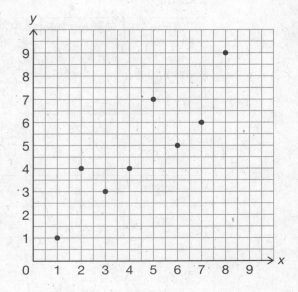

Determining and Interpreting the Correlation Coefficient

The correlation coefficient of a data set can be determined using this formula:

$$r = \frac{\sum_{i=1}^{n}(x_i - \bar{x})(y_i - \bar{y})}{\sqrt{\sum_{i=1}^{n}(x_i - \bar{x})^2}\ \sqrt{\sum_{i=1}^{n}(y_i - \bar{y})^2}}$$

A graphing calculator can also be used to determine the correlation coefficient.

Example

Hours of Video Games Played per Day	3	1	2	4	0
Hours of Sleep per Night	5	9	8	7	11

The correlation coefficient of this data set is -0.85. The correlation coefficient indicates that the data set has a negative association and is closer to being linear than not.

9.3 Creating Residual Plots

An additional method used to determine if a linear model is appropriate for a data set is to analyze the residuals. A residual is the distance between an observed data value and its predicted value using the regression equation. Once residuals are determined, this residual data can be used to create a residual plot. A residual plot is a scatter plot of the independent variable on the x-axis and the residuals on the y-axis.

Example

Time Exercised per Day (minutes)	Resting Heart Rate (beats per minute)	Predicted Resting Heart Rate (beats per minute)	Residual Value Actual Value − Predicted
10	90	$y = -0.26(10) + 86.23 = 83.63$	$90 - 83.63 = 6.37$
20	75	$y = -0.26(20) + 86.23 = 81.03$	$75 - 81.03 = -6.03$
30	80	$y = -0.26(30) + 86.23 = 78.43$	$80 - 78.43 = 1.57$
60	65	$y = -0.26(60) + 86.23 = 70.63$	$65 - 70.63 = -5.63$
90	67	$y = -0.26(90) + 86.23 = 62.83$	$67 - 62.83 = 4.17$

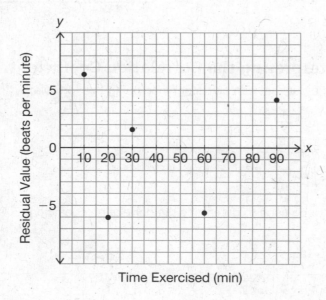

Analyzing the Shapes of Residual Plots

The shape of a residual plot can be useful when determining the most appropriate model for a data set. When a linear model is a good fit for the data, the shape of the residual plot is flat. When a linear model may not be the best fit for the data, the shape of the residual plot is a curve.

Examples

Data Set A

Scatter plot for Data A:
The scatter plot does not look like a linear model.

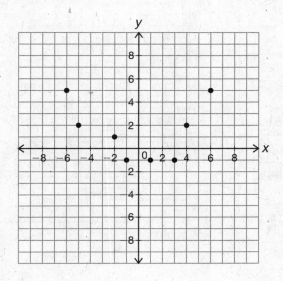

Data Set B

Scatter plot for Data B:
The scatter plot looks like a linear model.

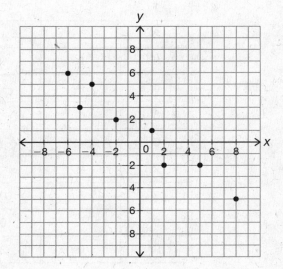

Residual plot for Data A:
The residual plot is curved, indicating a linear model may not be the best fit.

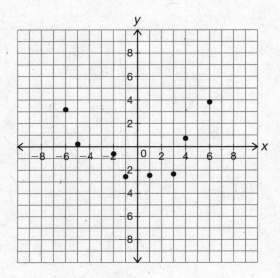

Residual plot for Data B:
The residual plot is flat, indicating a linear model may be a good fit.

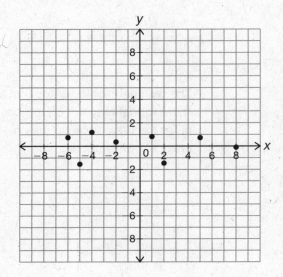

9.4 Determining Whether a Linear Regression Is a Good Fit for Data

To determine if a linear model is an appropriate fit for a data set, consider the shape of the scatter plot, the correlation coefficient, or the residual plot. It is always a good idea to look at the data in multiple ways because one measure may show you something that isn't obvious with another measure. If the points on a scatter plot appear to lie along a line, then a linear model may be appropriate. A correlation coefficient close to -1 or 1 indicates that a linear model may be appropriate. If the residual plot is curved, then a linear model may not be the most appropriate model for the data.

Example

x	y	Residual Value
1	1	2.164
2	1	1.327
3	0	−0.509
4	0	−1.345
5	1	−1.182
6	1	−2.018
7	2	−1.855
8	5	0.309
9	6	0.473
10	9	2.636

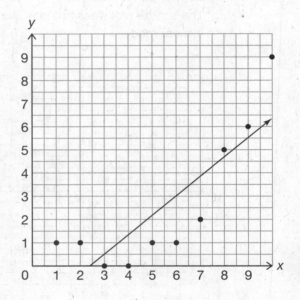

The regression equation is $y = 0.836x - 2$ and the r-value is 0.837.

From the scatter plot and the r-value, it seems like the regression equation is a good fit for the data.

The residual plot indicates that a linear model may not be the best fit for the data because the residual plot is not flat.

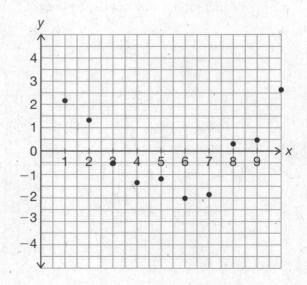

9.5 Examining Correlation Vs. Causation

When interpreting the correlation between two variables, you are looking at the association between the variables. While an association may exist, that does not mean there is causation between the variables. Causation is when one event causes a second event. A correlation is a necessary condition for causation, but a correlation is not a sufficient condition for causation.

Example

A group of college students conducted an experiment and found that more class absences correlated to rainy days. Therefore they concluded that rain causes students to be sick.

This correlation does not imply causation. Rain is neither a necessary condition (because students can get sick on days that do not rain) nor a sufficient condition (because not every student who is absent is necessarily sick) for students being sick.

Analyzing Data Sets for Two Categorical Variables

10

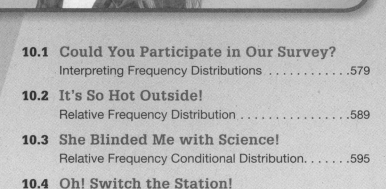

While many people listen to the radio to get their local news or listen to the latest hit songs, technology now allows us to listen to radio stations around the world. You can even create your own radio station and only listen to songs you like!

Could You Participate in Our Survey?

Interpreting Frequency Distributions

© 2012 Carnegie Learning

LEARNING GOALS

In this lesson, you will:

- Construct and interpret frequency and frequency marginal distributions displayed in two-way tables for two-variable categorical data.
- Create and interpret graphs of frequency distributions displayed in two-way tables.

KEY TERMS

- categorical data
- two-way frequency table
- frequency distribution
- joint frequency
- frequency marginal distribution

In order for many businesses to be successful they need one thing: money. If they do not have money, they have two choices—make more money or cut back on spending. While businesses have the opportunity to make more money, government-funded programs, such as schools or public libraries, do not have this option. In turn, these programs must figure out ways to cut back on their spending. So what do they do? These places must first prioritize and determine what areas need the most funding. For example, a school might desperately need new computers. Once these decisions are made, they must look at their budget and figure out where they can cut costs so that they have the money needed for these priorities. Oftentimes in schools this may mean getting rid of extra-curricular activities or limiting the school lunch menu.

Have you noticed any changes in your school? Do you think these changes are the result of school budget cuts? Do you have any ideas on how schools could cut costs without eliminating any programs?

Ms. Seymour is the school cafeteria supervisor at Williams High School. She has been asked to cut her food budget for the upcoming school year. One idea she has is to cut the number of meal choices during the week. However, determining which meal to cut will not be an easy decision. Ms. Seymour wonders if there is a difference in students' favorite cafeteria meals by grade level. She decides to survey the students in Mr. Kolbe's gym class, which consists of 9th and 10th graders. She recorded the results of her survey in the table shown.

Grade	Favorite Meal
9	Salad bar
10	Burgers
10	Pizza
10	Chicken nuggets
10	Chicken nuggets
9	Burgers
10	Salad bar
9	Salad bar
10	Chicken nuggets
9	Burgers
10	Pizza
9	Salad bar
9	Burgers
10	Burgers
9	Chicken nuggets
9	Salad bar
10	Chicken nuggets
10	Chicken nuggets
10	Salad bar
10	Burgers
10	Salad bar
9	Burgers
9	Pizza
10	Chicken nuggets
10	Salad bar
9	Salad bar
10	Pizza
9	Pizza
10	Chicken nuggets
9	Pizza

1. Analyze Ms. Seymour's data table.

   a. Can you summarize her findings just by looking at her data table? Explain why or why not.

   b. Identify the variables of the data from Ms. Seymour's survey. Are the variables in the table numerical? Explain your reasoning.

Categorical data can also be called qualitative data.

Previously, you explored the relationship between two variables that had data values that were quantitative, or numerical. Data that can be grouped into categories, such as favorite meals, are called **categorical data**.

One method of organizing categorical data is to use a *two-way frequency table*. A **two-way frequency table** displays categorical data by representing the number of occurrences that fall into each group for two variables. On the table, one variable is divided into rows and the other is divided into columns.

2. Identify the groups for the variable, grade level. How many groups are there for this variable?

3. Identify the groups for the variable, favorite meal. How many groups are there for this variable?

Remember, there *is* a difference between the variables in a data set and the groups in a data set.

4. Create a two-way frequency table of the data.

　　a. Enter the name of each group.

　　b. Record the favorite meal for each student in the appropriate row using tally marks. Then, write the frequency of each meal for each grade level.

Favorite Meals of Students

Grade Level				

5. What observations can you make from the data about the students' favorite meals?

The table you created is a *frequency distribution*. A **frequency distribution** displays the frequencies for categorical data in a two-way table. Each time you determined the frequency of one favorite meal of one of the grade levels, you recorded a *joint frequency*. Any frequency you record within the body of a two-way frequency table is known as a **joint frequency**.

A two-way frequency table is helpful in organizing each group's frequency in an efficient way. However, it is common to determine the total number of people surveyed just to ensure that a good survey was taken. Determining this total is also helpful to ensure that you recorded the data accurately within the table. For example, if you know 50 people took part in the survey, and the sum of the joint frequencies is 47, then you know that you are missing three data points from the data set.

6. Use the data from your frequency distribution to determine the total number of 9th graders and 10th graders, and to determine the total number of frequencies for each favorite meal category.

Favorite Meals of Students

		Burgers	Chicken Nuggets	Pizza	Salad Bar	Total
Grade Level	**9th grade**					
	10th grade					
	Total					

You just created a *frequency marginal distribution* of the data by determining the totals for each group. A **frequency marginal distribution** displays the total of the frequencies of the rows or columns of a frequency distribution.

7. Analyze the frequency marginal distribution to answer each question.

   a. How many 9th graders participated in the survey?

   b. How many students prefer burgers?

   c. How many students prefer chicken nuggets?

   d. How many 10th graders participated in the survey?

   e. How many students prefer salad bar?

8. What do you notice about the total number of students who prefer burgers, chicken nuggets, pizza, and salad bar; and the total number of 9th and 10th graders? Can you use this observation to determine if you correctly determined the frequency distribution?

9. Use the frequency marginal distribution to answer each question.

   a. Which meal is the least favorite of all students?

   b. Which meal is the least favorite of 9th graders?

   c. Which meal is the most favorite of all students?

    d. Which meal is the most favorite of the 10th graders?

 PROBLEM 2 Representing Data

While a two-way table shows a numerical summary of the data, a graph can help relay information about a survey in a visual way. Remember, every graph tells a story.

Recall that Ms. Seymour is trying to determine ways to cut the cafeteria budget for the upcoming school year. She has already gathered her data and organized it in a frequency distribution table. Ms. Seymour has a couple of ideas, but she would like to use a graph to visually display the ideas she has for cutting the cafeteria budget.

Ms. Seymour's data are displayed in the frequency distribution table shown.

Favorite Meals of Students

		Burgers	Chicken Nuggets	Pizza	Salad Bar
Grade Level	9th grade	4	1	3	5
	10th grade	3	7	3	4

1. Analyze the frequency distribution table.

   a. Determine which graphs would be appropriate to display Ms. Seymour's data. Justify your response.

   b. Determine which graphs would not be appropriate to display Ms. Seymour's data. Explain why these graphs would not be appropriate for displaying this data.

2. Construct a double bar graph of the frequencies. Let the *x*-axis represent the favorite meals, and let the *y*-axis represent the number of students.

Remember to create a key so you can identify what each bar represents!

3. What conclusions can you draw by examining the graph?

4. Use the graph to determine if you represented the data from the frequency distribution table accurately. Explain how you verified that the data in the graph matches the data in the frequency distribution table.

10

5. Construct a bar graph of the frequencies. This time, let the *x*-axis represent grade level.

6. What conclusions can you draw by examining the graph?

7. Does it matter which graph Ms. Seymour's uses to display her survey data? Why or why not.

PROBLEM 3 Putting It All Together

Ms. Seymour must decide on a plan for the upcoming school year. The principal of the school would like Ms. Seymour to present her data and a graph to justify her decision to cut costs.

1. Which meal choice would you cut according to the data? Explain why you would discontinue that meal choice. Then explain which graph you would recommend Ms. Seymour use when she presents her plan.

2. Ms. Seymour just thought of an idea, and she thinks it will help cut the cafeteria costs. She is recommending that two lunch periods be created: one for the 9th graders and one for the 10th graders. She thinks that if two lunch periods exist, she can keep all four meal choices, but just cook a lesser amount of certain choices; thus cutting costs.

    a. Do you think Ms. Seymour should present this idea to the principal? Use the data to justify your reasoning.

    b. Which graph would you recommend Ms. Seymour use to justify her solution? Explain your reasoning.

 Be prepared to share your solutions and methods.

It's So Hot Outside!
Relative Frequency Distribution

© 2012 Carnegie Learning

LEARNING GOALS

In this lesson, you will:

- Construct and interpret relative frequency distribution and relative frequency marginal distributions displayed in two-way tables for categorical data.
- Analyze and use relative frequency marginal distributions to make decisions for a problem situation.

KEY TERMS

- relative frequency distribution
- relative frequency marginal distribution

Humans are warm-blooded mammals. Normal human body temperature can range from 97°F to 99°F so anything significantly higher or lower than that can cause major issues. Hypothermia and hyperthermia are two conditions that can occur when the body's temperature is greatly different from normal body temperature. Hypothermia occurs when the body's temperature drops below 95°F. This occurs when the body is exposed to low temperatures for an extended period of time. Hyperthermia is the opposite of hypothermia and occurs when the body is exposed to high temperatures for a prolonged period of time. Hyperthermia occurs when the body produces more heat than it can emit and the body's temperature climbs to over 100°F.

While it seems like that is not much of a change in temperature, your body is well equipped to regulate its temperature and you can actually be exposed to heat or cold for some time before experiencing any hyperthermia or hypothermia symptoms.

The Northpointe community outreach director wants to plan special summer activities for the members of Northpointe. He posts a survey on the local newspaper's website to gather information on the favorite activities of the community members. Participants identified their age and then chose from four given activities. The responses gathered from the survey are shown.

Activities Preferred During Hot Weather

	Sports	Movies	Reading	Walking	Total
Students Age 18 Years Old and Under	20	30	22	8	
Adults Age 19 Thru 50 Years Old	10	32	25	43	
Adults Over 50 Years Old	5	20	35	30	
Total					

1. Complete the frequency marginal distribution for the data given.

While the raw data provides some information, it is often more efficient to use percents when analyzing data. The relative frequencies of each data entry can provide that information. Representing the relative frequencies for joint data displayed in a two-way table is called a *relative frequency distribution*. The **relative frequency distribution** provides the ratio of occurrences in each category to the total number of occurrences. Displaying the relative frequencies for the rows or columns is called a *relative frequency marginal distribution*. The **relative frequency marginal distribution** provides the ratio of total occurrences for each category to the total number of occurrences.

2. Construct a relative frequency distribution and relative frequency marginal distribution of the data.

Activities Preferred During Hot Weather

	Sports	Movies	Reading	Walking	Total
Students Age 18 Years Old and Under					
Adults Age 19 Thru 50 Years Old					
Adults Over 50 Years Old					
Total					

3. After creating the relative frequency distribution and relative frequency marginal distribution, the students in Mr. Thomas's class made the following statements.

 Marie

7.1% of students age 18 and under prefer playing sports in the hot weather.

 Shane

1.07% of adults over age 50 prefer walking in the hot weather.

 Isaac

29.3% of participants in the survey prefer watching movies or reading in the hot weather.

 Olivia

More adults over 50 responded to the survey than any other age group.

 Aaron

Playing sports is the least popular activity in the hot weather according to the survey results.

For each statement explain why the student is correct or incorrect. If the student is incorrect tell what the correct statement would be.

4. Which age group made up the smallest percent of people surveyed?

5. Which activity was preferred by the largest percent of people surveyed?

PROBLEM 2 How Does the Data Stack Up?

Previously, you used a bar graph to visually represent data. Another way to represent data is to use a stacked bar graph in which the bars are stacked on top of each other as opposed to sitting next to each other.

1. Construct a stacked bar graph of the relative frequency distribution. Let the *x*-axis represent age group.

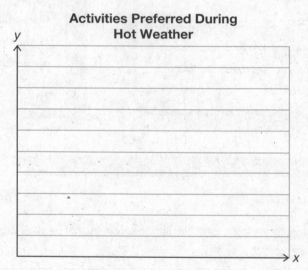

Activities Preferred During Hot Weather

2. What conclusions can you draw by examining the graph?

3. Construct a stacked bar graph of the relative frequency distribution. Let the *x*-axis represent the activities.

Activities Preferred During Hot Weather

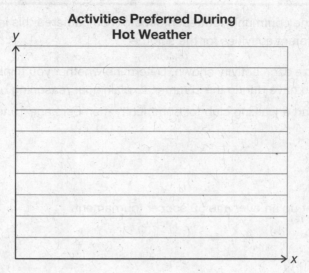

4. What conclusions can you draw by examining the graph?

5. Name some advantages of graphing the data by age group. Name some advantages of graphing the data by activity.

Now that the community outreach director has gathered this information, he wants to use it to plan different activities for the summer.

1. Analyze each activity shown. Determine whether you think the activity would be a good idea to have during the summer. Explain your reasoning based on the data.

   a. Start a walking club for community members age 19 to 50.

   b. Set up an over age 50 soccer tournament.

   c. Start an age 18 and under ultimate Frisbee league.

2. The community outreach director wants to offer one summer activity each week that will appeal to all ages of the community. Write a letter to the community outreach director recommending one activity and tell why the other activities may not be the best activities during the summer. Use the data to support your idea.

Be prepared to share your solutions and methods.

She Blinded Me with Science!
Relative Frequency Conditional Distribution

LEARNING GOALS

In this lesson, you will:

- Construct and interpret relative frequency conditional distributions displayed in two-way tables for categorical data.

KEY TERM

- relative frequency conditional distribution

Chances are pretty good you have taken some sort of science class every year since you started school. However, unlike elementary school science which was very general, you are probably now taking a more specific science class. The word science comes from the Latin word *scientia* which means knowledge and the study of science in the broadest sense has existed since humans began communicating knowledge to each other. In the Age of Enlightenment, which took place in the 17th and 18th centuries, there was rapid scientific advancement where scientists such as Descartes and Newton confirmed scientific thinking with experiments and mathematics. Today there are two major groups of sciences: natural sciences and social sciences. The natural sciences include topics such as astronomy, biology, chemistry, physics, and earth science. The social sciences include topics dealing with society and human behavior such as economics, geography, linguistics, and psychology.

Often scientists are belittled or questioned for their beliefs or ideas, such as when Galileo suggested the Earth traveled around the sun. However, without the work scientists have achieved we would have very little understanding about the world around us.

PROBLEM 1 Passing the Class

Mr. Lewis teaches three science classes at Matthews High School. He wants to compare the grades of the three classes of his students. He creates the following two-way frequency table shown.

Grades of Mr. Lewis's Science Students

Science Classes	A	B	C	D	F	Total
Biology	6	6	5	1	2	
Chemistry	4	8	12	4	2	
Physics	2	5	6	1	1	
Total						

1. Complete the frequency marginal distributions on Mr. Lewis's frequency table.

2. Complete the relative frequency and relative frequency marginal distributions for the data.

Grades of Mr. Lewis's Science Students

Science Classes	A	B	C	D	F	Total
Biology						
Chemistry						
Physics						
Total						

3. Write a paragraph interpreting the relative frequency distributions and relative frequency marginal distributions for the data.

4. Create a stacked bar grade to represent the percent of students passing in each class.

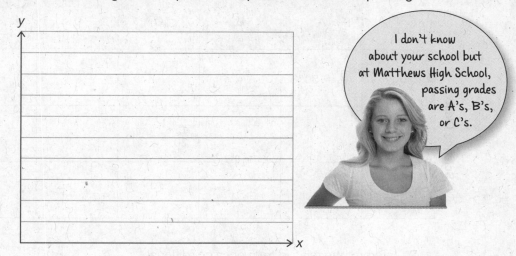

5. Campbell claims that the Chemistry class is the smartest because they have the greatest percent of students passing. Is Campbell's statement correct? Explain your reasoning.

PROBLEM 2 Which Is the Best?

Because each science class has a different number of students, the relative frequencies cannot help determine which class is doing the "best." Instead, you can use a *relative frequency conditional distribution* to determine this information. A **relative frequency conditional distribution** is the percent or ratio of occurrences of a category given the specific value of another category.

Let's construct a relative frequency conditional distribution of grades given the classes.

1. Use the information from Problem 1, Question 1 to determine the relative frequency for each grade given that particular class.

Grades of Mr. Lewis's Science Students

Science Classes	A	B	C	D	F	Total
Biology	$\frac{6}{20} = 30\%$					
Chemistry			$\frac{12}{30} = 40\%$			
Physics				$\frac{1}{15} \approx 6.7\%$		

2. Interpret the relative frequency conditional distributions of each class.

Since there are 20 students in biology, I must divide the number of students who got each grade by 20.

3. Use the relative frequency conditional distribution to answer each question.

   a. What percent of the biology students are passing?

   b. What percent of the chemistry students are passing?

   c. What percent of the physics students are passing?

   d. Which science class is doing the best according to their grades? Explain your reasoning.

   e. How does this compare to the statement Campbell made in Problem 1, *Passing the Class*, Question 5?

4. Which science class has the greatest percent of students failing?

10

Mr. Lewis also teaches two General Science classes. He wants to teach his students about a topic they are most interested in. He surveys his students and records the data in the table shown.

Science Classes	Matter	Plants and Animals	Astronomy	Anatomy	Genetics	Total
Class 1	5	3	10	3	4	25
Class 2	9	5	3	7	6	30
Total	14	8	13	10	10	55

5. Mr. Lewis wants to teach the same topic to both classes. Which topic would you recommend Mr. Lewis teach? Use the data to explain why you made your suggestion to Mr. Lewis.

Be prepared to share your solutions and methods.

Oh! Switch the Station!
Drawing Conclusions from Data

© 2012 Carnegie Learning

LEARNING GOALS

In this lesson, you will:

- Analyze different categorical data.
- Use categorical data to make decisions.

Have you ever gotten into a car, tuned to your favorite radio station, and then realized . . . it isn't the same station? It seems like overnight all of the on-air personalities and even the genre of music changed! Why does this happen? While there may be other factors, chances are your favorite radio station didn't have very high ratings. In the United States today there are over 10,000 AM and FM commercial radio stations. These stations earn most of their money from advertisements. Advertisers pay the radio stations to play their commercials in the hopes that people will hear the commercials and buy whatever they are selling. Companies want to make sure that there are many people listening to their commercials but if the ratings for a station are low, that means fewer people are listening. Companies will not give money to the station if the ratings are too low so, unfortunately for you, the radio station as you know it may be cancelled and something new will come on in its place in the hopes of attracting new listeners. Luckily today we have so many radio stations that you will probably be able to find a new favorite!

PROBLEM 1 Sifting Through Data to Make a Point

 Andres is a new radio station general manager at KYWN. The radio station unfortunately has sagging ratings and low advertising. He has been charged with making the station more popular in the hopes that with more popularity, more companies will want to advertise on KYWN. The station owners have given him the authority to do anything to turn around the ratings; however, if things don't change, he'll be doing overnight radio in the Gobi Desert!

Andres is considering changing the genre of the radio station. Currently, the station features country music. However, if he changes the genre, what will the new genre be?

Andres wants to target one of the highest demographics in radio listening: teenagers. He decides to sponsor the next dance at Rawlings High School. KYWN will provide the food, drinks, and most importantly, the music for the dance. Prior to the dance, he surveys the students. He will use this data to determine the new genre of KYWN.

| | Music Genre | | | | |
Grade Level	Rock (Classic/ Alternative)	Classical	Hip-Hop/Rap	Dance	Country
12				x	
9		x			
10				x	
10					x
9					x
11			x		
12		x			
10	x				
9					x
9				x	
10		x			
12				x	
11	x				
12				x	
11			x		
9	x				
9	x				
10					x
11	x				
9	x				
12				x	
12			x		
11			x		
10		x			

(Continued)

Music Genre					
Grade Level	Rock (Classic/Alternative)	Classical	Hip-Hop/Rap	Dance	Country
9			x		
12			x		
11				x	
9			x		
10	x				
10	x				
12					x
9				x	
9				x	
9					x
10		x			
12	x				
12	x				
12		x			
10		x			
10			x		
10				x	
11			x		
9				x	
9					x
10		x			
10		x			
12				x	
11	x				
12	x				
11	x				
11		x			
12				x	
12				x	
12		x			
11			x		
11					x

1. Analyze the data Andres collected.

   a. In looking at the data, can you determine which music genre is most preferred by the Rawlings High School students?

   b. How would you advise Andres to organize the data he gathered?

2. Organize the data to help Andres determine which music genre is most popular at Rawlings High School according to the survey he conducted.

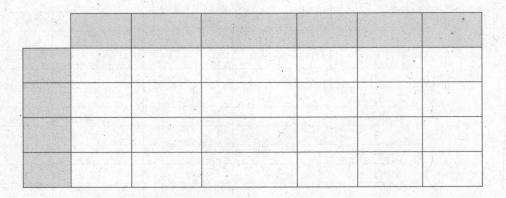

3. Analyze the table you created to organize Andres's data.

   a. How many students did Andres survey for the dance? How did you determine that you organized Andres data correctly?

   b. Can you determine which genre of music was the most popular from the table you created? Explain why or why not.

c. Do you think the results might be the same or different if Andres conducted another random survey at Rawlings High School? Explain your reasoning.

d. Based on the data you have analyzed, would you advise Andres to change the format of his station? If so, explain why. If not, explain why not. You may use graphs to better represent your advice to Andres.

PROBLEM 2 What if We Look at the Data *This* Way?

Data can be analyzed in many different ways, and then used to prove a point of an advertiser, a doctor, a scientist, or just about any occupation you can think of! How that data are interpreted can affect the decisions of people—for better or for worse.

Andres knows that one of the most sought after age groups is the age 18 to 35 group. Generally, if stations, magazines, blogs, and news websites can target and successfully attract viewers or users in this age range, they can then lure advertisers to buy air time or banners.

Knowing this, Andres decides to just use the data he gathered from the seniors he surveyed at Rawlings High School.

1. How could Andres use the table or graph(s) you created in Problem 1 to analyze the data for the seniors?

2. Analyze the tables and graphs you created.

   a. Do you think you can predict which music genre is most popular with the seniors at Rawlings High School using the data Andres collected? Explain why or why not.

   b. Predict (if possible) which music genre is the most popular for the Rawlings High School seniors. Explain how you came to your conclusion.

3. Suppose Andres decides to suggest a music format change for KYWN to dance music. What information would you advise Andres to use to strengthen his suggestion? You can use any of the data and can supply any graphs you think that will strengthen Andres's suggestion. Finally, explain why you chose the information.

4. Based on the information you analyzed regarding the seniors, would you change the advice you gave to Andres in Problem 1, Question 3, part (c)? Would you change KYWN's music format to match the Rawlings High School seniors' survey results? If yes, explain why using the data you have. If not, explain why not.

 Be prepared to share your solutions and methods.

Chapter 10 Summary

- categorical data (10.1)
- two-way frequency table (10.1)
- frequency distribution (10.1)
- joint frequency (10.1)

- frequency marginal distribution (10.1)
- relative frequency distribution (10.2)
- relative frequency marginal distribution (10.2)
- relative frequency conditional distribution (10.3)

10.1 Creating a Two-Way Frequency Table to Analyze Frequency Distribution

Data that can be grouped into categories, such as favorite foods, are called categorical data. One method of organizing categorical data is in a two-way frequency table. A two-way frequency table displays categorical data by representing the number of occurrences that fall into each group for two variables. On the table, one variable is divided into rows and the other is divided into columns. A frequency distribution displays the frequencies for categorical data in a two-way table. Any frequencies recorded within the body of a two-way frequency table are known as joint frequencies.

Example

Favorite Colors

		Blue	Red	Yellow	Green
Gender	**Girls**	┼┼┼┼ / / 7	/ / 2	/ / / / 4	/ / / 3
	Boys	/ / 2	┼┼┼┼ / / / 8	/ / / 3	/ 1

More girls liked the color blue than any other option and fewer girls liked red.

More boys liked red than any other option and fewer boys like green.

10.1 Creating and Analyzing a Frequency Marginal Distribution

A frequency marginal distribution displays the total of the frequencies of the rows or columns of a frequency distribution.

Example

		Favorite Colors				
		Blue	**Red**	**Yellow**	**Green**	**Total**
Gender	**Girls**	7	2	4	3	16
	Boys	2	8	3	1	14
	Total	9	10	7	4	30

Thirty children participated in the survey. Ten children liked red best; it is the most popular favorite color of those polled. Four children liked green best; it is the least popular favorite color of those polled.

10.1 Graphing and Interpreting Graphs of Frequency Distributions

A graph can help relay information from a two-way frequency table in a visual way. A bar graph, a double bar graph, or a stacked bar graph are all good choices for displaying this type of data. Remember a key is necessary to identify what each bar represents.

Example

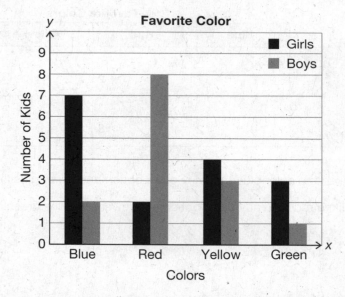

Red appears to be the most preferred by boys and blue is the most preferred by girls. Green appears to be the least favorite overall.

10.2 Creating and Analyzing Relative Frequency Distribution and Relative Frequency Marginal Distribution

A relative frequency is the ratio or percent of occurrences within a category to the total of the category. Representing the relative frequencies for joint data displayed in a two-way table is called a relative frequency distribution. The relative frequency distribution provides the ratio of occurrences in each category to the total number of occurrences. Displaying the relative frequencies for the rows or columns is called a relative frequency marginal distribution. The relative frequency marginal distribution provides the ratio of total occurrences for each category to the total number of occurrences.

Example

Preferred Movie Genre

	Animation	Comedy	Drama	Horror	Total
Movie Viewers ages 8 years and younger	$\frac{40}{240} \approx 16.7\%$	$\frac{18}{240} = 7.5\%$	$\frac{2}{240} \approx 0.8\%$	$\frac{0}{240} = 0\%$	$\frac{60}{240} = 25\%$
Movie Viewers ages 9 thru 16 years old	$\frac{20}{240} \approx 8.3\%$	$\frac{42}{240} = 17.5\%$	$\frac{13}{240} \approx 5.4\%$	$\frac{5}{240} \approx 2.1\%$	$\frac{80}{240} \approx 33.3\%$
Movie Viewers ages 17 and older	$\frac{5}{240} \approx 2.1\%$	$\frac{35}{240} \approx 14.6\%$	$\frac{32}{240} \approx 13.3\%$	$\frac{28}{240} \approx 11.7\%$	$\frac{100}{240} \approx 41.7\%$
Total	$\frac{65}{240} \approx 27.1\%$	$\frac{95}{240} \approx 39.6\%$	$\frac{47}{240} \approx 19.5\%$	$\frac{33}{240} \approx 13.8\%$	$\frac{240}{240} = 100\%$

Viewers ages 8 years and younger made up the smallest percent of participants.

Horror movies are the least popular type of movie overall.

Comedies are preferred by 39.6% of participants.

10.2 Graphing and Interpreting Graphs of Relative Frequency Distributions

A graph can help visually represent data. Use a stacked bar graph to represent relative frequency distributions. A stacked bar graph is a graph in which the bars are stacked on top of each other as opposed to sitting next to each other.

Example

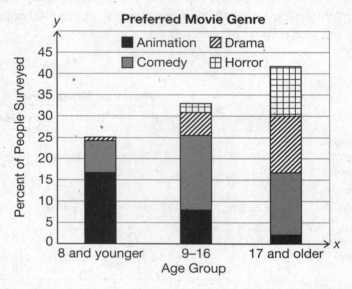

Animation appears to be the favorite genre of participants ages 8 and younger.

Comedy appears to be the favorite genre of participants ages 9 to 16.

Comedy, drama, and horror seem to be fairly evenly favored for participants ages 17 and older.

10.3 Creating and Analyzing a Relative Frequency Conditional Distribution

A relative frequency conditional distribution is the percent of proportion or occurrences of a category given the specific value of another category.

Example

Preferred Movie Genre

	Animation	Comedy	Drama	Horror	Total
Movie Viewers age 0–8	$\frac{40}{60} \approx 66.7\%$	$\frac{18}{60} = 30\%$	$\frac{2}{60} \approx 3.3\%$	$\frac{0}{60} = 0\%$	$\frac{60}{60} = 100\%$
Movie Viewers age 9–16	$\frac{20}{80} = 25\%$	$\frac{42}{80} = 52.5\%$	$\frac{13}{80} = 16.25\%$	$\frac{5}{80} = 6.25\%$	$\frac{80}{80} = 100\%$
Movie Viewers age 17+	$\frac{5}{100} = 5\%$	$\frac{35}{100} = 35\%$	$\frac{32}{100} = 32\%$	$\frac{28}{100} = 28\%$	$\frac{100}{100} = 100\%$

Of participants ages 8 and younger, only 3.3% preferred dramas.

Of participants ages 9 to 16, 52.5% preferred comedies.

Of participants ages 17 and older, only 5% preferred animated films.

10.4 Drawing Conclusions from Data

Raw data can be organized into a relative frequency marginal distribution table and graph. To further examine the trends within certain categories instead of the overall group, a relative frequency conditional distribution table and graph can be used.

Example

A hardware store chain collected some data on the departments within their store that are most frequented by different types of customers so they could target their advertising.

	Garden	Lumber	Paint	Tools	Total
Home Owners	$\frac{83}{615} \approx 13.5\%$	$\frac{12}{615} \approx 2.0\%$	$\frac{65}{615} \approx 10.6\%$	$\frac{45}{615} \approx 7.3\%$	$\frac{205}{615} \approx 33.3\%$
Contractors/ Professionals	$\frac{25}{615} \approx 4.1\%$	$\frac{95}{615} \approx 15.4\%$	$\frac{85}{615} \approx 13.8\%$	$\frac{45}{615} \approx 7.3\%$	$\frac{250}{615} \approx 40.7\%$
Landlords	$\frac{25}{615} \approx 4.1\%$	$\frac{25}{615} \approx 4.1\%$	$\frac{65}{615} \approx 10.6\%$	$\frac{45}{615} \approx 7.3\%$	$\frac{160}{615} \approx 26.0\%$
Total	$\frac{133}{615} \approx 21.7\%$	$\frac{132}{615} \approx 21.4\%$	$\frac{215}{615} \approx 35.0\%$	$\frac{135}{615} \approx 22.0\%$	$\frac{615}{615} = 100\%$

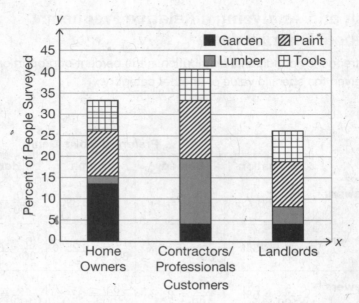

From the relative frequency marginal distribution shown, it looks like most customers frequent the Paint department, so the store should focus their advertising on the paints and paint services.

The CEO of the company feels that contractors and landlords are more likely to have wholesale connections, so she wants to focus their advertising on home owners.

	Garden	Lumber	Paint	Tools	Total
Home Owners	$\frac{83}{205} \approx 40.5\%$	$\frac{12}{205} \approx 5.9\%$	$\frac{65}{205} \approx 31.7\%$	$\frac{45}{205} \approx 22.0\%$	$\frac{205}{205} \approx 100\%$

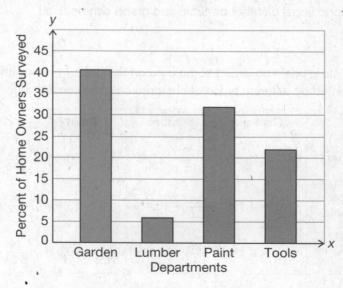

From the relative frequency conditional distribution shown, most home owners frequent the Garden department, so the store decides to focus their advertising on the Garden department.

Mathematical Modeling

The demand for gasoline seems to always be on the rise. This demand is sometimes seen in the rise in gas prices. However have there ever been dips in gas prices?

Let's Take a Little Trip
Every Graph Tells a Story

LEARNING GOALS

In this lesson, you will:

- Identify a linear piecewise function.
- Interpret the graph of a linear piecewise function.
- Determine intervals of increase and decrease for a linear piecewise function.
- Determine values from a graph of a linear piecewise function.
- Physically model the graphs of linear piecewise functions using technology.

While a person can describe the recent winning streak of a basketball team, or talk about a record number of tornados in certain parts of the country, data graphed on a coordinate plane enables people to *see* data. Graphs relay information about data in a visual way. These same graphs can also be used to make predictions. However, are these predictions accurate?

Often graphs used in textbooks are very organized as are the data sets they are created from. When a graph follows a "perfect" data set, predictions made from it will be accurate—but unfortunately, real life is not so perfect. There are very few examples of real life scenarios in which data sets are perfectly linear, exponential, or quadratic.

Why do you think textbooks use "perfect" data sets? Do you think predictions using real-life data are accurate? Why or why not?

The graph shows the relation between time in hours and Gulliver's distance from his house during a 10-hour period.

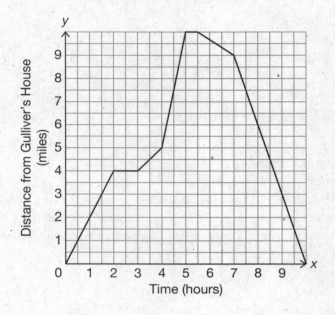

11

Use the graph to answer each question.

1. Is the relation a function? If so, explain why the relation is a function and identify the function family. If not, explain why the relation is not a function.

2. Identify if the relation has any absolute minimum or absolute maximum values. Explain what the absolute minimum or absolute maximum means in terms of this problem situation.

3. Determine the domain and range of this problem situation.

4. How far from home was Gulliver after:

    a. 2 hours?

    b. 2.5 hours?

    c. 6 hours?

    d. 8 hours?

    e. 10 hours?

5. After how many hours was Gulliver:

    a. 5 miles from home?

    b. 10 miles from home?

    c. 4 miles from home?

6. How far did Gulliver travel during the first two hours of the trip?

7. Consider Gulliver's speed during the trip.

    a. What was Gulliver's average speed during the first 2 hours of the trip?

    b. What was Gulliver's average speed between seven and ten hours?

    c. When was Gulliver traveling the fastest? Explain how you know.

d. What was Gulliver's average speed when he was traveling the fastest?

   e. When was Gulliver traveling the slowest? Explain how you know.

   f. What was Gulliver's average speed when he was traveling the slowest?

8. When was Gulliver traveling away from his house? Explain how you know.

9. When was Gulliver traveling toward his house? Explain how you know.

10. When was Gulliver not traveling? Explain how you know.

11. Write a paragraph describing Gulliver's travels.

PROBLEM 2   Acting Out a Linear Piecewise Function

You will need a graphing calculator, a Calculator-Based Ranger (CBR), and a connector cable for this activity. You will also need a meter stick and masking tape to mark off distance measures.

The step-by-step instructions shown tell how to create graphs of linear piecewise functions representing people walking. On these graphs, time can be represented on the x-axis, and distance can be represented on the y-axis. Your goal is to act out each graph by walking in the way that matches the graph. As you act out each graph, your motion will be plotted alongside the graph to monitor your performance.

Step 1: Prepare the workspace.

- Clear an area at least 1 meter wide and 4 meters long leading away from a wall.

- Measure the distances of 0.5, 1, 1.5, 2, 2.5, 3, 3.5, and 4 meters from the wall. Mark these distances on the floor using masking tape.

Step 2: Prepare the technology.

- Connect the CBR to a graphing calculator.

- Transfer the RANGER program from the CBR to the calculator. This only needs to be done the first time. It will then be stored in your calculator.

- Press **2nd LINK ⎯⎯→ ENTER**.

- Open the CBR and press the appropriate button on it for the type of calculator you are using. Your calculator screen will display **RECEIVING** and then **DONE**. The CBR will flash a green light and beep.

Step 3: Access the RANGER program.

- Press **PRGM** for program. Then scroll to **RANGER**. Press **ENTER**.

- Press **ENTER** to display the **MAIN MENU**.

- Scroll and choose **APPLICATIONS**, and then scoll and choose **METERS**.

- Next, scroll and choose **MATCH** or **DISTANCE MATCH**.

- Press **ENTER**. A graph will be displayed.

Step 4: Act out the graph.

- Examine each graph and plan your path. Use the scale to gauge where to begin in relation to the wall. Will you walk toward or away from the wall? Will you walk fast or slow?

- Hold the graphing calculator in one hand and the CBR in the other hand. The lid of the CBR should be aimed toward the wall.

- Press **ENTER**. Begin walking in a manner that matches the graph. Use the scale and floor markings as guides. You will hear a clicking sound and see a green light as your motion is plotted alongside the piecewise graph on the graphing calculator.

- When the time is finished, examine your performance. What changes should you make?

- Press **ENTER** to display the **OPTIONS** menu. Choose **SAME MATCH**.

- Press **ENTER** and try the walk a second time.

- Continue acting out walks by pressing **ENTER** and **NEW MATCH**.

- When you are finished, press **ENTER** and then scroll and choose **MAIN MENU** and finally **QUIT**.

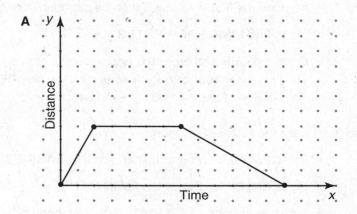

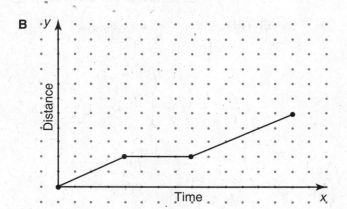

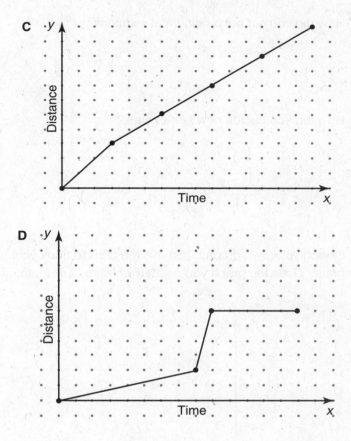

C

Distance / Time

D

Distance / Time

1. How did you decide where to stand when beginning to act out a graph?

2. How did you decide when to walk toward the wall and when to back away from the wall?

Did this activity help you make sense of the graphs?

3. How did you act out a horizontal segment?

4. How did you decide how fast to walk?

5. Sketch your own graph. Then use the CBR to track your motions as you act out the graph. Does the graph you created with the CBR match the graph you sketched?

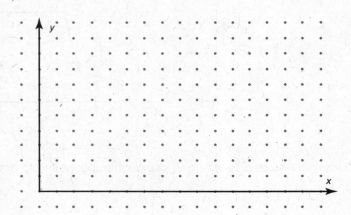

 Be prepared to share your solutions and methods.

Whodunit? The Function Family Line-Up

Modeling Data with Curves of Best Fit

LEARNING GOALS

In this lesson, you will:

- Model data from a scatter plot.
- Identify the function family to which a function belongs.
- Identify graphical behavior of a function.
- Use a model to predict values.
- Interpret parts of a graph.

If you work in technology, Moore's law can be a blessing—and at times, a curse! Moore's law describes a long-term trend in the history of computer hardware that claims that the number of transistors placed on a circuit doubles approximately every two years. What this basically means is that with more transistors comes the ability to make computers faster. The blessing is that technological products like phones and computers will always improve; thus giving the ability to sell new products every two years. The curse: trying to keep up with the technology and the demands of the market. Do you think that Moore's law is sustainable? Or might there be a point when technology can no longer improve its speed to do tasks.

PROBLEM 1 Gas Prices

The table shows the national average annual price of gasoline in the U.S in dollars per gallon for the years 2001 through 2011.

1. Create a scatter plot of the data on the grid shown.

U.S. National Annual Gas Price Average

Year	Dollars per gallon
2001	1.46
2002	1.36
2003	1.59
2004	1.88
2005	2.30
2006	2.59
2007	2.80
2008	3.27
2009	2.35
2010	2.79
2011	3.55

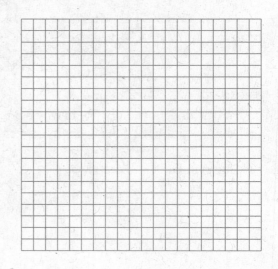

2. Sketch a function that best models the data. Then state the function family you sketched.

You can represent years with one- and two-digit numbers. Just think about the number of years since 2000!

3. Answer each question about the function you sketched in Question 2.

   a. State the domain and range of the function you sketched. How do they compare to the domain and range of this problem situation?

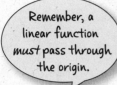

Remember, a linear function must pass through the origin.

   b. Does your function have an absolute minimum, absolute maximum, or neither? If so, describe what it means in terms of this problem situation.

   c. Is your function a smooth curve, or is it made up of one or more straight lines?

   d. Does your function represent continuous or discrete data? Explain your reasoning.

4. Use the function you sketched to answer each question.

    a. According to your function, what was the U.S. national annual average gasoline price per gallon in 2000?

    b. Predict what the U.S. national annual average gasoline price per gallon will be in 2014 using your function.

    c. Predict when the U.S national annual average gasoline price per gallon will be $5.00 using your function.

    d. Predict when the U.S. national average annual gasoline price will reach $10.00 per gallon using your function.

5. Write a brief summary about the national average annual gasoline prices in the U.S. In your summary, you may want to answer the following types of questions: What trends do you see from the data? Is your function a good model for the data, and why or why not? What predictions can you make? Are your predictions realistic? Professionals in what fields may find this type of information useful?

PROBLEM 2   Median Price of a Home

The table shows the median price of a single family home in the U.S for the years 2004 through 2010. A scatter plot of the data is also shown.

U.S. Median Home Price from 2004–2010

Year	Dollars
2004	122,100
2005	140,100
2006	168,800
2007	187,600
2008	178,900
2009	156,900
2010	140,300

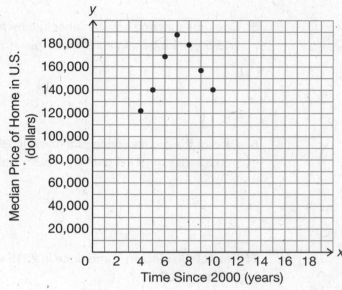

1. What do you notice about the median price of a home between the years 2004 and 2010?

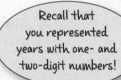

Recall that you represented years with one- and two-digit numbers!

2. Sketch a function that best models the data. Then state the function family you sketched.

3. State the domain and range of the function. How do they compare to the domain and range of this problem situation?

4. Estimate the function's *y*-intercept, and interpret its meaning in terms of this problem situation.

5. Does the function have an absolute minimum or maximum? If so, identify it and interpret its meaning in terms of this problem situation. If not, explain why not.

6. Predict the median price of a home in 2001 using your function. Does your prediction make sense in terms of this problem situation? Explain your reasoning.

7. Predict the median home price in 2015 using your function. Does this prediction make sense?

8. What do your answers tell you about the function you chose to model the data?

9. Do some research about the housing market from 2004 to 2010. Use your findings to write a paragraph that justifies the shape of the data and your model.

 Be prepared to share your solutions and methods.

People, Tea, and Carbon Dioxide

Modeling Using Exponential Functions

LEARNING GOALS

In this lesson, you will:

- Write exponential models from data sets.
- Use models to solve problems.

It can be amazing how many different historical events are connected in one way or another. For example, there are some environmentalists who claim that the increase in the world's population has led to an increase in atmospheric gases like carbon dioxide that have led to an overall global warming. In this event, population and environment collide in an issue that is on the minds of many people.

Of course, supporters and opponents of these theories can claim different statistics to support an opinion or contradict a theory. As some say, "facts are facts," but can these facts or statistics be reported in different ways to help support different theories? Do you think that some groups may only report some of the statistics, but not necessarily all of the statistics? Why might they do this?

The table shows the U.S. population in millions of people at 20-year intervals from 1815 to 1975.

U.S. Population 1815–1975

Year	Population (per 1 million people)
1815	8.3
1835	14.7
1855	26.7
1875	44.4
1895	68.9
1915	98.8
1935	127.1
1955	164.0
1975	214.3

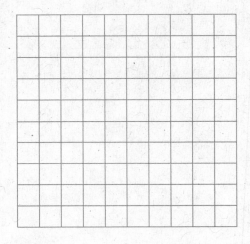

11

1. Create a scatter plot of the data on the grid shown. Then use a graphing calculator to determine the exponential regression equation and the value of the correlation coefficient. Finally define, write, and sketch a function to model this situation.

Remember to label your axes. Represent time as the number of years since 1815.

You can use a graphing calculator to determine the exponential regression equation for a data set.

Step 1: Press **STAT** and select **1:Edit**. Enter the data set with the independent variable in **L1** and the dependent variable in **L2**.

Step 2: Press **STAT** and scroll to **CALC**. Then scroll down to **0:ExpReg**. Press **ENTER** twice.

The calculator will display the values of each variable in the form $y = a \cdot b^x$.

Step 3: The r-value displayed represents the correlation coefficient.

2. State the domain and range of this function you sketched. How do they compare to the domain and range of this problem situation?

3. Use your function to predict the population of the United States in 1990.

4. The actual population of the United States in 1990 was 258 million. Compare your predicted population to the actual population. What do you notice? Why do you think this happens?

5. Use your function to predict the population of the United States in 1790.

 6. The population actually increased more rapidly after 1790 than what your function predicts. Do some research about U.S. history to explain why this may have happened.

Caroline loves green tea after a large meal. After dining out, she boiled water and sat in her kitchen to enjoy her tea.

The table shows the temperature of a cup of Caroline's tea over time.

Temperature of Caroline's Tea Over Time

Time (minutes)	Temperature (degrees Fahrenheit)
0	180
5	169
11	149
15	142
18	135
25	124
30	116
34	113
42	106
45	102
50	101

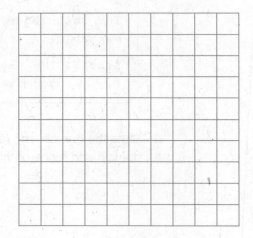

1. Create a scatter plot of the data on the grid shown. Then use a graphing calculator to determine the exponential regression equation and the value of the correlation coefficient. Finally define, write, and sketch a function to model this situation.

2. State the domain and range of the function you sketched. How do they compare to the domain and range of this problem situation?

3. Use your function to predict the temperature of Caroline's tea after 60 minutes.

4. Use your function to predict when Caroline's tea will reach room temperature, which is 72°F.

5. Use your function to predict the temperature of Caroline's tea after 240 minutes.

 6. Does your prediction make sense in terms of this problem situation? Explain your reasoning.

One measure of climate change is the amount of carbon dioxide in Earth's oceans. When the level of carbon dioxide in the atmosphere increases, the concentration of carbon dioxide in the ocean water also increases.

The table shows the carbon dioxide concentration in the Atlantic Ocean in parts per million from 1750 to 1975.

Carbon Dioxide in the Atlantic Ocean

Year	Carbon Dioxide Concentration (parts per million)
1750	277.0
1775	279.3
1800	282.9
1825	284.3
1850	285.2
1875	289.4
1900	296.7
1925	304.9
1950	312.0
1975	329.4

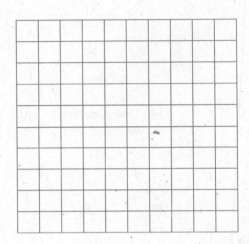

1. Create a scatter plot of the data on the grid shown. Then use a graphing calculator to determine the exponential regression equation and the value of the correlation coefficient. Finally define, write, and sketch a function to model this situation.

2. State the domain and range of the function you sketched. How do they compare to the domain and range of this problem situation?

3. Use your function to predict the concentration of carbon dioxide in the Atlantic Ocean in the year 2000.

4. Use your function to predict when the concentration of carbon dioxide in the Atlantic Ocean was 250 parts per million.

5. Use your function to predict when the concentration of carbon dioxide in the Atlantic Ocean was 100 parts per million.

6. Using your function, the concentration of carbon dioxide has been increasing exponentially over the past 250 years. What factors could have contributed to this behavior?

 Be prepared to share your solutions and methods.

11

BAC Is BAD News
Choosing the Best Function to Model Data

In this lesson, you will:

- Determine the type of regression equation that best fits a graph.
- Use a function to model a problem situation.
- Interpret characteristics of a function in terms of a problem situation.
- Analyze results to write a report.

Blood Alcohol Content, or BAC, is a way of measuring the amount of alcohol in a person's blood stream. BAC levels are measured in percentages. A BAC of 0.08 means that 0.08 percent of a person's blood is alcohol. That's not much! In fact, it is a lot less than 1%!

Most states in the United States define a driver that is 21 or older legally impaired at a BAC level of 0.08 or higher. For drivers under 21, *any* BAC level above 0.00 is illegal! So no high school students should ever be drinking alcohol!

There is a relationship between the relative probability of a driver causing a car accident and a driver's BAC. A driver with no alcohol in the blood system is defined as having a relative probability of 1 of causing a car accident. A relative probability is the number of times more than 1 that a car accident is likely to occur with alcohol in the blood system. For example, a relative probability of 2 for a driver that has alcohol in the blood system means that a car accident is twice as likely to occur as for a driver with no alcohol in the blood system.

Suppose that a recent study claims that a person with no alcohol in the blood system has a 1.8% chance of causing a car accident.

From this information, you can determine the relative probability of a person causing an accident if that person has any alcohol in the blood system.

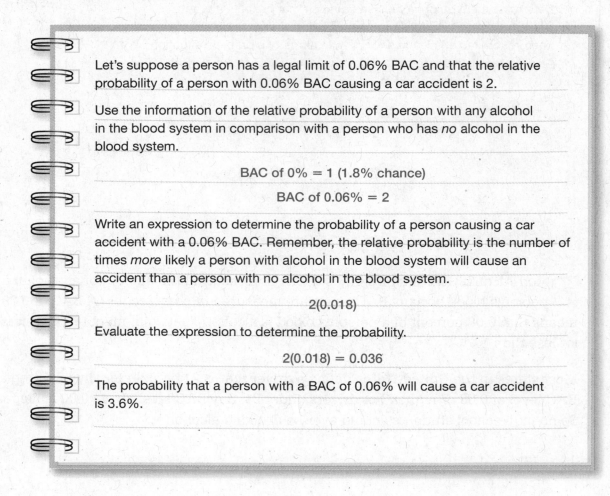

Let's suppose a person has a legal limit of 0.06% BAC and that the relative probability of a person with 0.06% BAC causing a car accident is 2.

Use the information of the relative probability of a person with any alcohol in the blood system in comparison with a person who has *no* alcohol in the blood system.

BAC of 0% = 1 (1.8% chance)

BAC of 0.06% = 2

Write an expression to determine the probability of a person causing a car accident with a 0.06% BAC. Remember, the relative probability is the number of times *more* likely a person with alcohol in the blood system will cause an accident than a person with no alcohol in the blood system.

2(0.018)

Evaluate the expression to determine the probability.

2(0.018) = 0.036

The probability that a person with a BAC of 0.06% will cause a car accident is 3.6%.

1. Use the given information in the worked example to answer each question.

   a. A person with a BAC of 0.10% is just over the legal driving limit. If the person's *relative* probability of causing an accident is 5, what is the probability that this person will cause a car accident?

b. A person with a BAC of 0.16% has twice the BAC of a driver that has just reached the legally impaired mark. If this person's *relative* probability of causing an accident is 25, what is the probability that this person will cause a car accident?

c. What do your answers in parts (a) and (b) tell you about the rate at which alcohol affects a person's ability to drive?

Many people may not realize how quickly a person's BAC can increase. Different factors affect a person's BAC, including weight, gender, the duration of consuming alcohol, and the amount of food the person eats.

According to the Virginia Tech Alcohol Abuse Prevention website, a typical 140-pound male who has one drink over a 40-minute period will have a BAC of 0.03%. If he has another drink over the next 40 minutes, his BAC rises to 0.05%. If he has one more drink, his BAC rises to 0.08%, which means he legally cannot drive.

The table shows the results of a study which examined a person's BAC level and the person's relative probability of causing an accident.

BAC Level (percent)	Relative Probability of Causing an Accident (percent)
0.02	1
0.04	1.8
0.06	2
0.08	3
0.10	5
0.12	8
0.14	15
0.16	25
0.18	33

2. Analyze the data in the table. What type(s) of function(s) model this situation? Explain your reasoning.

3. Create a scatter plot of the data.

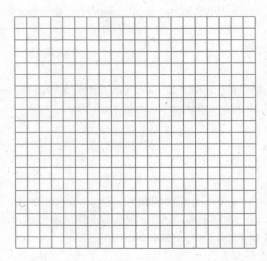

4. Consider the data in the table and your graph. What type(s) of function(s) model this situation based on these two representations? Explain your reasoning.

5. Based on your answer to Question 4, determine the appropriate regression equation. You may use your graphing calculator to determine the equation. Then sketch the function to model this situation.

6. Identify all the important key characteristics of your function in Question 5. Interpret what each means in terms of this problem situation. If applicable, include information about the domain, range, absolute minimums, absolute maximums, intervals of increase, intervals of decrease, *x*-intercepts, and *y*-intercepts.

7. Suppose that a driver is within the legal limit with a BAC of 0.075 percent. If a person with no alcohol in the blood system has a 1.8% chance of causing a car accident, predict the probability that a driver with a BAC of 0.075 percent will cause an accident. Do you think that this person is safe to drive, even though the person can legally drive? Explain why or why not. Show all your work.

8. Suppose that a driver has twice the BAC of the driver in Question 7. Predict the probability that this driver will cause an accident.

9. Suppose that a driver has three times the BAC of the driver in Question 7. Predict the probability that this driver will cause an accident.

10. Compare your answers in Question 7 through Question 9. What do you notice? Do they make sense in terms of this problem situation?

11. Write an article for the newsletter of the local chapter of S.A.D.D. (Students Against Destructive Decisions) that stresses the seriousness of drinking and driving. Use the results of this lesson to support your claims. You may want to include facts about the rate at which a driver's probability of causing an accident increases as their BAC increases, the definitions of legal limits in your state, and how a driver's motor skills are affected by alcohol.

 Be prepared to share your solutions and methods.

Chapter 11 Summary

Identifying Characteristics of Linear Piecewise Functions

A linear piecewise function is a piecewise-defined function whose pieces are linear. Characteristics such as domain and range and absolute minimum or absolute maximum can be determined from a piecewise function as well as information regarding the problem scenario.

Example

The graph shown describes a situation that represents the height of water in the bathtub over the 20 minutes that Parker is bathing her dog.

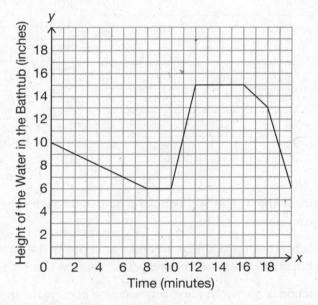

The domain is 0 to 20 minutes. The range is 6 to 15 inches. The absolute maximum is 15 inches, and it occurs between minutes 12 and 16. The absolute minimum is 6 inches, and it occurs between minutes 8 and 10 and at minute 16.

The height of the water decreased slowly between 0 and 8 minutes from 10 inches to 5 inches. It stayed at 5 inches for 2 minutes. The height of water then increased between minutes 10 and 12, when it increased 9 inches. It remained at this height for 4 minutes then slowly decreased for 2 minutes. Finally at 18 minutes, the water began decreasing more quickly.

Parker started her dog's bath with 10 inches of water in the tub. The water was slowly leaking out of the broken drain for the first 8 minutes of the bath. She realized the leak after 8 minutes and placed a washcloth over the drain to stop the leak. After 2 additional minutes, she ran the water for 2 minutes and increased the height of the water by 9 inches. The water held constant until the 16th minute, when the dog kicked the washcloth and slightly opened the drain. At 18 minutes, Parker opened the drain to start letting the water out of the bathtub.

Modeling Data with Curves of Best Fit

Real life data can be modeled using a scatter plot. Characteristics of the data such as increasing or decreasing over the domain, having an absolute maximum or absolute minimum, and being made of a smooth curve or straight lines can be used to identify the function family to which the function belongs.

Example

The table and graph display temperatures recorded during a 10-hour winter snow storm.

Time Since Start of Snow Storm (hours)	Temperature (°F)
1	26
2	24
3	18
4	16
5	10
6	12
7	14
8	20
9	23
10	27

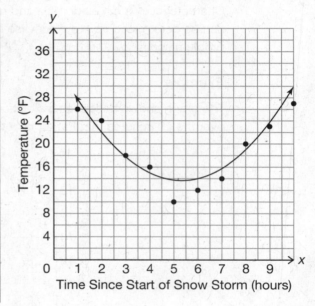

The function that is used to model the data decreases until about 5 hours and then the function increases.

This function has an absolute minimum at about (5, 14) which means the lowest temperature during the storm occurred about 5 hours after the storm began.

The function is a smooth curve representing continuous data. It is continuous because data exists in the time between hours.

Based on this information, this function belongs to the quadratic function family.

Writing Exponential Models from Data Sets

A graphing calculator can be used to determine an exponential regression equation to model real-world data. This regression equation can be used to predict future values.

Example

The table shows the weight of a golden retriever puppy as recorded during her growth. A scatter plot and regression equation of the data is shown.

Age (days)	Weight (pounds)
0	3.25
10	4.25
20	5.5
30	7
40	9
50	11.5
60	15
70	19

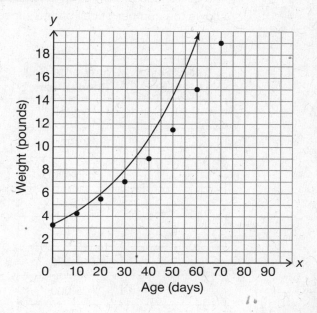

By using a graphing calculator, you can determine that the exponential regression equation for this scenario is $f(x) = 3.3(1.03)^x$. The correlation coefficient, r, is 0.9999. The equation can be used to predict the puppy's weight at 80 days.

$f(80) = 3.3(1.03)^{80}$
$f(80) = 35.1$

The exponential regression equation predicts that the puppy's weight will be approximately 35.1 pounds on day 80.

11.4 Determining the Type of Regression Equation that Best Fits a Graph

It is often difficult to tell the type of regression that best fits a data set. Calculating and graphing the regression equation can help determine which type of regression is the best fit.

Example

The cell phone use of Americans has increased dramatically since 1985. The data table shows the number of cell phone subscribers in the small town of Springfield.

Years Since 1985	Number of Cell Phone Users
0	285
1	498
3	1527
4	2672
6	8186
7	14,325
8	25,069

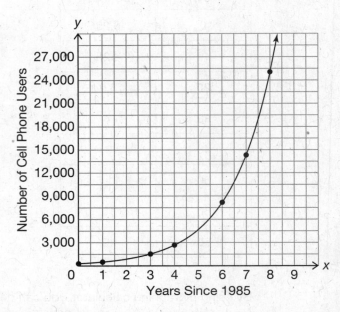

The number of cell phone users increases with the increase of each year. Increasing functions can be modeled by a linear or exponential function. However, because the number of cell phone users does not increase at a constant rate, the data cannot be modeled by a linear function. The exponential regression equation for the data is $f(x) = 285(1.75)^x$. This function when graphed closely models the data.

Geometry on the Coordinate Plane

12

The first transcontinental railroad in the U.S.—a railway connecting the Pacific and Atlantic Oceans—was completed in 1869. Today, there are over 200,000 miles of railroads in the U.S., carrying freight and passengers.

649

Let's Move!
Translating and Constructing Line Segments

© 2012 Carnegie Learning

LEARNING GOALS

In this lesson, you will:

- Determine the distance between two points.
- Use the Pythagorean Theorem to derive the Distance Formula.
- Apply the Distance Formula on the coordinate plane.
- Translate a line segment on the coordinate plane.
- Copy or duplicate a line segment by construction.

KEY TERMS

- Distance Formula
- transformation
- rigid motion
- translation
- image
- pre-image
- arc
- congruent line segments
- congruent

CONSTRUCTIONS

- copying a line segment
- duplicating a line segment

Are you better at geometry or algebra? Many students have a preference for one subject or the other. However, geometry and algebra are very closely related. While there are some branches of geometry that do not use much algebra, analytic geometry applies methods of algebra to geometric questions. Analytic geometry is also known as the study of geometry using a coordinate system. So anytime you are studying geometry and it involves a coordinate system, you are working on analytic geometry. Be sure to thank Descartes and his discovery of the coordinate plane for this!

What might be the pros and cons of analytic geometry compared to other branches of geometry? Does knowing about analytic geometry change how you feel about your own abilities in geometry or algebra?

Don, Freda, and Bert live in a town where the streets are laid out in a grid system.

1. Don lives 3 blocks east of Descartes Avenue and 5 blocks north of Elm Street. Freda lives 7 blocks east of Descartes Avenue and 2 blocks north of Elm Street. Plot points to show the locations of Don's house and Freda's house on the coordinate plane. Label each location with the student's name and the coordinates of the point.

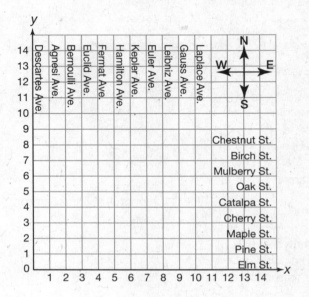

a. Name the streets that Don lives on.

b. Name the streets that Freda lives on.

2. Bert lives at the intersection of the avenue that Don lives on and the street that Freda lives on. Plot and label the location of Bert's house on the coordinate plane. Describe the location of Bert's house with respect to Descartes Avenue and Elm Street.

3. How do the x- and y-coordinates of Bert's house compare to the x- and y-coordinates of Don's house and Freda's house?

4. Use Don's and Bert's house coordinates to write and simplify an expression that represents the distance between their houses. Explain what this means in terms of the problem situation.

5. Use Bert's and Freda's house coordinates to write and simplify an expression that represents the distance between their houses. Explain what this means in terms of the problem situation.

6. All three friends are planning to meet at Don's house to hang out. Freda walks to Bert's house, and then Freda and Bert walk together to Don's house.

   a. Use the coordinates to write and simplify an expression that represents the total distance from Freda's house to Bert's house to Don's house.

   b. How far, in blocks, does Freda walk altogether?

7. Draw the direct path from Don's house to Freda's house on the coordinate plane. If Freda walks to Don's house on this path, how far, in blocks, does she walk? Explain how you determined your answer.

What shape do you see? How can that help you determine the distance of the direct path?

8. Complete the summary of the steps that you took to determine the direct distance between Freda's house and Don's house. Let d be the direct distance between Don's house and Freda's house.

Distance between Bert's house and Freda's house		Distance between Don's house and Bert's house		Direct distance between Don's house and Freda's house
$(\boxed{} - \boxed{})^2$	$+$	$(\boxed{} - \boxed{})^2$		$= \boxed{}$
$\boxed{}^2$	$+$	$\boxed{}^2$		$= \boxed{}$
$\boxed{}$	$+$	$\boxed{}$		$= \boxed{}$
			$\boxed{}$	$= \boxed{}$
			$\boxed{}$	$= \boxed{}$

Suppose Freda's, Bert's, and Don's houses were at different locations. You can generalize their locations by using x_1, x_2, y_1, and y_2 and still solve for the distances between their houses.

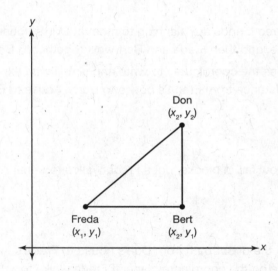

9. Use the graph to determine the distance from:

a. Don's house to Bert's house (*DB*).

b. Bert's house to Freda's house (*BF*).

Sure, they can be in different locations, but the points must still form a right triangle in order for us to generalize this, right?

12

10. Use the Pythagorean Theorem to determine the distance from Don's house to Freda's house (*DF*).

You used the Pythagorean Theorem to calculate the distance between two points on the coordinate plane. Your method can be written as the *Distance Formula*.

The **Distance Formula** states that if (x_1, y_1) and (x_2, y_2) are two points on the coordinate plane, then the distance d between (x_1, y_1) and (x_2, y_2) is given by

$$d = \sqrt{(x_2 - x_1)^2 + (y_2 - y_1)^2}.$$

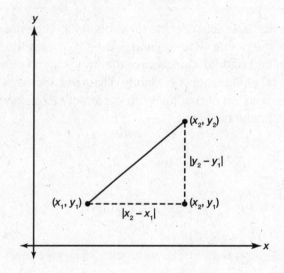

The absolute value symbols are used to indicate that the distance is always positive.

11. Do you think that it matters which point you identify as (x_1, y_1) and which point you identify as (x_2, y_2) when you use the Distance Formula? Explain your reasoning.

12. Calculate the distance between each pair of points. Round your answer to the nearest tenth if necessary. Show all your work.

    a. (1, 2) and (3, 7)   **b.** (−6, 4) and (2, −8)

    c. (−5, 2) and (−6, 10)

13. Carlos and Mandy just completed Question 12 parts (a) through (c). They need to calculate the distance between the points (−1, −2) and (−3, −7). They notice the similarity between this problem and part (a). Carlos says that the solution must be the negative of the solution of part (a) of Question 12. Mandy disagrees and says that the solution will be the same as the solution of part (a). Who is correct? Explain your reasoning and state the correct solution.

14. The distance between (x, 2) and (0, 6) is 5 units. Use the Distance Formula to determine the value of x. Show all your work.

1. Pedro's house is located at (6, 10). Graph this location on the coordinate plane and label the point *P*.

2. Jethro's house is located at (2, 3). Graph this location on the coordinate plane and label the point *J*.

3. Draw a line connecting the two houses to create line segment *PJ*.

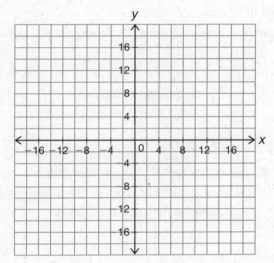

4. Determine the length of line segment *PJ*.

Length is the same as distance on the coordinate plane!

12

A **transformation** is the mapping, or movement, of all the points of a figure in a plane according to a common operation.

A **rigid motion** is a transformation of points in space.

A **translation** is a rigid motion that "slides" each point of a figure the same distance and direction. Sliding a figure left or right is a horizontal translation, and sliding it up or down is a vertical translation. The new figure created from the translation is called the **image**. The original figure is called the **pre-image**.

A line, or even a point, can be considered a figure.

5. Line segment *PJ* is horizontally translated 10 units to the left.

   a. Graph the new location of line segment *PJ*. Label the new points *P′* and *J′*.

   b. Identify the coordinates of *P′* and *J′*.

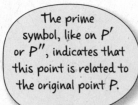

The prime symbol, like on *P′* or *P″*, indicates that this point is related to the original point *P*.

6. Line segment *P′J′* is vertically translated 14 units down.

   a. Graph the new location of line segment *P′J′*. Label the new points *P″* and *J″*.

   b. Identify the coordinates of *P″* and *J″*.

7. Line segment *P″J″* is horizontally translated 10 units to the right.

   a. Without graphing, predict the coordinates of *P‴* and *J‴*.

   b. Graph the new location of line segment *P″J″*. Label the new points *P‴* and *J‴*.

12

8. Describe the translation necessary on line segment $P'''J'''$ so that it returns to the location of PJ.

9. How do the lengths of the images compare to the lengths of the pre-images? Explain how you could verify your answer.

10. Analyze the coordinates of the endpoints of each line segment.

    a. Identify the coordinates of each line segment in the table.

Line Segments	PJ	$P'J'$	$P''J''$	$P'''J'''$
Coordinates of Endpoints				

    b. Describe how a horizontal translation changes the coordinates of the endpoints.

    c. Describe how a vertical translation changes the coordinates of the endpoints.

11. How many translations occurred for the line segment to return to its original location?

12. Does either a vertical or horizontal translation of a line segment alter the length of the line segment? Explain why or why not.

13. If both points on a line segment were not moved the same distance or direction, would the length of the line segment change? Would this still be considered a translation? Explain your reasoning.

PROBLEM 3 Copying Line Segments

In the previous problem, you translated line segments on the coordinate plane. The lengths of the line segments on the coordinate plane are measurable.

In this problem, you will translate line segments when measurement is not possible. This basic geometric construction is called **copying a line segment** or **duplicating a line segment.** The construction is performed using a compass and a straightedge.

One method for copying a line segment is to use circles. But before you can get to that, let's review how to draw perfect circles with a compass.

Remember that a compass is an instrument used to draw circles and arcs. A compass can have two legs connected at one end.

One leg has a point, and the other holds a pencil. Some newer compasses may be different, but all of them are made to construct circles by placing a point firmly into the paper and then spinning the top of the compass around, with the pencil point just touching the paper.

1. Use your compass to construct a number of circles of different sizes.

Take your time. It may take a while for you to be able to construct a clean, exact circle without doubled or smudged lines.

2. Point *C* is the center of a circle and line segment *CD* is the radius.

   a. Construct circle *C*.

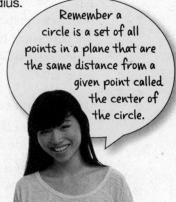

Remember a circle is a set of all points in a plane that are the same distance from a given point called the center of the circle.

C•————————•D

   b. Draw and label points *A*, *B*, *E*, and *F* anywhere on the circle.

   c. Construct $\overline{AC}$, $\overline{BC}$, $\overline{EC}$, and $\overline{FC}$.

   d. What conclusion can you make about all these line segments? Explain your reasoning.

   e. Do you think the line segments you constructed are also radii of the circle? How do you know?

An **arc** is a part of a circle. You can also think of an arc as the curve between two points on the circle.

3. Point *C* is the center of a circle and line segment *AC* is the radius.

   a. Construct an arc of circle *C*. Make your arc about one-half inch long. Construct the arc so that it does not pass through *A*.

     •C

   •
   A

   b. Draw and label two points *B* and *E,* on the arc and construct line segments *CE* and *CB*.

   c. What conclusion can you make about these line segments?

12

Line segments that have the same length are called **congruent line segments**. **Congruent** means to have the same size, shape, and measure. You can indicate that two line segments are congruent by using the congruence symbol, ≅, and writing the names of the line segments that are congruent on either side of it. For example, $\overline{CB} \cong \overline{CA}$ is read as "line segment CB is congruent to line segment CA."

4. Construct a circle with the center A and a radius of about 1 inch.

   a. Without changing the width of your compass, place the compass point on any point on the circle you constructed and then construct another circle.

   b. Draw a dot on a point where the two circles intersect. Place the compass point on that point of intersection of the two circles, and then construct another circle.

   c. Repeat this process until no new circles can be constructed.

   d. Connect the points of the circles' intersections with each other.

• A

   e. Describe the figure formed by the line segments.

12

Now let's use these circle-drawing skills to duplicate a line segment.

 5. Circle A is congruent to Circle A'.

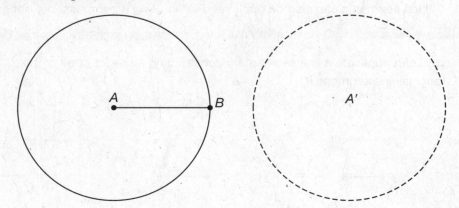

a. Duplicate line segment AB in Circle A'. Use point A' as the center of the circle, then label the endpoint of the duplicated segment as point B'.

b. Describe the location of point B'.

c. If possible, draw a second line segment in Circle A' that is a duplicate of line segment AB. Label the duplicate segment line segment A'C'. If it is not possible, explain why.

Line segments can also be duplicated while using a compass, but not drawing a circle.

You can duplicate a line segment by constructing an exact copy of the original line segment.

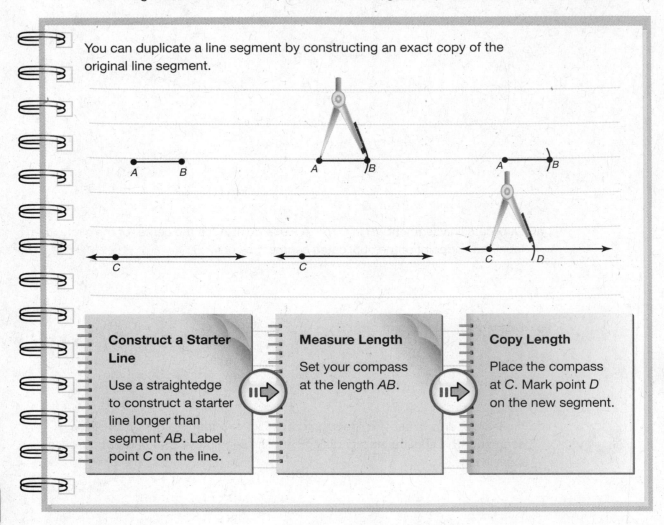

Construct a Starter Line

Use a straightedge to construct a starter line longer than segment AB. Label point C on the line.

Measure Length

Set your compass at the length AB.

Copy Length

Place the compass at C. Mark point D on the new segment.

1. Construct a line segment that is twice the length of line segment AB.

Make sure to construct a starter line first.

2. Duplicate each line segment using a compass and a straightedge.

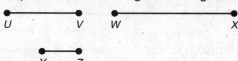

U   V   W   X

Y   Z

3. Dave and Sandy are duplicating the segment *AB*. Their methods are shown.

Dave

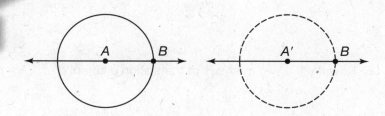

A   B   A'   B

Sandy

A   B   A'   B

Which method is correct? Explain your reasoning.

4. Which method do you prefer? Why?

Talk the Talk

Translating a line segment on the coordinate plane using coordinates and translating a line segment by construction using construction tools both preserve distance.

1. How are the two methods of translation similar?

2. How are the two methods of translation different?

Which method is more accurate?

Be prepared to share your solutions and methods.

Treasure Hunt
Midpoints and Bisectors

LEARNING GOALS

In this lesson, you will:

- Determine the midpoint of a line segment on a coordinate plane.
- Use the Midpoint Formula.
- Apply the Midpoint Formula on the coordinate plane.
- Bisect a line segment using patty paper.
- Bisect a line segment by construction.
- Locate the midpoint of a line segment.

KEY TERMS

- midpoint
- Midpoint Formula
- segment bisector

CONSTRUCTIONS

- bisecting a line segment

When you hear the phrase "treasure hunt," you may think of pirates, buried treasure, and treasure maps. However, there are very few documented cases of pirates actually burying treasure, and there are no historical pirate treasure maps! So where did this idea come from?

Robert Louis Stevenson's book *Treasure Island* is a story all about pirates and their buried gold, and this book greatly influenced public knowledge of pirates. In fact, it is Stevenson who is often credited with coming up with the concept of the treasure map and using an X to mark where a treasure is located.

Have you ever used a map to determine your location or the location of another object? Did you find it difficult or easy? How does the idea of a treasure map relate to a mathematical concept you are very familiar with?

PROBLEM 1 Locating the Treasure

Ms. Lopez, a kindergarten teacher, is planning a treasure hunt for her students. She drew a model of the playground on a coordinate plane as shown. She used this model to decide where to place items for the treasure hunt, and to determine how to write the treasure hunt instructions. Each grid square represents one square yard on the playground.

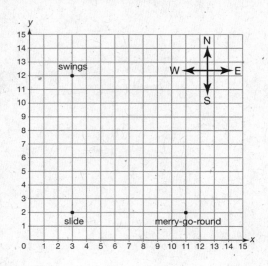

1. Determine the distance, in yards, between the merry-go-round and the slide. Show all your work.

2. Ms. Lopez wants to place a small pile of beads in the grass halfway between the merry-go-round and the slide. How far, in yards, should the beads be placed from the merry-go-round and the slide? Write the coordinates for the location exactly halfway between the merry-go-round and the slide.

3. Graph the location of the beads on the coordinate plane.

4. How do the coordinates of the location of the beads compare to the coordinates of the locations of the slide and merry-go-round?

5. Ms. Lopez wants to place a pile of kazoos in the grass halfway between the slide and the swings. What should the coordinates of the location of the kazoos be? Explain your reasoning. Plot and label the location of the kazoos on the coordinate plane.

6. How do the coordinates of the location of the kazoos compare to the coordinates of the locations of the slide and swings?

7. Ms. Lopez wants to place a pile of buttons in the grass halfway between the swings and the merry-go-round. Describe how you can determine the halfway point between the two locations.

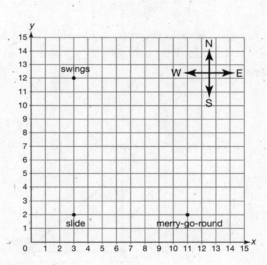

You can draw right triangles on the coordinate plane to figure out the *exact* location of the buttons. Do you see how?

8. How far, in yards, from the swings and the merry-go-round will the pile of buttons be? Plot the location of the buttons on the coordinate plane. Round your answer to the nearest tenth if necessary.

9. Verify your solution for Question 8.

    a. Use the Distance Formula to determine whether your answer in Question 8 is correct by calculating the distance between the buttons and the swings. Show all your work.

    b. Would it have mattered if you verified your answer by calculating the distance between the buttons and the merry-go-round? Explain your reasoning.

 Suppose the slide, the swings, and the merry-go-round were at different locations. You can generalize their locations by using x_1, x_2, y_1, and y_2, and then solve for the location between each.

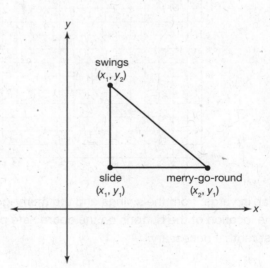

10. Use the diagram to describe these distances.

    a. the vertical distance from the *x*-axis to the slide

    b. the distance from the slide to the swings

    c. half the distance from the slide to the swings

    d. the vertical distance from the *x*-axis to the slide plus half the distance from the slide to the swings

11. Simplify the expression from Question 10, part (d).

12. Use the diagram to describe these distances.

    a. the horizontal distance from the *y*-axis to the slide

    b. the distance from the slide to the merry-go-round

    c. half the distance from the slide to the merry-go-round

    d. the horizontal distance from the *y*-axis to the slide plus half the distance from the slide to the merry-go-round

 13. Simplify the expression from Question 12, part (d).

The coordinates of the points that you determined in Questions 11 and 13 are **midpoints,** or points that are exactly halfway between two given points. The calculations you performed can be summarized in the *Midpoint Formula.*

The **Midpoint Formula** states that if (x_1, y_1) and (x_2, y_2) are two points on the coordinate plane, then the midpoint of the line segment that joins these two points is given by $\left(\dfrac{x_1 + x_2}{2}, \dfrac{y_1 + y_2}{2}\right)$.

14. Use the Midpoint Formula to determine the midpoint between the swings and the merry-go-round from Question 7.

15. Do you think it matters which point you identify as (x_1, y_1) and which point you identify as (x_2, y_2) when you use the Midpoint Formula? Explain why or why not.

16. Determine the midpoint of each line segment that has the given endpoints. Show all your work.

   a. (0, 5) and (4, 3)

   b. (8, 2) and (6, 0)

   c. (−3, 1) and (9, −7)

   d. (−10, 7) and (−4, −7)

Jack's Spare Key

Jack buried a spare key to his house in the backyard in case he ever locked himself out.

He remembers burying the key $\frac{1}{4}$ of the way between the back door and an oak tree. The

back door is located at point (2, 3), and the oak tree is located at point (12, 3).

 1. Plot and label the location of the back door and the oak tree on the coordinate plane.

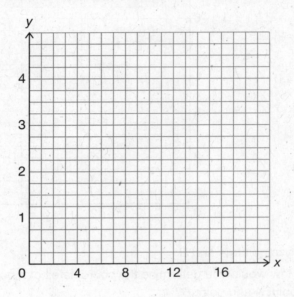

2. Determine the location of the key.

    a. How would you determine the coordinates of the location of the key?

     b. Determine the coordinates of the location of the key.

Using the Midpoint Formula Over and Over and Over Again

1. Plot and label points A (0, 4) and B (2, 10) on the coordinate plane.

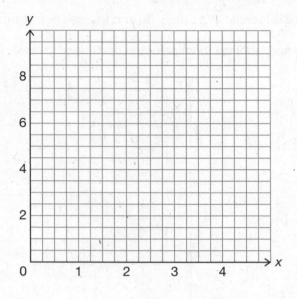

2. Analyze points A and B.

   a. How would you determine the coordinates of a point that is located halfway between point A and point B?

   b. Determine the coordinates of a point that is located halfway between point A and point B and graph the point.

   c. How would you determine the coordinates of a point that is located $\frac{1}{4}$ of the way between point A and point B?

d. Determine the coordinates of a point that is located $\frac{1}{4}$ of the way between point A and point B and graph the point.

e. How would you determine the coordinates of a point that is located $\frac{3}{4}$ of the way between point A and point B?

f. Determine the coordinates of a point that is located $\frac{3}{4}$ of the way between point A and point B and graph the point.

 3. Name other fractional divisions of a line segment possible to determine using the Midpoint Formula.

In the previous problem, you located the midpoint of a line segment on the coordinate plane. The lengths of the line segments on the plane are measurable.

In this problem, you will locate the midpoint of a line segment when measurement is not possible. This basic geometric construction used to locate a midpoint of a line segment is called **bisecting a line segment**. When bisecting a line segment, you create a *segment bisector*. A **segment bisector** is a line, line segment, or ray that divides a line segment into two line segments of equal measure, or two congruent line segments.

Just as with duplicating a line segment, there are a number of methods to bisect a line segment.

One method is to use tracing paper, which is sometimes known as patty paper.

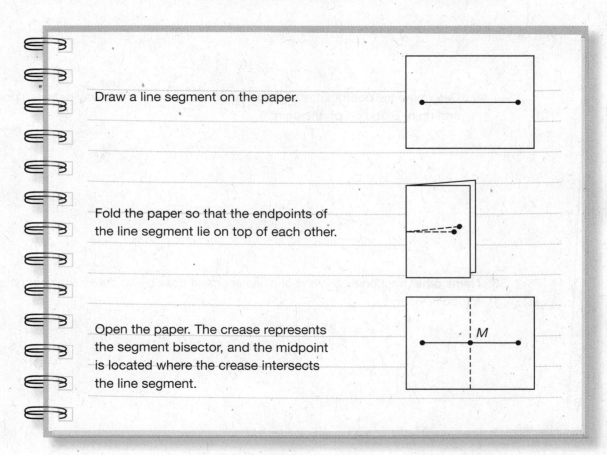

Draw a line segment on the paper.

Fold the paper so that the endpoints of the line segment lie on top of each other.

Open the paper. The crease represents the segment bisector, and the midpoint is located where the crease intersects the line segment.

1. Use patty paper to duplicate a line segment. How do you know your bisector and midpoint are accurate?

2. Thomas determined the midpoint of this line segment incorrectly.

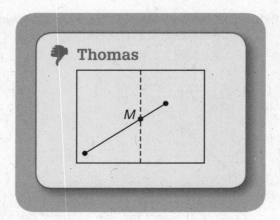

Explain what Thomas did incorrectly and how you can tell he is incorrect. Explain how he can correctly determine the midpoint.

Just as with other geometric constructions, a compass and straightedge can be used to determine a segment bisector.

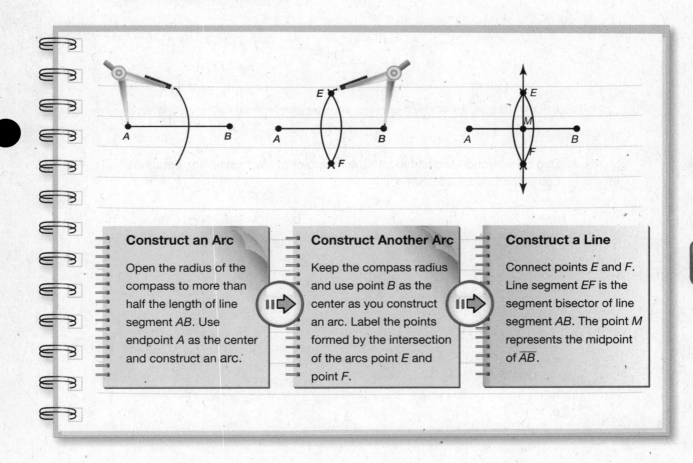

Construct an Arc

Open the radius of the compass to more than half the length of line segment *AB*. Use endpoint *A* as the center and construct an arc.

Construct Another Arc

Keep the compass radius and use point *B* as the center as you construct an arc. Label the points formed by the intersection of the arcs point *E* and point *F*.

Construct a Line

Connect points *E* and *F*. Line segment *EF* is the segment bisector of line segment *AB*. The point *M* represents the midpoint of $\overline{AB}$.

3. Aaron is determining the midpoint of line segment *RS*. His work is shown.

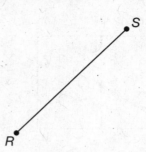

He states that because the arcs do not intersect this line segment does not have a midpoint. Kate disagrees and tells him he drew his arcs incorrectly and they must be redrawn to determine the midpoint. Who is correct? Explain your reasoning.

4. Use construction tools to locate the midpoint of each given line segment. Label each midpoint as *M*.

a.

A   *B*

b.

C

D

c.

F

G

12

5. When bisecting a line segment, does it make a difference which endpoint is used to draw the first arc? Explain your reasoning.

6. Explain how duplicating a line segment can be used to verify that the midpoint resulting from bisecting the line segment is truly the midpoint of the segment.

Talk the Talk

Two methods for locating the midpoint of a line segment are using the Midpoint Formula and constructing the bisector of a line segment.

1. How are the two methods similar?

2. How are the two methods different?

Be prepared to share your solutions and methods.

It's All About Angles
Translating and Constructing Angles and Angle Bisectors

LEARNING GOALS

In this lesson, you will:

- Translate an angle on the coordinate plane.
- Copy or duplicate an angle by construction.
- Bisect an angle by construction.

KEY TERMS

- angle
- angle bisector

CONSTRUCTIONS

- copying an angle
- duplicating an angle
- bisecting an angle

You may have never thought of it this way, but drawing and geometry are closely linked. Drawing is the process of deliberately arranging lines and curves to create an image. Most drawings have a number of different angles that are created through the intersection of these lines and curves. However, an art movement known as De Stijl limits the types of lines used when drawing to only horizontal and vertical lines. They also limit the colors used to the primary colors. While you may think this sounds restricting, many artists have created many works of art in this style. In fact, an architect even designed a house adhering to the De Stijl principles!

If De Stijl limits the artists to only using horizontal and vertical lines, what types of angles can be created in their art work? What types of angles cannot be created? What might be some challenges with drawing or painting in this style?

In a previous lesson, you practiced translating a line segment on the coordinate plane horizontally or vertically.

1. Describe how to translate a line segment on a coordinate plane.

An **angle** is formed by two rays that share a common endpoint. The sides of the angle are represented by the two rays. Each ray of an angle contains an infinite number of line segments. For the purposes of graphing an angle on the coordinate plane, you will label one line segment on each ray.

Remember that a ray has one endpoint and extends forever in one direction.

2. Analyze angle *DBM*. Describe how you would translate this angle on the coordinate plane.

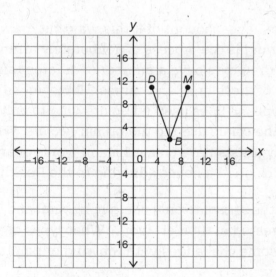

3. Complete the translations of angle *DBM*.

   a. Horizontally translate ∠*DBM* 13 units left. Label the image ∠*D'B'M'*.

   b. Vertically translate ∠*D'B'M'* 15 units down. Label the image ∠*D"B"M"*.

   c. Horizontally translate ∠*D"B"M"* 13 units right. Label the image ∠*D'''B'''M'''*.

   d. Use the graph to complete the tables.

Line Segments	MB	M'B'	M''B''	M'''B'''
Coordinates of Endpoints				

Line Segments	DB	D'B'	D''B''	D'''B'''
Coordinates of Endpoints				

4. Describe how a horizontal translation changes the coordinates of the angle endpoints.

5. Describe how a vertical translation changes the coordinates of the angle endpoints.

6. How many translations must occur for the angle to return to the location of the original figure?

An angle is measured using a protractor, and the measure of an angle is expressed in units called degrees.

7. Measure each angle on the coordinate plane. How do the measures of the images compare to the measures of the pre-images?

8. Does either a vertical or a horizontal translation of an angle alter the measure of the angle? Explain why or why not.

9. What is the result of moving only one angle endpoint a specified distance or direction? How does this affect the measure of the angle? Is this still considered a translation?

In the previous problem, you translated an angle on the coordinate plane using line segments that were associated with a measurement.

You can also translate an angle not associated with a measurement. This basic geometric construction is called **copying an angle** or **duplicating an angle**. The construction is performed using a compass and a straightedge.

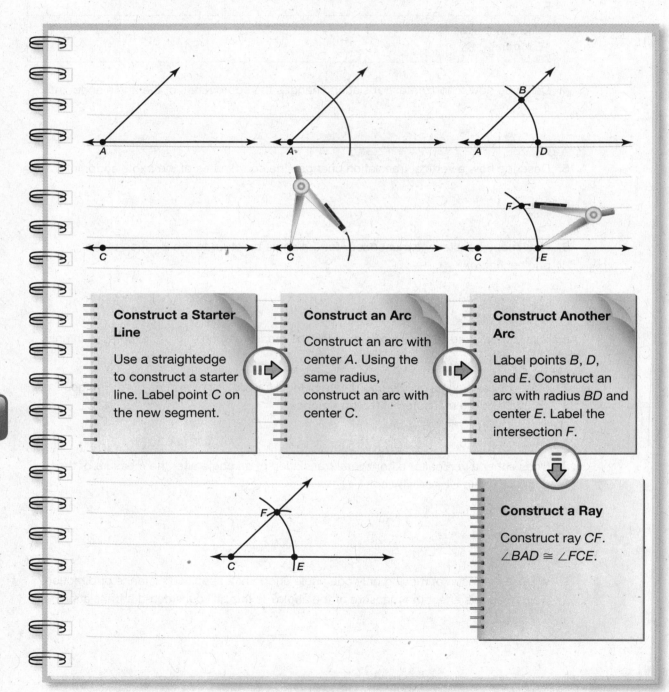

Construct a Starter Line

Use a straightedge to construct a starter line. Label point C on the new segment.

Construct an Arc

Construct an arc with center A. Using the same radius, construct an arc with center C.

Construct Another Arc

Label points B, D, and E. Construct an arc with radius BD and center E. Label the intersection F.

Construct a Ray

Construct ray CF.
∠BAD ≅ ∠FCE.

1. Construct an angle that is twice the measure of ∠A.

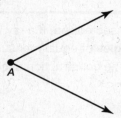

A

2. How is duplicating an angle similar to duplicating a line segment?
How is it different?

Just as line segments can be bisected, angles can be bisected too. If a ray is drawn through the vertex of an angle and divides the angle into two angles of equal measure, or two congruent angles, the ray is called an **angle bisector**. The construction used to create an angle bisector is called **bisecting an angle**.

One way to bisect an angle is using patty paper.

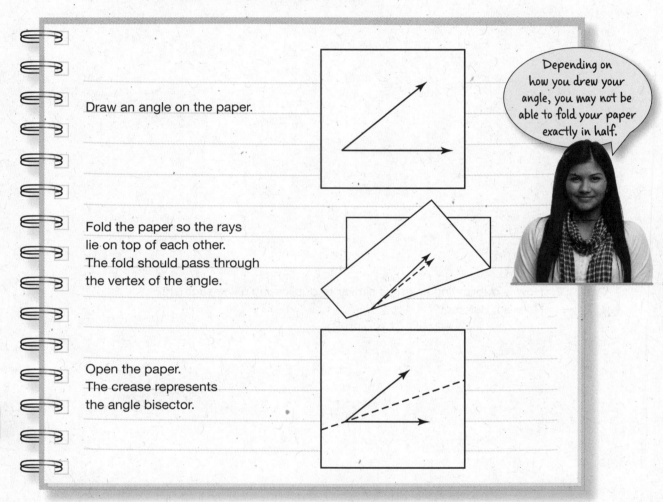

Draw an angle on the paper.

Fold the paper so the rays lie on top of each other. The fold should pass through the vertex of the angle.

Open the paper. The crease represents the angle bisector.

Depending on how you drew your angle, you may not be able to fold your paper exactly in half.

1. Angela states that as long as the crease goes through the vertex it is an angle bisector. Is she correct? Why or why not?

You can also bisect an angle using a compass and a straightedge.

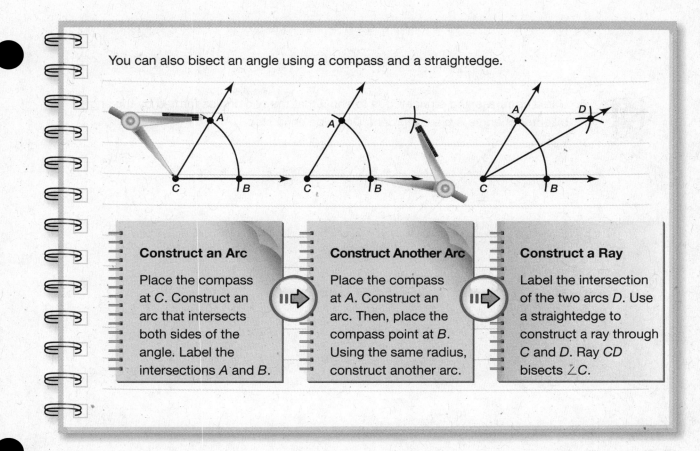

Construct an Arc

Place the compass at *C*. Construct an arc that intersects both sides of the angle. Label the intersections *A* and *B*.

Construct Another Arc

Place the compass at *A*. Construct an arc. Then, place the compass point at *B*. Using the same radius, construct another arc.

Construct a Ray

Label the intersection of the two arcs *D*. Use a straightedge to construct a ray through *C* and *D*. Ray *CD* bisects ∠*C*.

2. Construct the bisector of ∠*A*.

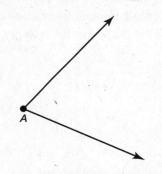

3. Construct an angle that is one-fourth the measure of ∠*H*.

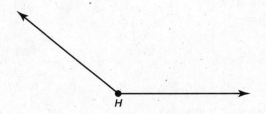

4. Describe how to construct an angle that is one-eighth the measure of angle *H*.

5. Use a compass and straightedge to show that the two angles formed by the angle bisector of angle *A* are congruent. Describe each step.

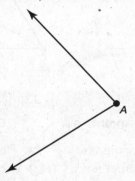

Talk the Talk

Translating an angle on the coordinate plane using coordinates and translating an angle by construction using construction tools both preserve the measure of the angle.

1. How are the two methods of translation similar?

2. How are the two methods of translation different?

Be prepared to share your solutions and methods.

© 2012 Carnegie Learning

Did You Find a Parking Space?

Parallel and Perpendicular Lines on the Coordinate Plane

LEARNING GOALS

In this lesson, you will:

- Determine whether lines are parallel.
- Identify and write the equations of lines parallel to given lines.
- Determine whether lines are perpendicular.
- Identify and write the equations of lines perpendicular to given lines.
- Identify and write the equations of horizontal and vertical lines.
- Calculate the distance between a line and a point not on the line.

KEY TERM

- point-slope form

They seem simple enough, but parking lots require a great deal of planning. Parking lots are designed by transportation engineers who use technology and science to plan, design, operate, and manage facilities for any mode of transportation. During the planning stage of a parking lot, these engineers must keep in mind the needs of the facility that will use the parking lot as well as the needs of the drivers. They must think about the entrances and exits as well as the surrounding streets and their traffic flow. Even the weather must be taken into account if the lot is being built somewhere with heavy rain or snow!

Only thinking about the cars and their drivers, what needs might affect an engineer's plans? What would make a parking lot "good" or "bad"? Can you think of anything else that might affect the planning of a parking lot other than the things mentioned above?

Large parking lots have line segments painted to mark the locations where vehicles are supposed to park. The layout of these line segments must be considered carefully so that there is enough room for the vehicles to move and park in the lot without other vehicles being damaged.

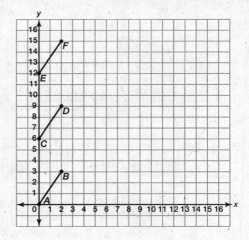

The line segments shown model parking spaces in a parking lot. One grid square represents one square meter.

1. What do you notice about the line segments that form the parking spaces?

2. What is the vertical distance between $\overline{AB}$ and $\overline{CD}$ and between $\overline{CD}$ and $\overline{EF}$?

3. Carefully extend $\overline{AB}$ to create line p, extend $\overline{CD}$ to create line q, and extend $\overline{EF}$ to create line r.

4. Use the graph to identify the slope of each line. What do you notice?

The **point-slope form** of the equation of the line that passes through (x_1, y_1) and has slope m is $y - y_1 = m(x - x_1)$.

5. Use the point-slope form to write the equations of lines p, q, and r. Then write the equations in slope-intercept form.

12

6. What do the y-intercepts tell you about the relationship between these lines in the problem situation?

Remember, parallel lines are lines that lie in the same plane and do not intersect no matter how far they extend! The symbol for parallel is ||.

7. If you were to draw $\overline{GH}$ above $\overline{EF}$ to form another parking space, predict what the slope and equation of the line will be without graphing the new line. How did you come to this conclusion?

8. In the *Parking Spaces* problem, all the slopes were equal and the y-intercepts were all multiples of the same number.

   a. Are the slopes of parallel lines on a coordinate plane always equal? Explain your reasoning.

   b. Are the y-intercepts of parallel lines on a coordinate plane always a multiple of the same number? Explain your reasoning.

9. Write equations for three lines that are parallel to the line given by $y = -2x + 4$. Explain how you determined your answers.

10. Write an equation for the line that is parallel to the line given by $y = 5x + 3$ and passes through the point (4, 0). Explain how you determined your answer.

12

11. Without graphing the equations, predict whether the lines given by $y - 2x = 5$ and $2x - y = 4$ are parallel.

12. Consider the graph shown.

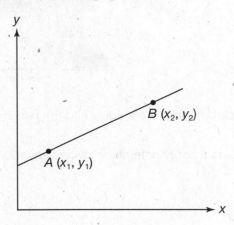

a. Use the graph to translate line segment *AB a* units up.

b. Identify the *x*- and *y*-coordinates of each corresponding point on the image.

c. Use the slope formula to calculate the slope of the pre-image.

d. Use the slope formula to calculate the slope of the image.

e. How does the slope of the image compare to the slope of the pre-image?

f. How would you describe the relationship between the graph of the image and the graph of the pre-image?

PROBLEM 2 More Parking Spaces

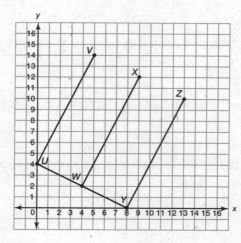

The line segments shown represent parking spaces in a truck parking lot. One grid square represents one square meter.

1. Use a protractor to determine the measures of ∠VUW, ∠XWY, and ∠ZYW. What similarity do you notice about the angles?

Remember how to use a protractor? Your answer must be in degrees!

2. Carefully extend $\overline{UY}$ to create line p, extend $\overline{UV}$ to create line q, extend $\overline{WX}$ to create line r, and extend $\overline{YZ}$ to create line s on the coordinate plane.

3. Determine whether the lines given are perpendicular or parallel.

   a. q, r, s

   b. p and q

   c. p and r

   d. p and s

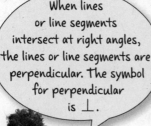

When lines or line segments intersect at right angles, the lines or line segments are perpendicular. The symbol for perpendicular is ⊥.

4. Predict how the slopes of the lines will compare. Do not actually calculate the slopes of the lines for your prediction.

5. Use the graph and the lines you drew to determine the slopes of lines p, q, r, and s.

6. Determine the product of the slopes of two perpendicular lines.

 7. Describe the difference between the slopes of two parallel lines and the slopes of two perpendicular lines.

When the product of two numbers is 1, the numbers are reciprocals of one another. When the product of two numbers is −1, the numbers are negative reciprocals of one another. So the slopes of perpendicular lines are negative reciprocals of each other.

 8. Do you think that the y-intercepts of perpendicular lines tell you anything about the relationship between the perpendicular lines? Explain your reasoning.

9. Write equations for three lines that are perpendicular to the line given by $y = -2x + 4$. Explain how you determined your answers.

10. Write an equation for the line that is perpendicular to the line given by $y = 5x + 3$ and passes through the point (4, 0). Show all your work and explain how you determined your answer.

11. Without graphing the equations, determine whether the lines given by $y + 2x = 5$ and $2x - y = 4$ are perpendicular. Explain how you determined your answer.

PROBLEM 3   Horizontal and Vertical

Consider the graph shown.

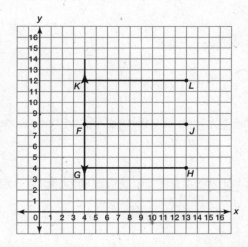

1. Carefully extend $\overline{GK}$ to create line p, extend $\overline{GH}$ to create line q, extend $\overline{FJ}$ to create line r, and extend $\overline{KL}$ to create line s.

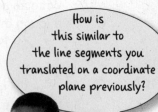

How is this similar to the line segments you translated on a coordinate plane previously?

12

2. Consider the three horizontal lines you drew for Question 1. For any horizontal line, if x increases by one unit, by how many units does y change?

3. What is the slope of any horizontal line? Explain your reasoning.

4. Consider the vertical line you drew in Question 1. Suppose that y increases by one unit. By how many units does x change?

5. What is the rise divided by the run? Does this make any sense? Explain why or why not.

6. Determine whether the statements are always, sometimes, or never true. Explain your reasoning.

   a. Vertical lines are always parallel.

   b. Horizontal lines are always parallel.

7. Describe the relationship between any vertical line and any horizontal line.

8. Write an equation for a horizontal line and an equation for a vertical line that pass through the point $(2, -1)$.

9. Write an equation for a line that is perpendicular to the line given by $x = 5$ and passes through the point $(1, 0)$.

10. Write an equation for a line that is perpendicular to the line given by $y = -2$ and passes through the point $(5, 6)$.

1. Sketch a line and a point not on the line. Describe the shortest distance between the point and the line.

2. The equation of the line shown on the coordinate plane is $f(x) = \frac{3}{2}x + 6$. Draw the shortest segment between the line and the point A (0, 12). Label the point where the segment intersects $f(x)$ as point B.

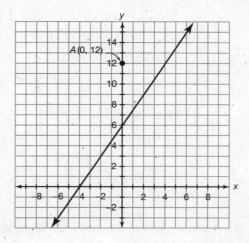

3. What information do you need in order to calculate the length of $\overline{AB}$ using the Distance Formula?

4. How can you calculate the intersection point of $\overline{AB}$ and the line $f(x) = \frac{3}{2}x + 6$ algebraically?

5. Write an equation for $\overline{AB}$.

6. Calculate the point of intersection of $\overline{AB}$ and the line $f(x) = \frac{3}{2}x + 6$.

7. Calculate the length of $\overline{AB}$.

8. What is the distance from the point (0, 12) to the line $f(x) = \frac{3}{2}x + 6$?

 Be prepared to share your solutions and methods.

Making Copies—Just as Perfect as the Original!

Constructing Perpendicular Lines, Parallel Lines, and Polygons

© 2012 Carnegie Learning

OBJECTIVES

In this lesson, you will:

- Construct a perpendicular line to a given line through a point on the line.
- Construct a perpendicular line to a given line through a point not on the line.
- Construct a parallel line to a given line through a point not on the line.
- Construct an equilateral triangle given the length of one side of the triangle.
- Construct an isosceles triangle given the length of one side of the triangle.
- Construct a square given the perimeter (as the length of a given line segment).
- Construct a rectangle that is not a square given the perimeter (as the length of a given line segment).

There's an old saying that you might have heard before: "They broke the mold when they made me!" A person says this to imply that they are unique. Of course, humans do not come from molds, but there are plenty of things that do.

For example, take a look at a dime if you have one handy. Besides some tarnish on the coin and the year the coin was produced, it is identical to just about every other dime out there. Creating and duplicating a coin a few billion times is quite a process involving designing the coin, creating multiple molds (and negatives of the molds), cutting the design onto metal, and on and on.

Can you think of any times when the "original" might be more important than a duplicate? Can you think of any examples where the "original" product might be more expensive than a generic brand of the same product?

In a previous lesson, you practiced bisecting a line segment and locating a midpoint of a line segment by construction. In fact, you were actually constructing a line segment perpendicular to the original line segment during the construction.

Follow the steps to construct a perpendicular line through a point on the line.

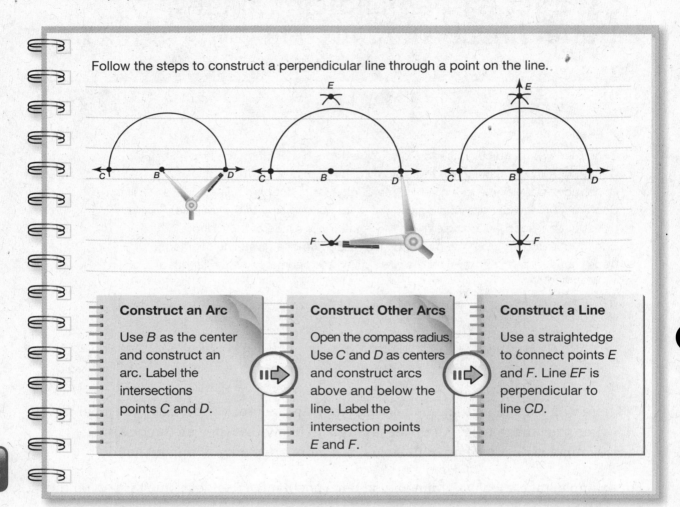

Construct an Arc

Use *B* as the center and construct an arc. Label the intersections points *C* and *D*.

Construct Other Arcs

Open the compass radius. Use *C* and *D* as centers and construct arcs above and below the line. Label the intersection points *E* and *F*.

Construct a Line

Use a straightedge to connect points *E* and *F*. Line *EF* is perpendicular to line *CD*.

1. Construct a line perpendicular to the given line through point *P*.

P

2. How is constructing a segment bisector and constructing a perpendicular line through a point on a line different?

3. Do you think that you can only construct a perpendicular line through a point that is on a line? Why or why not?

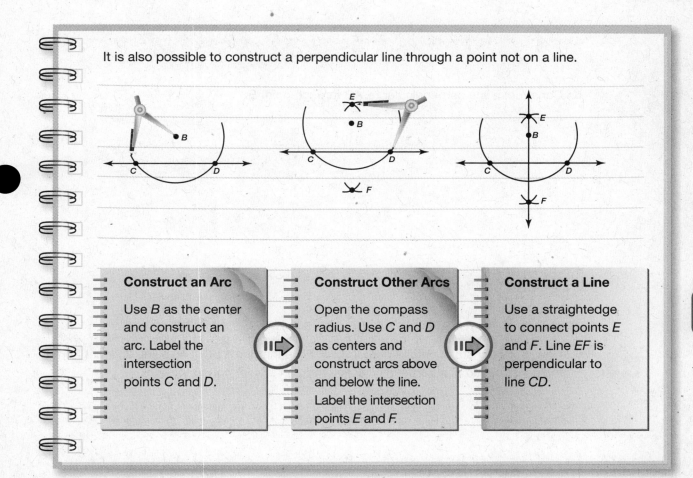

It is also possible to construct a perpendicular line through a point not on a line.

Construct an Arc

Use *B* as the center and construct an arc. Label the intersection points *C* and *D*.

Construct Other Arcs

Open the compass radius. Use *C* and *D* as centers and construct arcs above and below the line. Label the intersection points *E* and *F*.

Construct a Line

Use a straightedge to connect points *E* and *F*. Line *EF* is perpendicular to line *CD*.

4. Amos claims that it is only possible to construct a perpendicular line through horizontal and vertical lines because the intersection of the points must be right angles. Loren claims that a perpendicular line can be constructed through any line and any point on or not on the line. Who is correct? Correct the rationale of the student who is *not* correct.

5. Construct a line perpendicular to $\overleftrightarrow{AG}$ through point *B*.

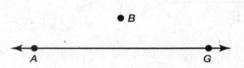

6. How is the construction of a perpendicular line through a point on a line different from the construction of a perpendicular line through a point not on the line?

PROBLEM 2   Constructing Parallel Lines

You can construct a line parallel to a given line. Of course, to ensure that the constructed line is parallel, you must use a perpendicular line.

1. Analyze the figure shown.

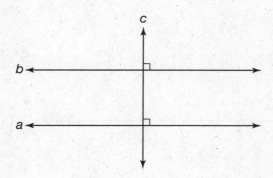

Describe the relationship between the lines given.

a. *a* and *c*

b. *b* and *c*

c. *a* and *b*

2. Use line *d* to construct line *e* parallel to line *d*. Then, describe the steps you performed for the construction.

← ————————————→ *d*

12

PROBLEM 3 Constructing an Equilateral Triangle

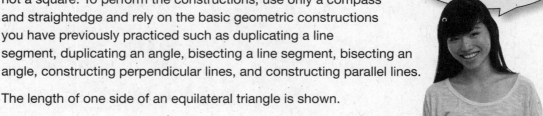

Remember, an equilateral triangle is a triangle that has three congruent sides.

In the rest of this lesson, you will construct an equilateral triangle, an isosceles triangle, a square, and a rectangle that is not a square. To perform the constructions, use only a compass and straightedge and rely on the basic geometric constructions you have previously practiced such as duplicating a line segment, duplicating an angle, bisecting a line segment, bisecting an angle, constructing perpendicular lines, and constructing parallel lines.

The length of one side of an equilateral triangle is shown.

●————●

1. What do you know about the other two sides of the equilateral triangle you will construct given the line segment shown?

2. Write a paragraph explaining how you will construct this equilateral triangle.

3. Construct the equilateral triangle using the starter line given.

⟵————————————⟶

12

4. Sophie claims that she can construct an equilateral triangle by duplicating the line segment three times and having the endpoints of all three line segments intersect. Roberto thinks that Sophie's method will not result in an equilateral triangle. Who is correct? Explain why the incorrect student's rationale is not correct.

PROBLEM 4 Constructing an Isosceles Triangle

The length of one side of an isosceles triangle that is not an equilateral triangle is shown.

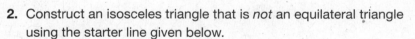

Remember, an isosceles triangle is a triangle that has at least two sides of equal length.

1. Write a paragraph to explain how you will construct this isosceles triangle that is not an equilateral triangle.

2. Construct an isosceles triangle that is *not* an equilateral triangle using the starter line given below.

3. Explain how you know your construction resulted in an isosceles triangle that is not an equilateral triangle.

PROBLEM 5   Constructing a Square Given the Perimeter

Now you will construct a square using a given perimeter.

 1. The perimeter of a square is shown by $\overline{AB}$.

A   B

    a. Write a paragraph to explain how you will construct this square.

     b. Construct the square.

12

PROBLEM 6 Constructing a Rectangle Given the Perimeter

1. The perimeter of a rectangle is shown by $\overline{AB}$.

A •————————————————————————• B

    a. Write a paragraph to explain how you will construct this rectangle that is not a square.

    b. Construct the rectangle that is not a square.

 Be prepared to share your solutions and methods.

Chapter 12 Summary

KEY TERMS

- Distance Formula (12.1)
- transformation (12.1)
- rigid motion (12.1)
- translation (12.1)
- image (12.1)
- pre-image (12.1)
- arc (12.1)
- congruent line segments (12.1)
- congruent (12.1)
- midpoint (12.2)
- Midpoint Formula (12.2)
- segment bisector (12.2)
- angle (12.3)
- angle bisector (12.3)
- point-slope form (12.4)

CONSTRUCTIONS

- copying a line segment (12.1)
- duplicating a line segment (12.1)
- bisecting a line segment (12.2)
- copying an angle (12.3)
- duplicating an angle (12.3)
- bisecting an angle (12.3)

12.1 Applying the Distance Formula

The Distance Formula can be used to calculate the distance between two points on the coordinate plane. The Distance Formula states that if (x_1, y_1) and (x_2, y_2) are two points on the coordinate plane, then the distance d between (x_1, y_1) and (x_2, y_2) is given by $d = \sqrt{(x_2 - x_1)^2 + (y_2 - y_1)^2}$.

Example

Calculate the distance between the points $(3, -2)$ and $(-5, 1)$.

$x_1 = 3, y_1 = -2, x_2 = -5, y_2 = 1$

$d = \sqrt{(x_2 - x_1)^2 + (y_2 - y_1)^2}$

$d = \sqrt{(-5 - 3)^2 + [1 - (-2)]^2}$

$d = \sqrt{(-8)^2 + (3)^2}$

$d = \sqrt{64 + 9}$

$d = \sqrt{73}$

$d \approx 8.5$

The distance between the points $(3, -2)$ and $(-5, 1)$ is $\sqrt{73}$ units, or approximately 8.5 units.

12

12.1 Translating Line Segments on the Coordinate Plane

A translation is a rigid motion that slides each point of a figure the same distance and direction. A horizontal translation of a line segment on the coordinate plane changes the *x*-coordinates of both endpoints while leaving the *y*-coordinates the same. A vertical translation changes the *y*-coordinates of both endpoints while leaving the *x*-coordinates the same.

Example

Line segment *PQ* is translated horizontally 10 units to the left to create *P'Q'*. Line segment *P'Q'* is translated vertically 8 units down to create line segment *P"Q"*.

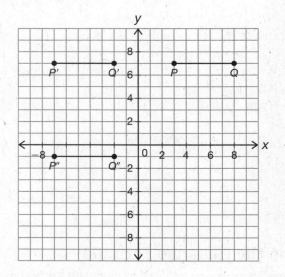

Line Segment	PQ	P'Q'	P"Q"
Coordinates of Endpoints	(3, 7) (8, 7)	(−7, 7) (−2, 7)	(−7, −1) (−2, −1)

The lengths of the images and the pre-images remain the same after each translation.

12.1 Duplicating a Line Using Construction Tools

A straightedge and compass can be used to duplicate a line.

Example

Line segment *JK* can be duplicated using a straightedge and compass by drawing a starter line and then copying a line segment that is the same length as $\overline{JK}$.

12.2 Applying the Midpoint Formula

A midpoint is a point that is exactly halfway between two given points. The Midpoint Formula can be used to calculate the coordinates of a midpoint. The Midpoint Formula states that if (x_1, y_1) and (x_2, y_2) are two points on the coordinate plane, then the midpoint of the line segment that joins these two points is given by $\left(\dfrac{x_1 + x_2}{2}, \dfrac{y_1 + y_2}{2} \right)$.

Example

Calculate the midpoint of a line segment with the endpoints $(-8, -3)$ and $(4, 6)$.

$x_1 = -8, y_1 = -3, x_2 = 4, y_2 = 6$

$$\left(\frac{x_1 + x_2}{2}, \frac{y_1 + y_2}{2} \right) = \left(\frac{-8 + 4}{2}, \frac{-3 + 6}{2} \right)$$

$$= \left(\frac{-4}{2}, \frac{3}{2} \right)$$

$$= \left(-2, \frac{3}{2} \right)$$

The midpoint of the line segment is $\left(-2, \dfrac{3}{2} \right)$.

12.2 Bisecting a Line Segment Using Construction Tools

Construction tools can be used to bisect a line segment.

Example

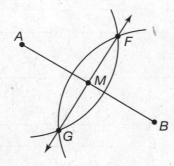

Open the radius of the compass to more than half the length of the original line segment. Construct an arc using one endpoint as the center. Keeping the compass at the same radius, construct an arc using the other endpoint as center. Label and connect the points created by the intersection of the arcs. Line segment *FG* bisects line segment *AB*.

12

Translating an Angle on the Coordinate Plane

Translating an angle on the coordinate plane is a rigid motion that slides the angle, either horizontally or vertically, on the coordinate plane. Because it is a rigid motion, the angle measures of the image and the pre-image are the same. Horizontal translations only impact the *x*-coordinates of the endpoints; vertical translations only impact the *y*-coordinates of the endpoints.

Example

Angle *JDL* is translated horizontally 11 units right to form angle *J′D′L′*. Angle *J′D′L′* is translated vertically 12 units down to create angle *J″D″L″*.

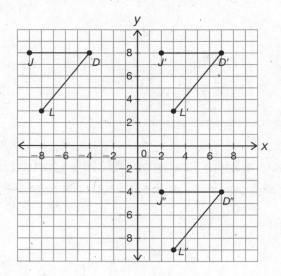

Line Segment	JD	J′D′	J″D″
Coordinates of Endpoints	(−9, 8) (−4, 8)	(2, 8) (7, 8)	(2, −4) (7, −4)

Line Segment	DL	D′L′	D″L″
Coordinates of Endpoints	(−4, 8) (−8, 3)	(7, 8) (3, 3)	(7, −4) (3, −9)

The measure of the angle images and pre-images remain the same after each translation.

12.3 Bisecting an Angle Using Construction Tools

An angle bisector is a ray drawn through the vertex of an angle that divides the angle into two angles of equal measure.

Example

Angle F can be bisected using construction tools.

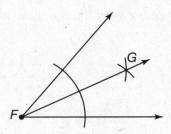

Place the compass on the vertex of the angle. Construct an arc that intersects both sides of the angle. Place the compass at one of the intersection points and construct an arc, then using the same radius of the compass construct an arc using the other intersection point. Construct a ray connecting the vertex to the intersection of the arcs. Ray FG bisects angle F.

12.4 Determining Whether Lines Are Parallel or Perpendicular

The slopes of parallel lines are equal. The slopes of perpendicular lines are negative reciprocals of each other. When the product of two numbers is -1, the numbers are negative reciprocals of each other.

Example

The equation of line p is $y = 2x + 6$, the equation of line q is $y = 2x - 10$, and the equation of line r is $y = -\frac{1}{2}x$. The slopes of lines p and q are equal, so lines p and q are parallel.

The slopes of lines p and r are negative reciprocals of each other, so lines p and r are perpendicular. Also, the slopes of lines q and r are negative reciprocals of each other, so lines q and r are also perpendicular.

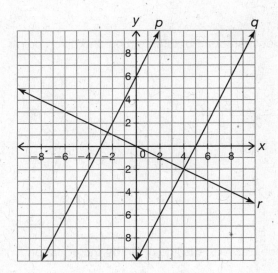

12.4 Determining the Distance Between Lines and Points

The shortest distance between any line and a point not on that line is the length of the perpendicular segment drawn from the point to the line. The shortest distance between a line and a point not on the line can be determined using the equation of the perpendicular segment drawn from the point to the line, the equation of the original line, and the Distance Formula.

Example

Calculate the distance between the line given by the equation $f(x) = \frac{4}{3}x + 2$ and the point $(-4, 5)$.

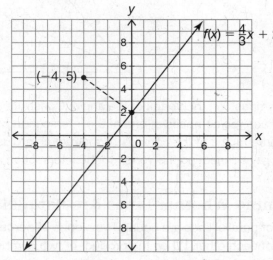

Equation of perpendicular segment:

$y = mx + b$

$5 = -\frac{3}{4}(-4) + b$

$5 = 3 + b$

$2 = b$

$y = -\frac{3}{4}x + 2$

Point of intersection:

$\frac{4}{3}x + 2 = -\frac{3}{4}x + 2$

$16x = -9x$

$25x = 0$

$x = 0$

$y = \frac{4}{3}(0) + 2$

$y = 2$

$(0, 2)$

Distance between point of intersection and given point:

$x_1 = 0, y_1 = 2, x_2 = -4, y_2 = 5$

$d = \sqrt{(x_2 - x_1)^2 + (y_2 - y_1)^2}$

$d = \sqrt{(-4 - 0)^2 + (5 - 2)^2}$

$d = \sqrt{(-4)^2 + (3)^2}$

$d = \sqrt{16 + 9}$

$d = \sqrt{25}$

$d = 5$

The distance between the line given by the equation $f(x) = \frac{4}{3}x + 2$ and the point $(-4, 5)$ is 5 units.

12.5 Constructing Perpendicular Lines

Perpendicular lines can be constructed through a given point using construction tools.

Example

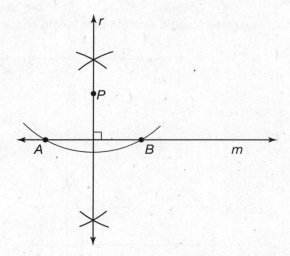

Use the given point *P* as the center and construct an arc that passes through the given line. Open the compass radius. Construct an arc above and below the given line using one of the intersection points just created. Keeping the radius the same, construct an arc above and below the given line using the other intersection point. Connect the intersection points of the arcs which should also pass through the given point. Line *r* is perpendicular to line *m*.

12.5 Constructing Equilateral Triangles

Equilateral triangles have 3 congruent sides. Construction tools can be used to construct an equilateral triangle given the length of one side.

Example

Construct an equilateral triangle with the side length shown.

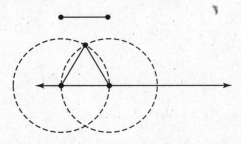

Construct a starter line and duplicate the given segment onto the starter line. Construct a circle using an endpoint of the line segment as the center. Then construct another circle using the other endpoint as the center. Connect the point of intersection of the circles to each endpoint using line segments.

12.5 Constructing Isosceles Triangles

An isosceles triangle is a triangle that has at least two sides of equal length.

Example

Construct an isosceles triangle with the side length shown.

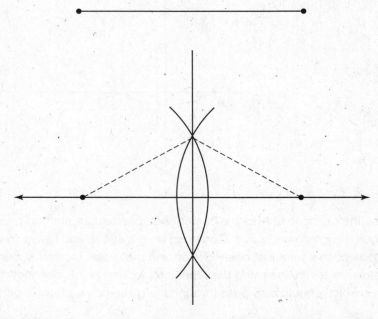

Construct a starter line and duplicate the given line segment. Then construct a perpendicular bisector through the line segment. Connect the endpoints of each line segment to a point on the bisector.

12.5 Constructing Squares

A square can be constructed using construction tools.

Example

Construct a square using the perimeter given.

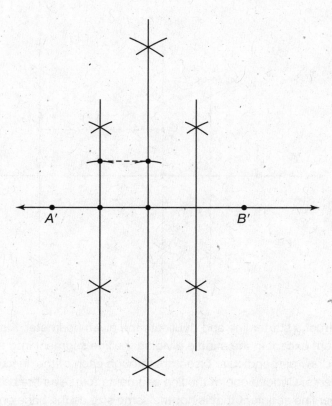

Construct a starter line and duplicate the given perimeter. Bisect the line segment using a perpendicular bisector. Then bisect each of the created line segments to create 4 line segments of equal length. Duplicate one of the line segments along two perpendicular bisectors to create the height of the square. Connect the two endpoints of the line segments representing the height to complete the square.

12

Constructing Rectangles That Are Not Squares

A rectangle can be constructed in a similar method to constructing a square using a given perimeter of the rectangle.

Example

Construct a rectangle using the perimeter given.

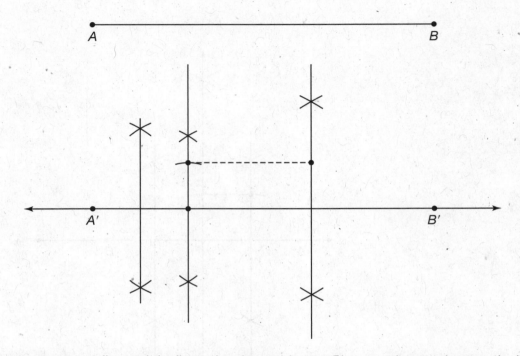

Construct a starter line and duplicate the given perimeter. Place a point anywhere on the line segment except in the middle dividing the line segment into two unequal line segments. Then draw perpendicular bisectors through each of the line segments to create four line segments. Choose one of the line segments to use as the base of the rectangle. Duplicate another line segment that is not the same size as the base on two of the perpendicular bisectors to use as the height of the rectangle. Finally, connect the endpoints of the line segments representing the height to create a rectangle.

Congruence Through Transformations

The Louvre (pronounced Loov) Pyramid in Paris, France, serves as the entrance to the world famous Louvre museum. It was constructed using 673 rhombus-shaped and triangular glass segments.

719

Slide, Flip, Turn: The Latest Dance Craze?

Translating, Rotating, and Reflecting Geometric Figures

© 2012 Carnegie Learning

OBJECTIVES

In this lesson, you will:

- Translate geometric figures on a coordinate plane.
- Rotate geometric figures on a coordinate plane.
- Reflect geometric figures on a coordinate plane.

KEY TERMS

- rotation
- point of rotation
- angle of rotation
- reflection
- line of reflection

Did you know that most textbooks are translated from English into at least one other language, usually Spanish? And in some school districts, general memos and letters to parents may be translated to up to 5 different languages! Of course, *translating* a language means something completely different from *translating* in geometry.

The same can be said for reflection. A "reflection pool" is a place where one can "reflect" on one's thoughts, while also admiring reflections in the pool of still water.

How about rotation? What do you think the term *rotation* means in geometry? Is this different from its meaning in common language?

13

To begin this chapter, cut out the figure shown.

You will use this trapezoid throughout this lesson so don't lose it!

13

13

1. Graph trapezoid *ABCD* by plotting the points *A* (3, 9), *B* (3, 4), *C* (11, 4), and *D* (11, 10).

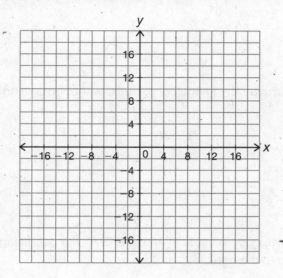

Use the model you cut out to help with the translations.

2. Translate the trapezoid on the coordinate plane. Graph the image and record the vertex coordinates in the table.

   a. Translate trapezoid *ABCD* 15 units to the left to form trapezoid *A'B'C'D'*.

   b. Translate trapezoid *ABCD* 12 units down to form trapezoid *A"B"C"D"*.

Trapezoid *ABCD* (coordinates)	Trapezoid *A'B'C'D'* (coordinates)	Trapezoid *A"B"C"D"* (coordinates)
A (3, 9)		
B (3, 4)		
C (11, 4)		
D (11, 10)		

13

Let's consider translations without graphing.

3. The vertices of parallelogram DEFG are D (−9, 7), E (−12, 2), F (−3, 2), and G (0, 7).

   a. Determine the vertex coordinates of image D'E'F'G' if parallelogram DEFG is translated 14 units down.

   b. How did you determine the image coordinates without graphing?

   c. Determine the vertex coordinates of image D"E"F"G" if parallelogram DEFG is translated 8 units to the right.

   d. How did you determine the image coordinates without graphing?

PROBLEM 2 Rotating Geometric Figures on the Coordinate Plane

Another transformation that exists in geometry is a *rotation*. A **rotation** is a rigid motion that turns a figure about a fixed point, called the **point of rotation**. The figure is rotated in a given direction for a given angle, called the *angle of rotation*. The **angle of rotation** is the measure of the amount the figure is rotated about the point of rotation. The direction of a rotation can either be clockwise or counterclockwise.

© 2012 Carnegie Learning

13

Let's rotate a point about the origin. The origin will be the point of rotation and you will rotate the point 90°, 180°, and 270°.

First, let's rotate the point 90° counterclockwise about the origin.

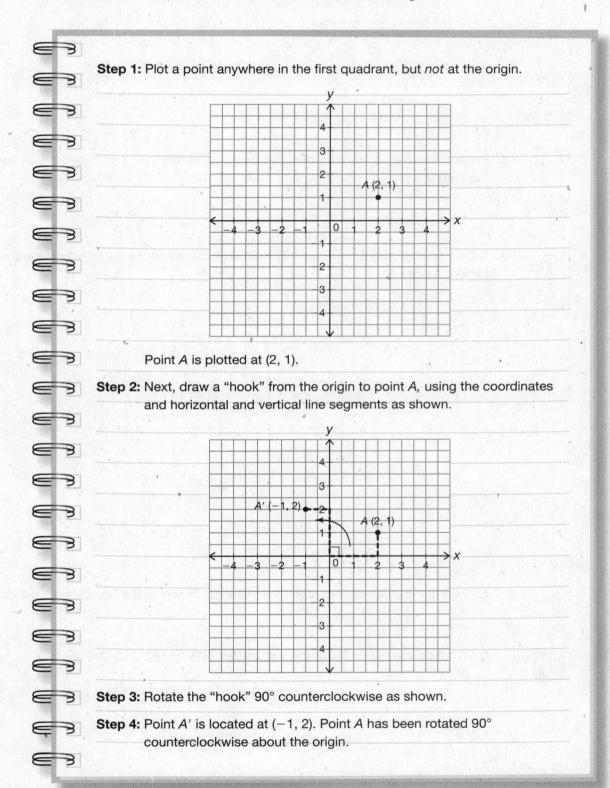

Step 1: Plot a point anywhere in the first quadrant, but *not* at the origin.

Point A is plotted at (2, 1).

Step 2: Next, draw a "hook" from the origin to point A, using the coordinates and horizontal and vertical line segments as shown.

Step 3: Rotate the "hook" 90° counterclockwise as shown.

Step 4: Point A' is located at (−1, 2). Point A has been rotated 90° counterclockwise about the origin.

1. What do you notice about the coordinates of point *A* and the coordinates of point *A'*?

2. Predict what the coordinates of *A"* will be if you rotate *A'* 90° counterclockwise about the origin.

3. Rotate point *A'* about the origin 90° counterclockwise on the coordinate plane shown. Label the point *A"*.

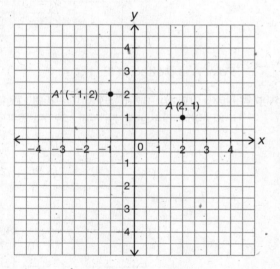

a. What are the coordinates of *A"*? Was your prediction for the coordinates of *A"* correct?

b. What do you notice about the coordinates of *A* and *A"*? How are the two points related?

13

You may have noticed that the values of the *x*- and *y*-coordinates seem to switch places for every 90° rotation about the origin. You may have also noticed that the rotation from *A* to *A″* is a 180° counterclockwise rotation about the origin. In this case, the coordinates of point *A″* are the opposite of the coordinates of point *A*.

You can use the table shown to determine the coordinates of any point after a 90° and 180° counterclockwise rotation about the origin.

Original Point	Coordinates After a Rotation About the Origin 90° Counterclockwise	Coordinates After a Rotation About the Origin 180° Counterclockwise
(x, y)	$(-y, x)$	$(-x, -y)$

Verify that the information in the table is correct by using a test point. You will plot a point on a coordinate plane and rotate it 90° and 180° counterclockwise about the origin.

4. Graph and label point *Q* at (5, 7) on the coordinate plane.

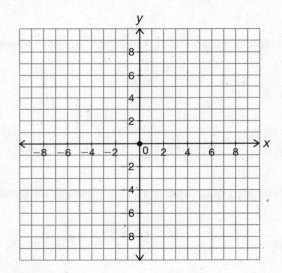

Remember that these are *values* for the coordinates, but coordinates for a plotted point are always in the form (*x, y*)!

13

5. Use the origin (0, 0) as the point of rotation.

   a. Rotate Q 90° counterclockwise about the origin. Label the image Q'.

   b. Determine the coordinates of Q', then describe how you determined the location of image Q'.

   c. Rotate Q 180° counterclockwise about the origin. Label the image Q".

   d. Determine the coordinates of Q", then describe how you determined the location of image Q".

13

You have been rotating points about the origin on a coordinate plane. However, do you think polygons can also be rotated on the coordinate plane?

You can use models to help show that you *can* rotate polygons on a coordinate plane. However, before we starting modeling the rotation of a polygon on a coordinate plane, let's graph the trapezoid to establish the pre-image.

6. Graph trapezoid *ABCD* by plotting the points *A* (−12, 9), *B* (−12, 4), *C* (−4, 4), and *D* (−4, 10).

Now that you have graphed the pre-image, you are ready to model the rotation of the polygon on the coordinate plane.

- First, fold a piece of tape in half and tape it to both sides of the trapezoid you cut out previously.

- Then, take your trapezoid and set it on top of trapezoid *ABCD* on the coordinate plane, making sure that the tape covers the origin (0, 0).

- Finally, put a pin or your pencil point through the tape at the origin and rotate your model counterclockwise. The 90° rotation of trapezoid *ABCD* is shown.

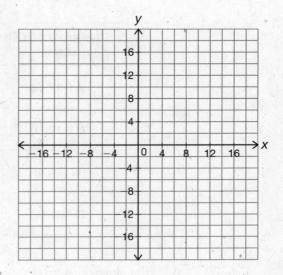

The rotation of trapezoid *ABCD* 90° counterclockwise is shown.

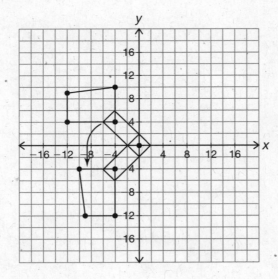

7. Rotate trapezoid *ABCD* about the origin for each given angle of rotation. Graph and label each image on the coordinate plane and record the coordinates in the table.

   a. Rotate trapezoid *ABCD* 90° counterclockwise about the origin to form trapezoid *A'B'C'D'*.

   b. Rotate trapezoid *ABCD* 180° counterclockwise about the origin to form trapezoid *A"B"C"D"*.

Trapezoid *ABCD* (coordinates)	Trapezoid *A'B'C'D'* (coordinates)	Trapezoid *A"B"C"D"* (coordinates)
A (–12, 9)		
B (–12, 4)		
C (–4, 4)		
D (–4, 10)		

8. What similarities do you notice between rotating a single point about the origin and rotating a polygon about the origin?

13

Let's consider rotations without graphing.

9. The vertices of parallelogram *DEFG* are *D* (−9, 7), *E* (−12, 2), *F* (−3, 2), and *G* (0, 7).

   a. Determine the vertex coordinates of image *D′E′F′G′* if parallelogram *DEFG* is rotated 90° counterclockwise about the origin.

   b. How did you determine the image coordinates without graphing?

   c. Determine the vertex coordinates of image *D″E″F″G″* if parallelogram *DEFG* is rotated 180° counterclockwise about the origin.

   d. How did you determine the image coordinates without graphing?

10. Dante claims that if he is trying to determine the coordinates of an image that is rotated 180° about the origin, it does not matter which direction the rotation occurred. Desmond claims that the direction is important to know when determining the image coordinates. Who is correct? Explain why the correct student's rationale is correct.

13

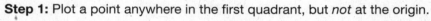

There is a third transformation that can move geometric figures within the coordinate plane. Figures that are mirror images of each other are called *reflections*. A **reflection** is a rigid motion that reflects, or "flips," a figure over a given line called *a line of reflection*. A **line of reflection** is a line over which a figure is reflected so that corresponding points are the same distance from the line.

Let's reflect a point over the *y*-axis.

Step 1: Plot a point anywhere in the first quadrant, but *not* at the origin.

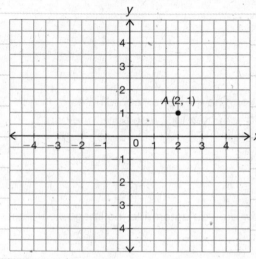

Point *A* is plotted at (2, 1).

Step 2: Next, count the number of *x*-units from point *A* to the *y*-axis.

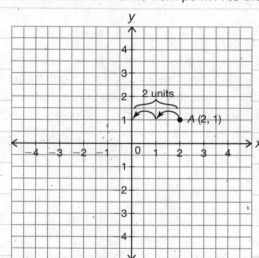

Point *A* is 2 units from the *y*-axis.

13

Step 3: Then, count the same number of x-units on the opposite side of the y-axis to locate the reflection of point A. Label the point A′.

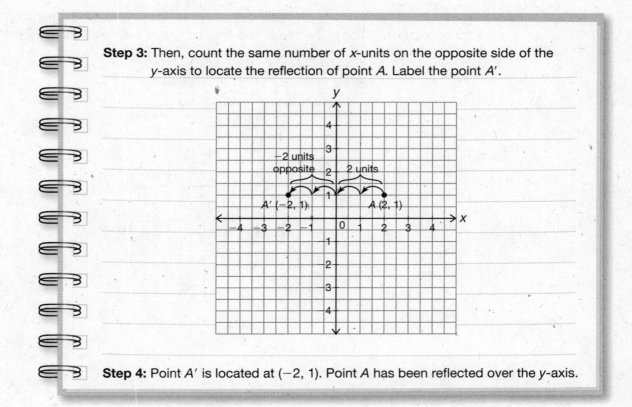

Step 4: Point A′ is located at (−2, 1). Point A has been reflected over the y-axis.

1. What do you notice about the coordinates of point A and the coordinates of image A′?

2. Predict the coordinates of A″ if point A is reflected over the x-axis. Explain your reasoning.

13

3. Reflect point *A* over the *x*-axis on the coordinate plane shown. Verify whether your prediction for the location of the image was correct. Graph the image and label it *A"*.

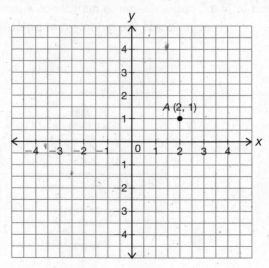

4. What do you notice about the coordinates of *A* and *A"*?

The coordinates of a pre-image reflected over either the *x*-axis or the *y*-axis can be used to determine the coordinates of the image.

You can use the table shown as an efficient way to determine the coordinates of an image reflected over the *x*- or *y*-axis.

Original Point	Coordinates of Image After a Reflection Over the *x*-axis	Coordinates of Image After a Reflection Over the *y*-axis
(x, y)	(x, −y)	(−x, y)

Does this table still make sense if the line of reflection is not the *x*- or *y*-axis?

13

5. Graph point *J* at (5, 7) on the coordinate plane shown.

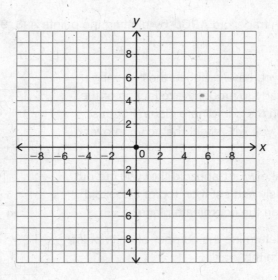

6. Reflect point *J* over the *y*-axis on the coordinate plane. Label the image *J'*.

7. Determine the coordinates of *J'*. Then describe how you determined the location of image *J'*.

8. Reflect point *J* over the *x*-axis on the coordinate plane. Label the image *J"*.

9. Determine the coordinates of *J"*. Then describe how you determined the location of image *J"*.

13

You can also reflect polygons on the coordinate plane. You can model the reflection of a polygon across a line of reflection. Just as with rotating a polygon on a coordinate plane, you will first need to establish a pre-image.

10. Graph trapezoid *ABCD* by plotting the points *A* (3, 9), *B* (3, 4), *C* (11, 4), and *D* (11, 10).

Now that you have graphed the pre-image, you are ready to model the reflection of the polygon on the coordinate plane. For this modeling, you will reflect the polygon over the *y*-axis.

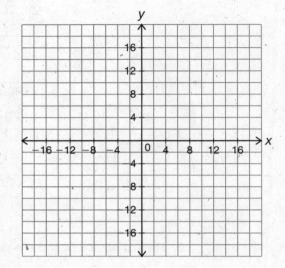

• First, take your trapezoid that you cut out previously and set it on top of trapezoid *ABCD* on the coordinate plane.

• Next, determine the number of units point *A* is from the *y*-axis.

• Then count the same number of units on the opposite side of the *y*-axis to determine where to place the image in Quadrant II.

• Finally, physically flip the trapezoid over the *y*-axis like you are flipping a page in a book.

The reflection of trapezoid *ABCD* over the *y*-axis is shown.

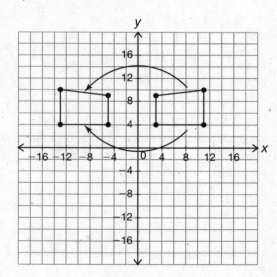

13

11. Reflect trapezoid *ABCD* over each given line of reflection. Graph and label each image on the coordinate plane and record each image's coordinates in the table.

   a. Reflect trapezoid *ABCD* over the *x*-axis to form trapezoid *A'B'C'D'*.

   b. Reflect trapezoid *ABCD* over the *y*-axis to form trapezoid *A"B"C"D"*.

Trapezoid *ABCD* (coordinates)	Trapezoid *A'B'C'D'* (coordinates)	Trapezoid *A"B"C"D"* (coordinates)
A (3, 9)		
B (3, 4)		
C (11, 4)		
D (11, 10)		

12. What similarities do you notice between reflecting a single point over the *x*- or *y*-axis and reflecting a polygon over the *x*- or *y*-axis?

Let's consider reflections without graphing.

13. The vertices of parallelogram *DEFG* are *D* (−9, 7), *E* (−12, 2), *F* (−3, 2), and *G* (0, 7).

   a. Determine the vertex coordinates of image *D'E'F'G'* if parallelogram *DEFG* is reflected over the *x*-axis.

   b. How did you determine the image coordinates without graphing?

13

c. Determine the vertex coordinates of image $D''E''F''G''$ if parallelogram $DEFG$ is reflected over the y-axis.

d. How did you determine the image coordinates without graphing?

Talk the Talk

1. The vertices of rectangle $PQRS$ are P (6, 8), Q (6, 2), R (−3, 2), and S (−3, 8). Describe the translation used to form each rectangle given each image's coordinates. Explain your reasoning.

   a. P' (1, 8), Q' (1, 2), R' (−8, 2), and S' (−8, 8)

   b. P'' (6, 14.5), Q'' (6, 8.5), R'' (−3, 8.5), and S'' (−3, 14.5)

2. The vertices of rectangle $JKLM$ are J (6, 8), K (6, 2), $L.$(−3, 2), and M (−3, 8). Describe the rotation used to form each rectangle. Explain your reasoning.

   a. J' (−8, 6), K' (−2, 6), L' (−2, −3), and M' (−8, −3)

   b. J'' (−6, −8), K'' (−6, −2), L'' (3, −2), and M'' (3, −8)

13

3. The vertices of rectangle *NOPQ* are *N* (8, 8), *O* (8, 2), *P* (−3, 2), and *Q* (−3, 8). Describe the reflection used to form each rectangle. Explain your reasoning.

  a. *N′* (−8, 8), *O′* (−8, 2), *P′* (3, 2), and *Q′* (3, 8)

  b. *N″* (8, −8), *O″* (8, −2), *P″* (−3, −2), and *Q″* (−3, −8)

4. Complete this sentence:

Images that result from a translation, rotation, or reflection are (always, sometimes, or never) congruent to the original figure.

 Be prepared to share your solutions and methods.

13

All the Same to You
Congruent Triangles

LEARNING GOALS

In this lesson, you will:

- Identify corresponding sides and corresponding angles of congruent triangles.
- Explore the relationship between corresponding sides of congruent triangles.
- Explore the relationship between corresponding angles of congruent triangles.
- Write statements of triangle congruence.
- Identify and use rigid motion to create new images.

KEY TERMS

- congruent angles
- corresponding sides
- corresponding angles

In mathematics, when a geometric figure is transformed, the size and shape of the figure do not change. However, in physics, things are a little different. An idea known as length contraction explains that when an object is in motion, its length appears to be slightly less than it really is. This cannot be seen with everyday objects because they do not move fast enough. To truly see this phenomenon you would have to view an object moving close to the speed of light. In fact, if an object was moving past you at the speed of light, the length of the object would seem to be practically zero!

This theory is very difficult to prove and yet scientists came up with the idea in the late 1800s. How do you think scientists test and prove length contraction? Do you think geometry is used in these verifications?

In a previous lesson, you determined that when you translate, rotate, or reflect a figure, the resulting image is the same size and the same shape as the pre-image. Therefore, the image and the pre-image are said to be congruent.

Recall that congruent line segments are line segments that have the same length. Congruent triangles are triangles that are the same size and the same shape.

If the length of line segment AB is equal to the length of line segment DE, the relationship can be expressed using symbols.

- $AB = DE$ is read as "the distance between A and B is equal to the distance between D and E."

- $m\overline{AB} = m\overline{DE}$ is read as "the measure of line segment AB is equal to the measure of line segment DE."

- $\overline{AB} \cong \overline{DE}$ is read as "line segment AB is congruent to line segment DE."

Congruent angles are angles that are equal in measure.

If the measure of angle A is equal to the measure of angle D, the relationship can be expressed using symbols.

- $m\angle A = m\angle D$ is read as "the measure of angle A is equal to the measure of angle D."

- $\angle A \cong \angle D$ is read as "angle A is congruent to angle D."

© 2012 Carnegie Learning

13

Let's explore the properties of congruent triangles.

1. Graph triangle *ABC* by plotting the points *A* (8, 10), *B* (1, 2), and *C* (8, 2).

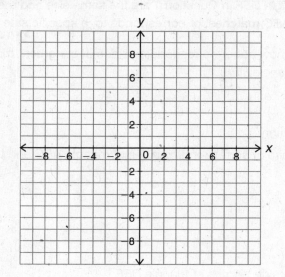

In this lesson, you will use different letters to name different triangles.

a. Classify triangle *ABC*. Explain your reasoning.

b. Use the Pythagorean Theorem to determine the length of side *AB*.

How do you know you can use the Pythagorean Theorem?

2. Translate triangle *ABC* 10 units to the left to form triangle *DEF*. Graph triangle *DEF* and list the coordinates of points *D*, *E*, and *F*.

13

Corresponding sides are sides that have the same relative positions in corresponding geometric figures.

Triangle *ABC* and triangle *DEF* in Question 1 are the same size and the same shape. Each side of triangle *ABC* matches, or corresponds to, a specific side of triangle *DEF*.

3. Given what you know about corresponding sides of congruent triangles, predict the side lengths of triangle *DEF*.

4. Verify your prediction.

   a. Identify the pairs of corresponding sides of triangle *ABC* and triangle *DEF*.

   b. Determine the side lengths of triangle *DEF*.

Would there ever be a time when corresponding sides of figures would not be congruent?

   c. Compare the lengths of the sides of triangle *ABC* to the lengths of the corresponding sides of triangle *DEF*. What do you notice?

5. In general, what can you conclude about the relationship between the corresponding sides of congruent triangles?

13

Use triangle *ABC* and triangle *DEF* from Question 1 to answer each question.

6. Use a protractor to determine the measures of ∠*A*, ∠*B*, and ∠*C*.

Each angle in triangle *ABC* corresponds to a specific angle in triangle *DEF*. **Corresponding angles** are angles that have the same relative positions in corresponding geometric figures.

7. What would you predict to be true about the measures of corresponding angles of congruent triangles?

8. Verify your prediction.

  a. Identify the corresponding angles of triangle *ABC* and triangle *DEF*.

  b. Use a protractor to determine the measures of angles *D*, *E*, and *F*.

  c. Compare the measures of the angles of triangle *ABC* to the measures of the corresponding angles of triangle *DEF*.

So, what can you say about corresponding sides and corresponding angles of congruent triangles?

 9. In general, what can you conclude about the relationship between the corresponding angles of congruent triangles?

13

PROBLEM 2 Statements of Triangle Congruence

1. Consider the congruence statement △*JRB* ≅ △*MNS*.

    a. Identify the congruent angles.   **b.** Identify the congruent sides.

Remember, the ≅ means "is congruent to."

2. Analyze the two triangles shown.

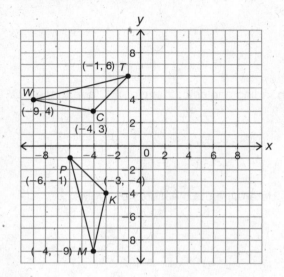

a. Determine the transformation used to create triangle *PMK*.

b. Does the transformation preserve the size and shape of the triangle in this problem situation? Why or why not?

c. Write a triangle congruence statement for the triangles.

d. Identify the congruent angles.   **e.** Identify the congruent sides.

© 2012 Carnegie Learning

13

3. Analyze the two triangles shown.

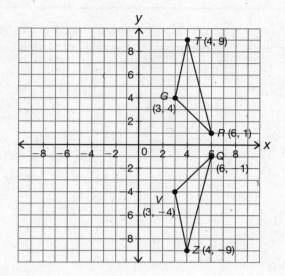

a. Determine the transformation used to create triangle *ZQV*.

b. Does the transformation preserve the size and shape of the triangle in this problem situation? Why or why not?

c. Write a triangle congruence statement for the triangles shown.

d. Identify the congruent angles.

e. Identify the congruent sides.

13

Talk the Talk

1. Given any triangle on a coordinate plane, how can you create a different triangle that you know will be congruent to the original triangle?

2. Describe the properties of congruent triangles.

Be prepared to share your solutions and methods.

Side-Side-Side
SSS Congruence Theorem

© 2012 Carnegie Learning

LEARNING GOALS

In this lesson, you will:

- Explore the Side-Side-Side Congruence Theorem through constructions.
- Explore the Side-Side-Side Congruence Theorem on the coordinate plane.

KEY TERMS

- theorem
- postulate
- Side-Side-Side Congruence Theorem

Have you ever tried to construct something from scratch—a model car or a bird house, for example? If you have, you have probably discovered that it is a lot more difficult than it looks. To build something accurately, you must have a plan in place. You must think about materials you will need, measurements you will make, and the amount of time it will take to complete the project. You may need to make a model or blueprint of what you are building. Then, when the actual building begins, you must be very precise in all your measurements and cuts. The difference of half an inch may not seem like much, but it could mean the wall of your bird house is too small and now you may have to start again!

You will be constructing triangles throughout the next 4 lessons. While you won't be cutting or building anything, it is still important to measure accurately and be precise. Otherwise, you may think your triangles are accurate even though they're not!

In mathematics you often have to prove a solution is correct. In geometry, *theorems* are used to verify statements. A **theorem** is a statement that can be proven true using definitions, *postulates*, or other theorems. A **postulate** is a mathematical statement that cannot be proved but is considered true.

While you can assume that all duplicated or transformed triangles are congruent, mathematically, you need to use a theorem to prove it.

The *Side-Side-Side Congruence Theorem* is one theorem that can be used to prove triangle congruence. The **Side-Side-Side Congruence Theorem** states that if three sides of one triangle are congruent to the corresponding sides of another triangle, then the triangles are congruent.

1. Use the given line segments to construct triangle *ABC*. Then, write the steps you performed to construct the triangle.

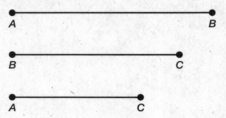

2. Analyze the triangle you created.

   a. Classify △*ABC*. Explain your reasoning.

13

b. Compare your triangle to your classmates' triangles. Are the triangles congruent? Why or why not?

c. How many different triangles can be formed given the lengths of three distinct sides?

3. Rico compares his triangle with his classmate Annette's. Rico gets out his ruler and protractor to verify the triangles are congruent. Annette states he does not need to do that. Who is correct? Explain your reasoning.

In the previous problem, you proved that two triangles are congruent if three sides of one triangle are congruent to the corresponding sides of another triangle. When dealing with triangles on the coordinate plane, measurement must be used to prove congruence.

1. Graph triangle *ABC* by plotting the points *A* (8, −5), *B* (4, −12), and *C* (12, −8).

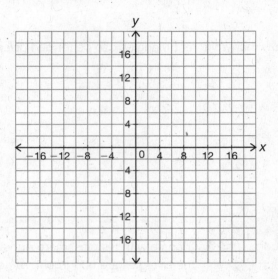

2. How can you determine the length of each side of this triangle?

3. Calculate the length of each side of triangle *ABC*. Record the measurements in the table.

Use exact measurements when determining the lengths.

Side of Triangle *ABC*	Length of Side
$\overline{AB}$	
$\overline{BC}$	
$\overline{AC}$	

13

4. Translate line segments *AB*, *BC*, and *AC* up 7 units to form triangle *A'B'C'*. Graph the image.

5. Calculate the length of each side of triangle *A'B'C'*. Record the measurements in the table.

Side of Triangle *A'B'C'*	Length of Side
$\overline{A'B'}$	
$\overline{B'C'}$	
$\overline{A'C'}$	

6. Are the corresponding sides of the pre-image and image congruent? Explain your reasoning.

7. Do you need to determine the measures of the angles to verify that the triangles are congruent? Explain why or why not.

© 2012 Carnegie Learning

1. Graph triangle *ABC* using the same coordinates as in Problem 1.

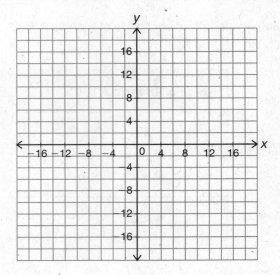

2. Reflect line segments *AB*, *BC*, and *AC* over the *x*-axis to form triangle *A"B"C"*.

3. Calculate the length of each side of triangle *A'B'C'*. Record the measurements in the table.

Side of Triangle *D'E'F'*	Length of Side
$\overline{A'B'}$	
$\overline{B'C'}$	
$\overline{A'C'}$	

4. Are the triangles congruent? Explain your reasoning.

 Be prepared to share your solutions and methods.

13

13

Side-Angle-Side
SAS Congruence Theorem

OBJECTIVES

In this lesson, you will:

- Explore Side-Angle-Side Congruence Theorem using constructions.
- Explore Side-Angle-Side Congruence Theorem on the coordinate plane.

KEY TERMS

- Side-Angle-Side Congruence Theorem
- included angle

The smaller circle you see here has an infinite number of points. And the larger circle has an infinite number of points. But since the larger circle is, well, larger, shouldn't it have more points than the smaller circle?

Mathematicians use one-to-one correspondence to determine if two sets are equal. If you can show that each object in a set corresponds to one and only one object in another set, then the two sets are equal.

Look at the circles. Any ray drawn from the center will touch only two points—one on the smaller circle and one on the larger circle. This means that both circles contain the same number of points! Can you see how correspondence was used to come up with this answer?

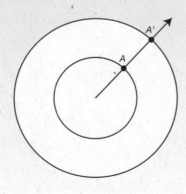

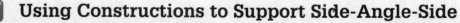

PROBLEM 1   Using Constructions to Support Side-Angle-Side

So far in this chapter, you have determined the congruence of two triangles by proving that if the sides of one triangle are congruent to the corresponding sides of another triangle, then the triangles are congruent.

There is another way to determine if two triangles are congruent that does not involve knowledge of three sides. You will prove the *Side-Angle-Side Congruence Theorem*.

The **Side-Angle-Side Congruence Theorem** states that if two sides and the *included angle* of one triangle are congruent to the corresponding sides and the included angle of the second triangle, then the triangles are congruent. An **included angle** is the angle formed by two sides of a triangle.

First, let's prove this theorem through construction.

1. Construct △*ABC* using the two line segments and included angle shown. Then, write the steps you performed to construct the triangle.

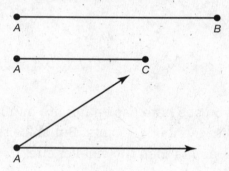

13

2. How does the length of side *BC* compare to the length of your classmates' side *BC*?

3. Use a protractor to measure angle *B* and angle *C* in triangle *ABC*.

4. How do the measures of your corresponding angles compare to the measures of your classmates' corresponding angles?

5. Is your triangle congruent to your classmates' triangles? Why or why not?

6. If you were given one of the non-included angles, ∠*C* or ∠*B*, instead of ∠*A*, do you think everyone in your class would have constructed an identical triangle? Explain your reasoning.

13

Through your construction, you and your classmates constructed congruent triangles using two given sides and the included angle of a triangle.

Let's now try to prove the Side-Angle-Side Theorem on the coordinate plane using algebra.

 1. Graph triangle *ABC* by plotting the points *A* (5, 9), *B* (2, 3), and *C* (7, 2).

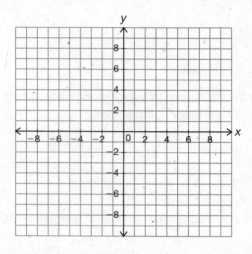

2. Calculate the length of each side of triangle *ABC* and record the measurements in the table. Record exact measurements.

Side of Triangle *ABC*	Length of Side
$\overline{AB}$	
$\overline{BC}$	
$\overline{AC}$	

Do you remember the difference between exact and approximate solutions?

13

3. Rotate side *AB*, side *BC,* and included angle *B*, in triangle *ABC* 270° counterclockwise. Then connect points *A'* and *C'* to form triangle *A'B'C'*. Use the table to record the image coordinates.

Triangle *ABC* (coordinates)	Triangle *A'B'C'* (coordinates)
A (5, 9)	
B (2, 3)	
C (14, 3)	

Before you graph, think! In which quadrant will the rotated image appear?

4. Calculate the length of each side of triangle *A'B'C'* and record the measurements in the table. Record exact measurements.

Side of Triangle *A'B'C'*	Length of Side
$\overline{A'B'}$	
$\overline{B'C'}$	
$\overline{A'C'}$	

13

5. What do you notice about the corresponding side lengths of the pre-image and the image?

6. Use a protractor to measure angle B of triangle ABC and angle B′ of triangle A′B′C′.

   a. What are the measures of each angle?

   b. What does this information tell you about the corresponding angles of the two triangles?

You have shown that the corresponding sides of the image and pre-image are congruent. Therefore, the triangles are congruent by the SSS Congruence Theorem.

You have also used a protractor to verify that the corresponding included angles of each triangle are congruent.

In conclusion, when two side lengths of one triangle and the measure of the included angle are equal to the two corresponding side lengths and the measure of the included angle of another triangle, the two triangles are congruent by the SAS Congruence Theorem.

7. Use the SAS Congruence Theorem and a protractor to determine if the two triangles drawn on the coordinate plane shown are congruent. Use a protractor to determine the measures of the included angles.

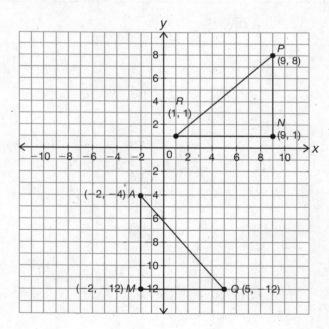

Congruent line segments and congruent angles are often denoted using special markers, rather than given measurements.

Slash markers can be used to indicate congruent line segments. When multiple line segments contain a single slash marker, this implies that all of those line segments are congruent. Double and triple slash markers can also be used to denote other line segment congruencies.

Arc markers can be used to indicate congruent angles. When multiple angles contain a single arc marker, this implies that those angles are congruent. Double and triple arc markers can also be used to denote other angle congruencies.

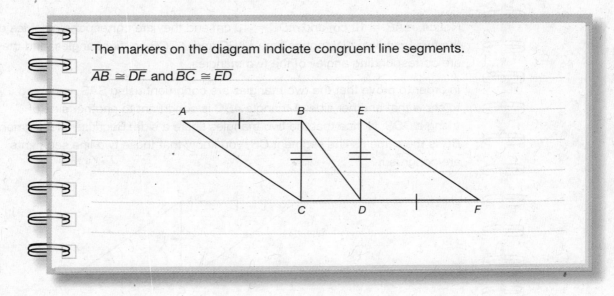

The markers on the diagram indicate congruent line segments.

$\overline{AB} \cong \overline{DF}$ and $\overline{BC} \cong \overline{ED}$

1. Write the congruence statements represented by the markers in each diagram.

a.

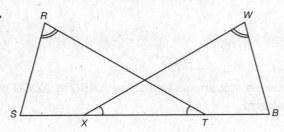

b.

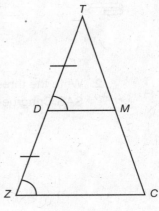

13

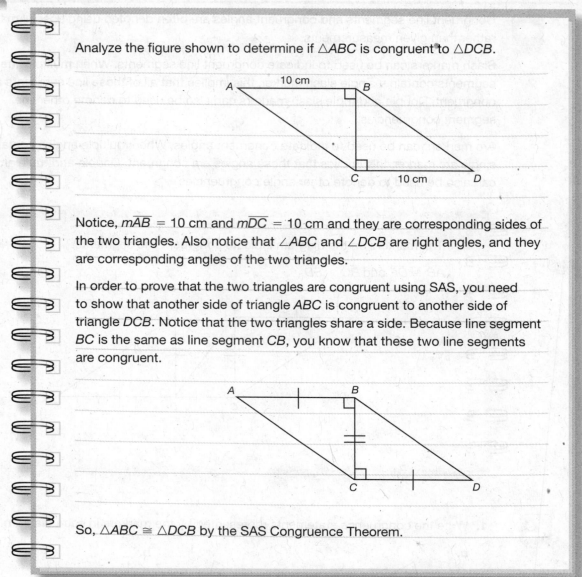

Analyze the figure shown to determine if △ABC is congruent to △DCB.

Notice, m$\overline{AB}$ = 10 cm and m$\overline{DC}$ = 10 cm and they are corresponding sides of the two triangles. Also notice that ∠ABC and ∠DCB are right angles, and they are corresponding angles of the two triangles.

In order to prove that the two triangles are congruent using SAS, you need to show that another side of triangle ABC is congruent to another side of triangle DCB. Notice that the two triangles share a side. Because line segment BC is the same as line segment CB, you know that these two line segments are congruent.

So, △ABC ≅ △DCB by the SAS Congruence Theorem.

2. Write the three congruence statements that show △ABC ≅ △DCB by the SAS Congruence Theorem.

13

3. Determine if there is enough information to prove that the two triangles are congruent by SSS or SAS. Write the congruence statements to justify your reasoning.

a. $\triangle ABC \overset{?}{\cong} \triangle ADC$

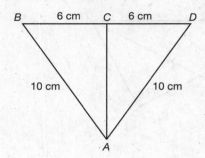

Use markers to identify all congruent line segments and angles.

b. $\triangle ABC \overset{?}{\cong} \triangle DEF$

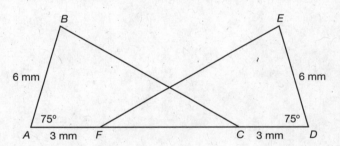

13

4. Simone says that since the two triangles shown have two pairs of congruent corresponding sides and congruent corresponding angles, then the triangles are congruent by SAS. Is Simone correct? Explain your reasoning.

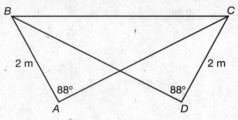

  Be prepared to share your solutions and methods.

13

You Shouldn't Make Assumptions

Angle-Side-Angle Congruence Theorem

LEARNING GOALS

In this lesson, you will:

- Explore the Angle-Side-Angle Congruence Theorem using constructions.
- Explore the Angle-Side-Angle Congruence Theorem on the coordinate plane.

KEY TERMS

- Angle-Side-Angle Congruence Theorem
- included side

"Don't judge a book by its cover." What does this saying mean to you? Usually it is said to remind someone not to make assumptions. Just because something (or someone!) looks a certain way on the outside, until you really get into it, you don't know the whole story. Often in geometry it is easy to make assumptions. You assume that two figures are congruent because they look congruent. You assume two lines are perpendicular because they look perpendicular. Unfortunately, mathematics and assumptions do not go well together. Just as you should not judge a book by its cover, you should not assume anything about a measurement just because it looks a certain way.

Have you made any geometric assumptions so far in this chapter? Was your assumption correct or incorrect? Hopefully it will only take you one incorrect assumption to learn to not assume!

So far you have looked at the Side-Side-Side and Side-Angle-Side Congruence Theorems. But are there other theorems that prove triangle congruence as well?

1. Use the given two angles and line segment to construct triangle *ABC*. Then, write the steps your performed to construct the triangle.

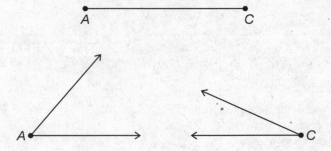

2. Compare your triangle to your classmates' triangles. Are the triangles congruent? Why or why not?

13

3. Wendy says that if the line segment and angles had not been labeled, then all the triangles would not have been congruent. Ian disagrees and says that there is only one way to put two angles and a side together to form a triangle whether they are labeled or not. Who is correct? Explain your reasoning.

You just used construction to prove the *Angle-Side-Angle Congruence Theorem*. The **Angle-Side-Angle Congruence Theorem** states that if two angles and the *included side* of one triangle are congruent to the corresponding two angles and the included side of another triangle, then the triangles are congruent. An **included side** is the side between two angles of a triangle.

PROBLEM 2 How Did You Get There?

1. Analyze triangles *ABC* and *DEF*.

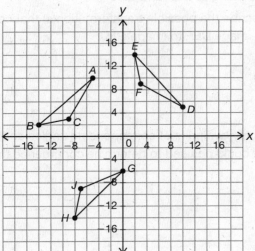

a. Describe the possible transformation(s) that could have occurred to transform pre-image *ABC* into image *DEF*.

13

    b. Identify two pairs of corresponding angles and a pair of corresponding included sides that could be used to determine congruence through the ASA Congruence Theorem.

    c. Use the ASA Congruence Theorem and a protractor to determine if the two triangles are congruent.

2. Analyze triangles *DEF* and *GHJ*.

    a. Describe the possible transformation(s) that could have occurred to transform pre-image *DEF* to image *GHJ*.

    b. Identify two pairs of corresponding angles and a pair of corresponding included sides that could be used to determine congruence through the ASA Congruence Theorem.

13

c. Use the ASA Congruence Theorem and a protractor to determine if the two triangles are congruent.

3. Based on your solution to Question 2, part (c), what can you conclude about the relationship between triangle *ABC* and triangle *GHJ*? Explain your reasoning.

 Be prepared to share your solutions and methods.

13

Ahhhhh...We're Sorry We Didn't Include You!

Angle-Angle-Side Congruence Theorem

© 2012 Carnegie Learning

OBJECTIVES

In this lesson, you will:

- Explore Angle-Angle-Side Congruence Theorem using constructions.
- Explore Angle-Angle-Side Congruence Theorem on the coordinate plane.

KEY TERMS

- Angle-Angle-Side Congruence Theorem
- non-included side

Sometimes, good things must come to an end, and that can be said for determining if triangles are congruent given certain information.

You have used many different theorems to prove that two triangles are congruent based on different criteria. Specifically,

- Side-Side-Side Congruence Theorem
- Side-Angle Side Congruence Theorem
- and Angle-Side-Angle Congruence Theorem.

So, do you think there are any other theorems that must be used to prove that two triangles are congruent? Here's a hint: we have another lesson—so there must be at least one more congruence theorem!

There is another way to determine if two triangles are congruent that is different from the congruence theorems you have already proven. You will prove the *Angle-Angle-Side Congruence Theorem*.

The **Angle-Angle-Side Congruence Theorem** states that if two angles and a *non-included side* of one triangle are congruent to the corresponding angles and the corresponding non-included side of a second triangle, then the triangles are congruent. The **non-included side** is a side that is *not* located between the two angles.

First, you will prove this theorem through construction.

13

© 2012 Carnegie Learning

1. Construct triangle *ABC* given line segment *AB* and angles *A* and *C*. Then, write the steps you performed to construct the triangle.

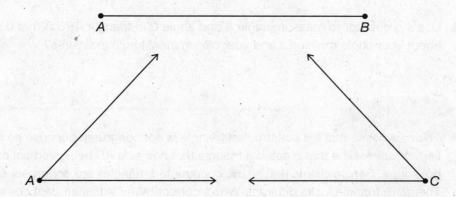

13

2. How does the length of side *AB* compare to the length of your classmates' side *AB*?

3. Use a protractor to measure angle *A* and angle *C* in triangle *ABC*. What do you notice about your angle measures and your classmates' angle measures?

4. Thomas claims that his constructed triangle is not congruent because he drew a vertical starter line that created a triangle that has side *AB* being vertical rather than horizontal. Denise claims that all the constructed triangles are congruent even though Thomas's triangle looks different. Who's correct? Why is this student correct?

 5. Is your triangle congruent to your classmates' triangles? Why or why not?

PROBLEM 2 **Using Reflection to Support AAS**

 If two angles and the non-included side of a triangle are reflected is the image of the triangle congruent to the pre-image of the triangle?

1. Graph triangle *ABC* by plotting the points *A* (−3, −6), *B* (−9, −10), and *C* (−1, −10).

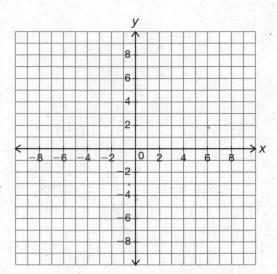

2. Use the Distance Formula to calculate the length of each side of triangle *ABC*. Record the exact measurements in the table.

Side of Triangle *ABC*	Length of Side
$\overline{AB}$	
$\overline{BC}$	
$\overline{AC}$	

3. Reflect angle *A*, angle *B*, and side *BC* over the line of reflection $y = -2$ to form angle *D*, angle *E*, and side *EF*. Then connect points *D* and *E* to form triangle *DEF*. Record the image coordinates in the table.

Triangle *ABC* (coordinates)	Triangle *DEF* (coordinates)
A (−3, −6)	
B (−9, −10)	
C (−1, −10)	

4. Use the Distance Formula to calculate the length of each side of triangle *DEF*. Record the exact measurements in the table.

Side of Triangle *DEF*	Length of Side
DE	
EF	
DF	

13

5. Compare the corresponding side lengths of the pre-image and image. What do you notice?

You have shown that the corresponding sides of the image and pre-image are congruent. Therefore, the triangles are congruent by the SSS Congruence Theorem. However, you are proving the Angle-Angle-Side Congruence Theorem. Therefore, you need to verify if angle *A* and angle *C* are congruent to the corresponding angles in triangle *DEF*.

6. Use a protractor to determine the angle measures of each triangle.

    a. What is the measure of angle *A* and angle *C*?

    b. Which angles in triangle *DEF* correspond to angle *A* and angle *C*?

    c. What do you notice about the measures of the corresponding angles in the triangles? What can you conclude from this information?

You have used a protractor to verify that the corresponding angles of the two triangles are congruent.

In conclusion, when the measure of two angles and the length of the non-included side of one triangle are equal to the measure of the two corresponding angles and the length of the non-included side of another triangle, the two triangles are congruent by the AAS Congruence Theorem.

13

Determine if there is enough information to prove that the two triangles are congruent by ASA or AAS. Write the congruence statements to justify your reasoning.

1. △ABS $\stackrel{?}{\cong}$ △AVF

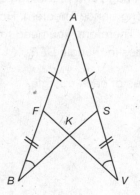

2. △GAB $\stackrel{?}{\cong}$ △SBA

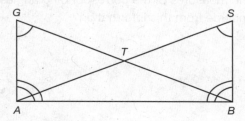

13

3. △EQD $\overset{?}{\cong}$ △DWE

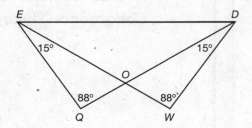

 4. △ABC $\overset{?}{\cong}$ △PQR

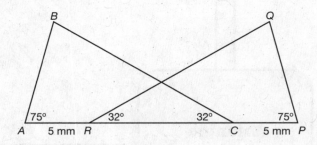

Talk the Talk

 This chapter focused on four methods that you can use to prove that two triangles are congruent. Complete the graphic organizer by providing an illustration of each theorem.

Use markers to show congruent sides and congruent angles.

 Be prepared to share your solutions and methods.

13

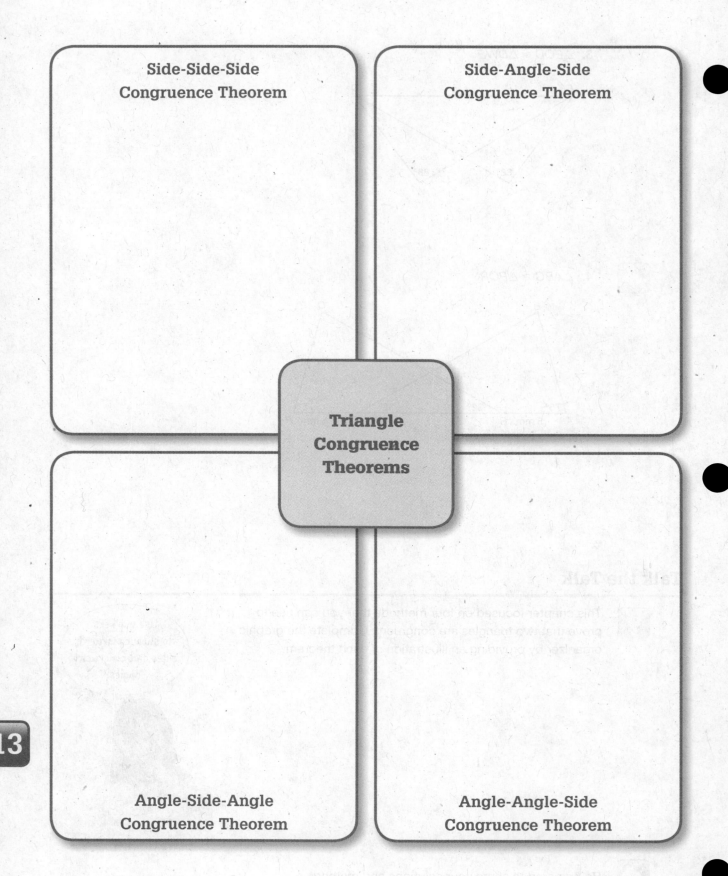

Side-Side-Side
Congruence Theorem

Side-Angle-Side
Congruence Theorem

Triangle
Congruence
Theorems

Angle-Side-Angle
Congruence Theorem

Angle-Angle-Side
Congruence Theorem

13

Chapter 13 Summary

- rotation (13.1)
- point of rotation (13.1)
- angle of rotation (13.1)
- reflection (13.1)
- line of reflection (13.1)
- congruent angles (13.2)
- corresponding sides (13.2)

- corresponding angles (13.2)
- theorem (13.3)
- postulate (13.3)
- Side-Side-Side Congruence Theorem (13.3)
- Side-Angle-Side Congruence Theorem (13.4)

- included angle (13.4)
- Angle-Side-Angle Congruence Theorem (13.5)
- included side (13.5)
- Angle-Angle-Side Congruence Theorem (13.6)
- non-included side (13.6)

13.1 Translating Triangles on the Coordinate Plane

A translation is a rigid motion that slides each point of a figure the same distance and direction.

Example

Triangle *ABC* has been translated 10 units to the left and 2 units down to create triangle *A'B'C'*.

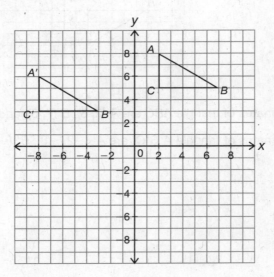

The coordinates of triangle *ABC* are *A* (2, 8), *B* (7, 5), and *C* (2, 5).

The coordinates of triangle *A'B'C'* are *A'* (−8, 6), *B'* (−3, 3), and *C'* (−8, 3).

13

13.1 Rotating Triangles in the Coordinate Plane

A rotation is a rigid motion that turns a figure about a fixed point, called the point of rotation. The figure is rotated in a given direction for a given angle, called the angle of rotation. The angle of rotation is the measure of the amount the figure is rotated about the point of rotation. The direction of a rotation can either be clockwise or counterclockwise. To determine the new coordinates of a point after a 90° counterclockwise rotation, change the sign of the y-coordinate of the original point and then switch the x-coordinate and the y-coordinate. To determine the new coordinates of a point after a 180° rotation, change the signs of the x-coordinate and the y-coordinate of the original point.

Example

Triangle *ABC* has been rotated 180° counterclockwise about the origin to create triangle *A'B'C'*.

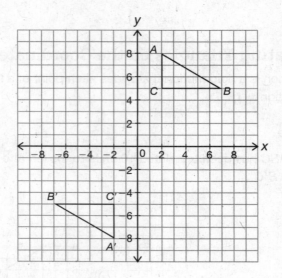

The coordinates of triangle *ABC* are *A* (2, 8), *B* (7, 5), and *C* (2, 5).

The coordinates of triangle *A'B'C'* are *A'* (−2, −8), *B'* (−7, −5), and *C'* (−2, −5).

13.1 **Reflecting Triangles on a Coordinate Plane**

A reflection is a rigid motion that reflects or "flips" a figure over a given line called a line of reflection. Each point in the new triangle will be the same distance from the line of reflection as the corresponding point in the original triangle. To determine the coordinates of a point after a reflection across the *x*-axis, change the sign of the *y*-coordinate of the original point. The *x*-coordinate remains the same. To determine the coordinates of a point after a reflection across the *y*-axis, change the sign of the *x*-coordinate of the original point. The *y*-coordinate remains the same.

Example

Triangle *ABC* has been reflected across the *x*-axis to create triangle *A'B'C'*.

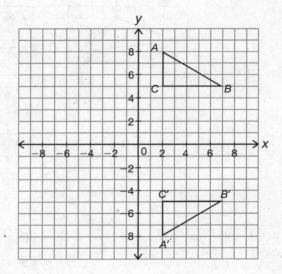

The coordinates of triangle *ABC* are *A* (2, 8), *B* (7, 5), and *C* (2, 5).

The coordinates of triangle *A'B'C'* are *A'* (2, −8), *B'* (7, −5), and *C'* (2, −5).

13

13.3 Using the SSS Congruence Theorem to Identify Congruent Triangles

The Side-Side-Side (SSS) Congruence Theorem states that if three sides of one triangle are congruent to the corresponding sides of another triangle, then the triangles are congruent.

Example

Use the SSS Congruence theorem to prove $\triangle CJS$ is congruent to $\triangle C'J'S'$.

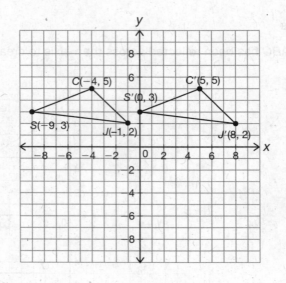

$$SC = \sqrt{[-4-(-9)]^2 + (5-3)^2}$$
$$= \sqrt{5^2 + 2^2}$$
$$= \sqrt{25 + 4}$$
$$SC = \sqrt{29}$$

$$S'C' = \sqrt{(5-0)^2 + (5-3)^2}$$
$$= \sqrt{5^2 + 2^2}$$
$$= \sqrt{25 + 4}$$
$$S'C' = \sqrt{29}$$

$$CJ = \sqrt{[-1-(-4)]^2 + (2-5)^2}$$
$$= \sqrt{3^2 + (-3)^2}$$
$$= \sqrt{9 + 9}$$
$$CJ = \sqrt{18}$$

$$C'J' = \sqrt{(8-5)^2 + (2-5)^2}$$
$$= \sqrt{3^2 + (-3)^2}$$
$$= \sqrt{9 + 9}$$
$$C'J' = \sqrt{18}$$

$$SJ = \sqrt{[-1-(-9)]^2 + (2-3)^2}$$
$$= \sqrt{8^2 + (-1)^2}$$
$$= \sqrt{64 + 1}$$
$$SJ = \sqrt{65}$$

$$S'J' = \sqrt{(8-0)^2 + (2-3)^2}$$
$$= \sqrt{8^2 + (-1)^2}$$
$$= \sqrt{64 + 1}$$
$$S'J' = \sqrt{65}$$

The lengths of the corresponding sides of the pre-image and the image are equal, so the corresponding sides of the image and the pre-image are congruent. Therefore, the triangles are congruent by the SSS Congruence Theorem.

13.4 Using the SAS Congruence Theorem to Identify Congruent Triangles

The Side-Angle-Side (SAS) Congruence Theorem states that if two sides and the included angle of one triangle are congruent to the corresponding two sides and the included angle of a second triangle, then the triangles are congruent. An included angle is the angle formed by two sides of a triangle.

Example

Use the SAS Congruence Theorem to prove that $\triangle AMK$ is congruent to $\triangle A'M'K'$.

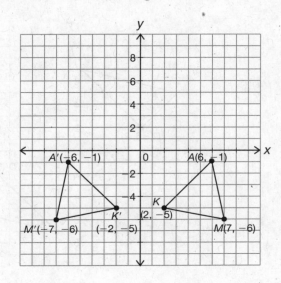

$$KA = \sqrt{(6-2)^2 + [-1-(-5)]^2}$$
$$= \sqrt{4^2 + 4^2}$$
$$= \sqrt{16 + 16}$$
$$= \sqrt{32}$$

$$K'A' = \sqrt{[-5-(-1)]^2 + [-2-(-6)]^2}$$
$$= \sqrt{(-4)^2 + 4^2}$$
$$= \sqrt{16 + 16}$$
$$= \sqrt{32}$$

$$KM = \sqrt{(7-2)^2 + [-6-(-5)]^2}$$
$$= \sqrt{5^2 + (-1)^2}$$
$$= \sqrt{25 + 1}$$
$$= \sqrt{26}$$

$$K'M' = \sqrt{[-7-(-2)]^2 + [-6-(-5)]^2}$$
$$= \sqrt{(-5)^2 + (-1)^2}$$
$$= \sqrt{25 + 1}$$
$$= \sqrt{26}$$

$m\angle K = 58°$

$m\angle K' = 58°$

The lengths of the pairs of the corresponding sides and the measures of the pair of corresponding included angles are equal. Therefore, the triangles are congruent by the SAS Congruence Theorem.

13.5 Using the ASA Congruence Theorem to Identify Congruent Triangles

The Angle-Side-Angle (ASA) Congruence Theorem states that if two angles and the included side of one triangle are congruent to the corresponding two angles and the included side of another triangle, then the triangles are congruent. An included side is the line segment between two angles of a triangle.

Example

Use the ASA Congruence Theorem to prove that $\triangle DLM$ is congruent to $\triangle D'L'M'$.

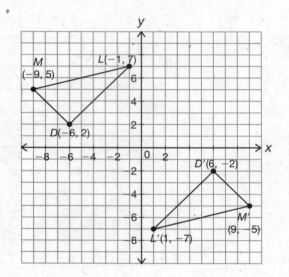

$DM = \sqrt{[-9 - (-6)]^2 + (5 - 2)^2}$

$= \sqrt{(-3)^2 + 3^2}$

$= \sqrt{9 + 9}$

$= \sqrt{18}$

$D'M' = \sqrt{(9 - 6)^2 + [-5 - (-2)]^2}$

$= \sqrt{3^2 + (-3)^2}$

$= \sqrt{9 + 9}$

$= \sqrt{18}$

$m\angle D = 90°$

$m\angle D' = 90°$

$m\angle M = 60°$

$m\angle M' = 60°$

The measures of the pairs of corresponding angles and the lengths of the corresponding included sides are equal. Therefore, the triangles are congruent by the ASA Congruence Theorem.

© 2012 Carnegie Learning

13.6 Using the AAS Congruence Theorem to Identify Congruent Triangles

The Angle-Angle-Side (AAS) Congruence Theorem states that if two angles and a non-included side of one triangle are congruent to the corresponding two angles and the corresponding non-included side of a second triangle, then the triangles are congruent.

Example

Use the AAS Congruence Theorem to prove $\triangle LSK$ is congruent to $\triangle L'S'K'$.

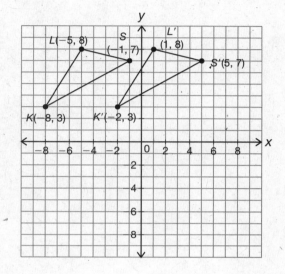

$m\angle L = 108°$

$m\angle L' = 108°$

$m\angle K = 30°$

$m\angle K' = 30°$

$KS = \sqrt{[-1 - (-8)]^2 + (7 - 3)^2}$
$= \sqrt{7^2 + 4^2}$
$= \sqrt{49 + 16}$
$= \sqrt{65}$

$K'S' = \sqrt{[5 - (-2)]^2 + (7 - 3)^2}$
$= \sqrt{7^2 + 4^2}$
$= \sqrt{49 + 16}$
$= \sqrt{65}$

The measures of the two pairs of corresponding angles and the lengths of the pair of corresponding non-included sides are equal. Therefore, the triangles are congruent by the AAS Congruence Theorem.

13

13

Perimeter and Area of Geometric Figures on the Coordinate Plane

There are more than 200 national flags in the world. One of the largest is the flag of Brazil flown in Three Powers Plaza in Brasilia. This flag has an area of over 8500 square feet!

Transforming to a New Level!

Using Transformations to Determine Perimeter and Area

© 2012 Carnegie Learning

LEARNING GOALS

In this lesson, you will:

- Determine the perimeter and area of non-square rectangles on a coordinate plane.
- Determine the perimeter and area of squares on a coordinate plane.
- Connect transformations of geometric figures with number sense and operation.
- Determine perimeters and areas of rectangles using transformations.

Did you know that every baseball game has a "seventh-inning stretch" that gives people an opportunity to get up and stretch their legs? While stretching the legs is good for humans—especially at long sporting events—stretching is not helpful when determining the perimeter and area of geometric figures.

As you learned previously, translations, rotations, and reflections are transformations. And for a transformation to be a transformation, all the points need to be transformed—not just *some* of the points.

What do you think might happen if you try to translate a figure by moving only one point? What would this "stretching" do to the geometric figure's perimeter and area?

PROBLEM 1   Determining the Outside and Inside

Previously, you determined the congruency of geometric figures. Now, you will determine the perimeter and the area of geometric figures.

1. Graph rectangle *ABCD* with vertices *A*(4, 3), *B*(10, 3), *C*(10, 5), and *D*(4, 5).

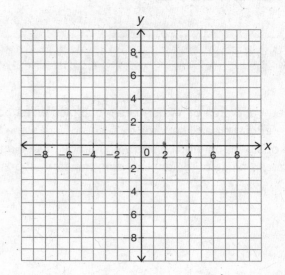

Remember that the perimeter of a geometric figure is calculated by adding the side lengths.

a. Determine the perimeter of rectangle *ABCD*.

b. Determine the area of rectangle *ABCD*.

Don't forget! The formula for area of a rectangle is *A* = *bh*, where *A* represents the area, *b* represents the base, and *h* represents the height.

© 2012 Carnegie Learning

14

2. Horace says that he determined the area of rectangle *ABCD* by determining the product *CD*(*CB*). Bernice says that Horace is incorrect because he needs to use the base of the rectangle and that the base is *AB*, not *CD*. Horace responded by saying that *CD* is one of the bases. Who's correct? Explain why the correct student's rationale is correct.

The perimeter or area of a rectangle can be determined efficiently by using the distance formula or by simply counting units on the coordinate plane.

3. Analyze rectangle *RSTU* on the coordinate plane shown.

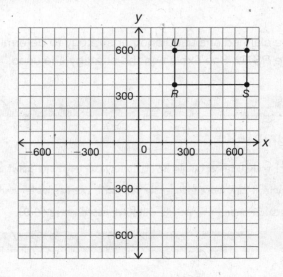

a. What are the increments for the *x*- and *y*-axes?

b. List some strategies you can use to determine the perimeter and area of rectangle *RSTU*.

14

c. Determine the coordinates of the vertices of rectangle *RSTU*. Then, calculate the perimeter and area of rectangle *RSTU*.

4. Shantelle claimed she used another strategy to determine the perimeter and area of rectangle *RSTU*. She explained the strategy she used.

> **Shantelle**
>
> If I translate rectangle RSTU to have at least one point of image R'S'T'U' on the origin, I can more efficiently calculate the perimeter and area of rectangle RSTU because one of the points will have coordinates (0,0).

Explain why Shantelle's rationale is correct or incorrect.

5. If you perform a transformation of rectangle *RSTU* as Shantelle describes, will the image of rectangle *RSTU* have the same area and perimeter as the pre-image *RSTU*? Explain your reasoning.

As you learned previously, transformations are rigid motions that leave a geometric figure unchanged. The pre-image and the image are congruent because in a transformation, *all* vertices must be rigidly moved from one location to another location.

If you are determining the length of a line segment, you can graph the line segment above a number line to determine the length. Segment *LM* is shown.

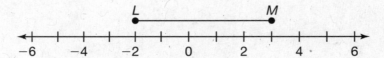

While you can count the number of intervals between −2 and 3, you can also just translate the segment to have the entire segment on the positive side of the number line. Or, you can translate the segment to have the entire segment on the negative side of the number line.

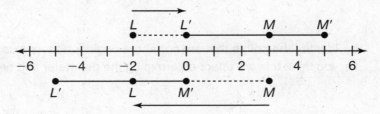

As you can see, segment *LM* and segment *L'M'* are congruent. Thus, the lengths are equal.

So, you know that the lengths of the sides of rectangle *RSTU* will be preserved if the rectangle is translated. That means that the perimeter of the rectangle is preserved when translated.

6. Once again, analyze rectangle *RSTU*.

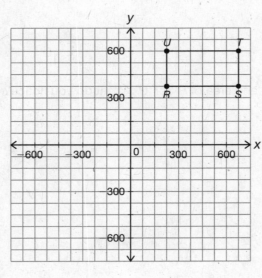

a. Explain how you can transform the rectangle so that point *R* is located at the origin.

14

b. Graph rectangle $R'S'T'U'$ on the coordinate plane with point R at the origin. Then, list the coordinates of rectangle $R'S'T'U'$.

c. Identify the points that are *not* at the origin, on the *x*-axis, or on the *y*-axis. How do you think this will affect determining the perimeter and area of rectangle $R'S'T'U'$?

d. Determine the perimeter and area of $R'S'T'U'$. What do you notice?

You translated a rectangle to allow one vertex to sit at the origin. As a result of the translation, two points also were translated onto the *x*- or *y*-axis, making it possible to use mental calculations to determine the perimeter and area of rectangle *RSTU*.

While making the calculation of perimeter and area more efficient, you actually uncovered yet another way that mathematics maintains balance between different parts of a mathematical problem. Recall that when you use the Distributive Property in a mathematical expression, you must distribute both the value and the operation to all parts of the expression. The same can be said when performing a transformation of a geometric figure.

If a transformation is performed on a geometric figure, not only are the pre-image and the image congruent, but the pre-image's and image's perimeters and areas are equal. Knowing this information will help you make good decisions on how to work more efficiently with geometric figures.

1. Analyze the graph of square *WXYZ* shown on the coordinate plane.

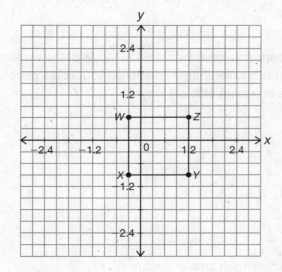

Remember, all squares are considered rectangles. However, the sides of a square are all congruent.

© 2012 Carnegie Learning

a. Determine the coordinates of square *WXYZ*'s vertices.

b. Do you think that using a transformation could make determining the perimeter and area more efficient? Explain why or why not.

c. Suppose you will perform a transformation to move all the vertices of square *WXYZ* into Quadrant I. Explain which transformation(s) you would perform to determine the perimeter and area in a more efficient way.

 d. Determine the perimeter and area of square *WXYZ*.

14

2. Analyze the graph of the polygon on the coordinate plane shown.

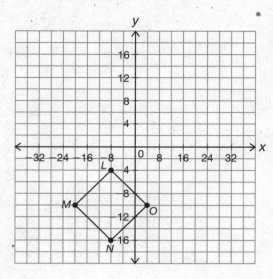

a. Without performing any calculations, predict whether the polygon graphed is a square. Explain how you determined your answer.

b. Determine each vertex coordinate of the polygon. Algebraically verify your prediction. Then determine the perimeter and area.

Be prepared to share your solutions and methods.

14

14

Looking at Something Familiar in a New Way

Area and Perimeter of Triangles on the Coordinate Plane

LEARNING GOALS

In this lesson, you will:

- Determine the perimeter of triangles on the coordinate plane.
- Determine the area of triangles on the coordinate plane.
- Explore the effects doubling the area has on the properties of a triangle.

Your brain can often play tricks on your eyes, and your eyes can play tricks on your brain! Many brain teasers are pictures in which your brain is certain it sees one image; however, by adjusting the way you are looking at the it, suddenly the picture is something totally different! In the early 1990s a series of books was published called *Magic Eye.* These books were autostereograms which are designed to create the illusion of a 3D scene from a 2D image in our brains. When looking at an autostereogram, your eyes send a message to your brain that it is looking at a repeated 2D pattern. However, your eyes are viewing the pattern from slightly different angles so your brain cannot make sense of the pattern. Once you find that correct angle, you can trick your brain into seeing the picture. While many people have fun trying to get the picture to "pop out at them," eye doctors and vision therapists have actually used these autostereograms in the treatment of some different vision disorders.

Are you able to trick your brain into seeing an image in a different way? When your brain is processing the information differently, is the actual image changing at all? How can you be sure?

PROBLEM 1   Area of a Triangle

1. The formula for the area of a triangle can be determined from the formula for the area of a rectangle.

   a. Explain how the formula for the area of a triangle is derived using the given rectangle.

   b. Write the formula used to determine the area of a triangle.

2. Graph triangle ABC with vertices $A(-7.5, 2)$, $B(-5.5, 13)$, and $C(2.5, 2)$. Then, determine its perimeter.

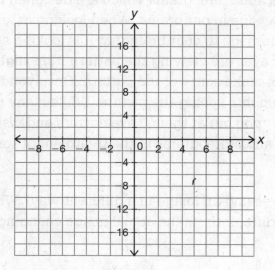

© 2012 Carnegie Learning

3. Determine the area of triangle *ABC*.

a. What information is needed about triangle *ABC* to determine its area?

b. Arlo says that line segment *AB* can be used as the height. Trisha disagrees and says that line segment *BC* can be used as the height. Randy disagrees with both of them and says that none of the line segments currently on the triangle can be used as the height. Who is correct? Explain your reasoning.

c. Draw a line segment representing the height of triangle *ABC*. Label the segment *BD*. Then, determine the height of triangle *ABC*.

Do I use *AC* or *DC* as the length of the base?

d. Determine the area of triangle *ABC*.

14

4. Let's see if there is a more efficient way to determine the area and perimeter of this triangle.

   a. Transform triangle *ABC* on the coordinate plane. Label the image *A'B'C'*. Describe the transformation(s) completed and explain your reasoning.

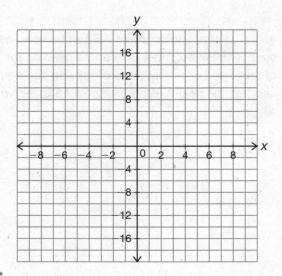

   b. Determine the perimeter of triangle *A'B'C'*.

c. Determine the area of triangle $A'B'C'$. Be sure to label the height on the coordinate plane as $B'D'$.

5. Compare the perimeters and areas of triangles ABC and $A'B'C'$.

   a. What do you notice about the perimeters and areas of both triangles?

   b. Use what you know about transformations to explain why this occurs.

14

6. Mr. Young gives his class triangle *DEF* and asks them to determine the area and perimeter.

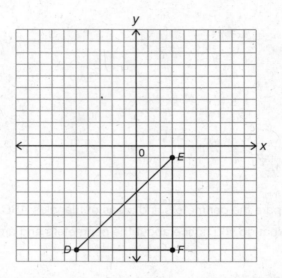

Four of his students decide to first transform the figure and then determine the perimeter and area. Their transformations are shown.

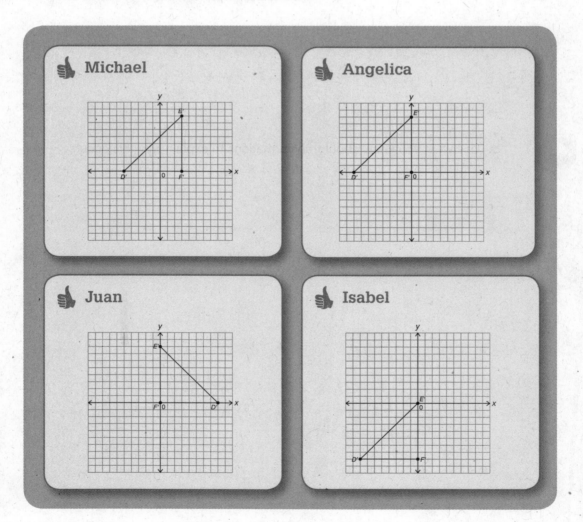

a. Describe the transformation(s) each student made to triangle *DEF*.

b. Whose method is most efficient? Explain your reasoning.

c. What do you know about the perimeter and area of all the triangles? Explain your reasoning.

14

PROBLEM 2   Which Way Is Up?

1. Graph triangle *ABC* with vertices *A*(2, 5), *B* (10, 9), and *C*(6, 1). Determine the perimeter.

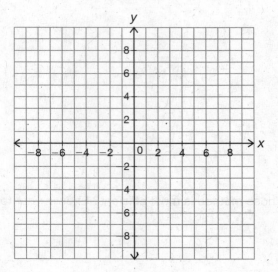

2. To determine the area, you will need to determine the height. How will determining the height of this triangle be different from determining the height of the triangle in Problem 1?

14

To determine the height of this triangle, you must first understand the relationship between the base and the height. Remember that the height must always be perpendicular to the base.

> **Remember, the slopes of perpendicular lines are negative reciprocals.**

Let's use AC as the base of triangle ABC.

Calculate the slope of the base.	$m = \dfrac{y_2 - y_1}{x_2 - x_1} = \dfrac{1 - 5}{6 - 2} = \dfrac{-4}{4}$ $m = -1$
Determine the slope of the height.	$m = 1$

	Height BD	Base AC
Determine the equation of the base and the equation of the height.	$B(10, 9), m = 1$ $(y - y_1) = m(x - x_1)$ $(y - 9) = 1(x - 10)$ $y = x - 1$	$A(5, 2), m = -1$ $(y - y_1) = m(x - x_1)$ $(y - 2) = -1(x - 5)$ $y = -x + 7$
Solve the system of equations to determine the coordinates of the point of intersection.	$x - 1 = -x + 7$ $2x = 8$ $x = 4$	$y = x - 1$ $y = 4 - 1$ $y = 3$

3. Identify the coordinates of the point of intersection. Graph this point on the coordinate plane and label it point D. Draw line segment BD to represent the height.

4. Determine the area of triangle ABC.

   a. Determine the height of the triangle.

   b. Determine the area of the triangle.

5. You know that any side of a triangle can be thought of as the base of the triangle. Predict whether using a different side as the base will result in a different area of the triangle. Explain your reasoning.

Let's consider your prediction.

6. Triangle *ABC* is given on the coordinate plane. This time let's consider side *AB* as the base.

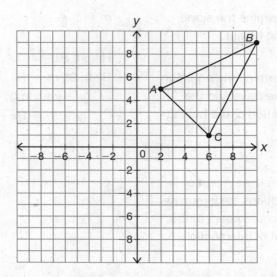

   a. Let point *D* represent the intersection point of the height, *CD*, and the base. Determine the coordinates of point *D*.

14

b. Determine the height of triangle *ABC*.

c. Determine the area of triangle *ABC*.

14

7. Triangle *ABC* is graphed on the coordinate plane. Determine the area of triangle *ABC* using *BC* as the base.

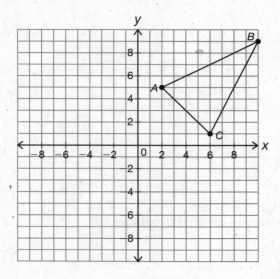

14

8. Compare the three areas you determined for triangle *ABC*. Was your prediction in Question 5 correct?

PROBLEM 3 Double Trouble

1. Graph triangle *ABC* with vertices *A*(−14, 2), *B*(−4, 2), and *C*(−12, 5). Determine the area.

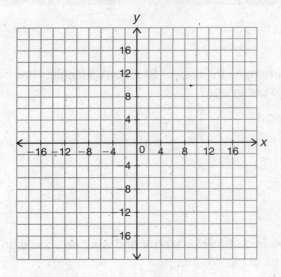

14

2. Brandon's teacher asks his class to double the area of triangle *ABC* by manipulating the pre-image. Brandon's work is shown.

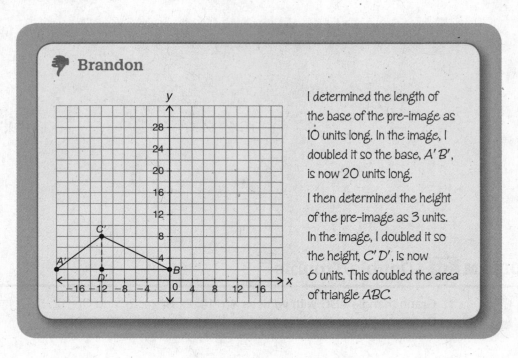

👎 Brandon

I determined the length of the base of the pre-image as 10 units long. In the image, I doubled it so the base, *A′B′*, is now 20 units long.

I then determined the height of the pre-image as 3 units. In the image, I doubled it so the height, *C′D′*, is now 6 units. This doubled the area of triangle *ABC*.

a. Determine the area of Brandon's triangle. How does this relate to the area of the pre-image?

b. Describe Brandon's error and what he should do to draw a triangle that is double the area of the pre-image.

3. Triangle *ABC* is given. Double the area of triangle *ABC* by manipulating the height. Label the image *ABC'*.

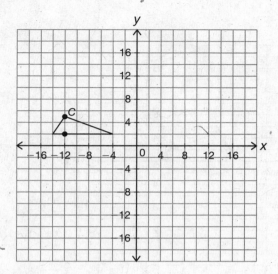

a. Paul identified the coordinates of point *C'* as (−12, 8). Olivia disagrees with him and identifies the coordinates of point *C'* as (−12, −4). Who is correct? Explain your reasoning.

b. Determine the area of triangle *ABC'*.

4. Triangle *ABC* is given. Double the area of triangle *ABC* by manipulating the base. Label the image, identify the coordinates of the new point, and determine the area.

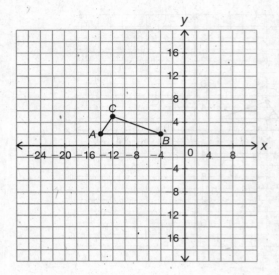

14

5. Emilio's class is given triangle *ABC*. They are asked to double the area of this triangle by manipulating the height. They must identify the coordinates of the new point, *A'*, and then determine the area. Emilio decides to first translate the triangle so it sits on grid lines to make his calculations more efficient. His work is shown.

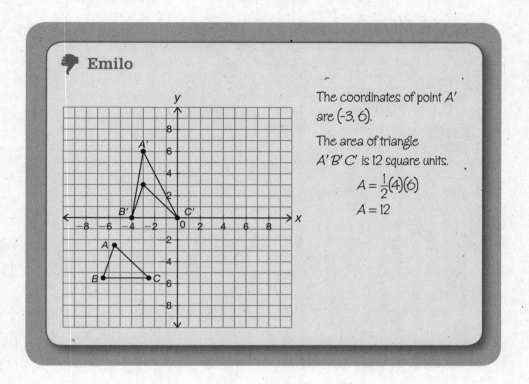

Emilo

The coordinates of point *A'* are (-3, 6).

The area of triangle *A'B'C'* is 12 square units.

$$A = \frac{1}{2}(4)(6)$$

$$A = 12$$

Emilio is shocked to learn that he got this answer wrong. Explain to Emilio what he did wrong. Determine the correct answer for this question.

Be prepared to share your solutions and methods.

14

14

One Figure, Many Names

Area and Perimeter of Parallelograms on the Coordinate Plane

LEARNING GOALS

In this lesson, you will:

- Determine the perimeter of parallelograms on a coordinate plane.
- Determine the area of parallelograms on a coordinate plane.
- Explore the effects doubling the area has on the properties of a parallelogram.

A parallelogram is a quadrilateral with two pairs of parallel sides. However, this is a pretty simple definition when it comes to the many figures we work with in geometry. There are actually different types of parallelograms depending on special features it may have. A parallelogram with four angles of equal measure is known as a rectangle. A parallelogram with four sides of equal length is known as a rhombus. A parallelogram with four sides of equal length and four angles of equal measure is a . . . well, you should know that one.

While working with the parallelograms in the following lesson, try to determine whether they are a certain type of parallelogram. How might knowing a parallelogram is a rectangle or square help you when determining the area or perimeter? But remember, you should never assume a figure has certain measures unless you can prove it!

PROBLEM 1   Rectangle or Parallelogram?

You know the formula for the area of a parallelogram. The formula, $A = bh$, where A represents the area, b represents the length of the base, and h represents the height is the same formula that is used when determining the area of a rectangle. But how can that be if they are different shapes?

1. Use the given parallelogram to explain how the formula for the area of a parallelogram and the area of a rectangle can be the same.

2. Analyze parallelogram *ABCD* on the coordinate plane.

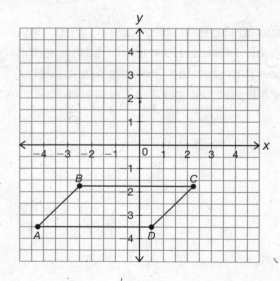

Could I transform this parallelogram to make these calculations easier?

© 2012 Carnegie Learning

a. Determine the perimeter of parallelogram *ABCD*.

b. To determine the area of *ABCD*, you must first determine the height. Describe how to determine the height of *ABCD*.

c. Ms. Finch asks her class to identify the height of *ABCD*. Peter draws a perpendicular line from point *B* to line segment *AD*, stating that the height is represented by line segment *BE*. Tonya disagrees. She draws a perpendicular line from point *B* to line segment *BC*, stating that the height is represented by line segment *DF*. Who is correct? Explain your reasoning.

14

d. Determine the height of *ABCD*.

e. Determine the area of *ABCD*.

PROBLEM 2   Stand Up Straight!

1. Graph parallelogram *ABCD* with vertices *A*(1, 1), *B*(7, −7), *C*(8, 0), and *D*(2, 8). Determine the perimeter.

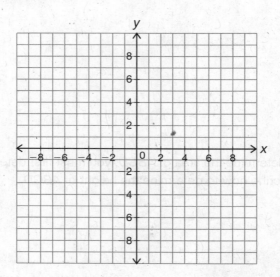

2. Determine the area of parallelogram *ABCD*.

    a. Using *CD* as the base, how will determining the height of this parallelogram be different from determining the height of the parallelogram in Problem 1?

These steps will be similar to the steps you took to determine the height of a triangle.

    b. Using *CD* as the base, explain how you will locate the coordinates of point *E*, the point where the base and height intersect.

    c. Determine the coordinates of point *E*. Label point *E* on the coordinate plane.

© 2012 Carnegie Learning

14

d. Determine the height of parallelogram *ABCD*.

e. Determine the area of parallelogram *ABCD*.

 3. You determined earlier that any side of a parallelogram can be thought of as the base. Predict whether using a different side as the base will result in a different area of the parallelogram. Explain your reasoning.

14

Let's consider your prediction.

4. Parallelogram *ABCD* is given on the coordinate plane. This time let's consider side *BC* as the base.

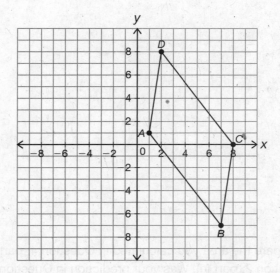

a. Let point *E* represent the intersection point of the height, *AE*, and the base. Determine the coordinates of point *E*.

b. Determine the area of parallelogram *ABCD*.

 5. Compare the area you calculated in Question 4, part (b) with the area you calculated in Question 2, part (e). Was your prediction in Question 3 correct?

PROBLEM 3 **Double Trouble**

 1. Graph parallelogram *ABCD* with the vertices *A*(−7, 8), *B*(−3, 11), *C*(5, 11), and *D*(1, 8).

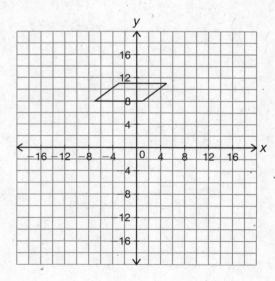

14

a. Determine the area of parallelogram *ABCD*.

b. You want to double the area of parallelogram *ABCD* by manipulating the base. Describe how you would move the points to represent this on the coordinate plane.

c. Manipulate parallelogram *ABCD* on the coordinate plane as you described above to double the area. Label the image and identify the coordinates of the new point(s).

d. Determine the area of the manipulated triangle.

14

2. Parallelogram *ABCD* is given. Double the area of parallelogram *ABCD* by manipulating the height. Label the image, identify the coordinates of the new point(s), and determine the area.

Be prepared to share your solutions and methods.

Let's Go Halfsies!
Determining the Perimeter and Area of Trapezoids and Composite Figures

LEARNING GOALS

In this lesson, you will:

- Determine the perimeter and area of trapezoids and hexagons on a coordinate plane.
- Use composite figures to determine the perimeter on a coordinate plane.

KEY TERMS

- bases of a trapezoid
- legs of a trapezoid
- regular polygon
- composite figure

You've probably heard it before: "let's go halfsies" when you and a friend of yours want something, but there is only one left. It can even be more annoying if your guardian tells you that you have to "go halfsies" with your sibling!

Of course, for some reason, when you split a bill, the term is *not* "halfsies," but this is called "going dutch." Wow! This can get confusing!

So, what area formulas seem to go "halfsies" with another area formula. Here's a hint: it might have to do something with triangles!

PROBLEM 1 Well, It's the Same, But It's Also Different!

So far, you have determined the perimeter and area of rectangles, squares, and parallelograms. However, there is one last quadrilateral you will discover and you will determine its perimeter and area. Can you name the mysterious quadrilateral?

1. Plot each point on the coordinate plane shown:

   • *A* (−5, 4)

   • *B* (−5, −4)

   • *C* (6, −4)

   • *D* (0, 4)

   Then, connect the points in alphabetical order.

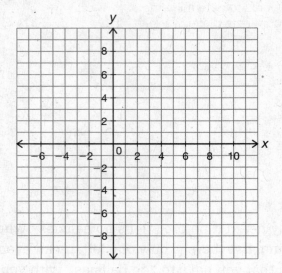

2. What quadrilateral did you graph? Explain how you know.

© 2012 Carnegie Learning

14

The final quadrilateral you will work with is the trapezoid. The trapezoid is unique in the quadrilateral family because it is a quadrilateral that has *exactly* one pair of parallel sides. The parallel sides are known as the **bases of the trapezoid**, while the non-parallel sides are called the **legs of the trapezoid**.

3. Using the trapezoid you graphed, identify:

   a. the bases.

   b. the legs.

Like the other quadrilaterals in this chapter, you can use various methods to determine the perimeter and area of a trapezoid.

4. Analyze trapezoid *ABCD* that you graphed on the coordinate plane.

   a. Describe a way that you can determine the perimeter of trapezoid *ABCD* without using the distance formula.

Think: Can you transform the figure so that a base and at least one leg is on the x- and y-axis?

   b. Determine the perimeter of trapezoid *ABCD* using the strategy you described in part (a). First, perform a transformation of trapezoid *ABCD* on the coordinate plane and then calculate the perimeter of the image.

14

In the last lesson, you learned how to calculate the area of parallelograms. You can use this knowledge to calculate the area of a trapezoid.

So, what similarities exist when determining the area of a parallelogram and a trapezoid?

1. Analyze parallelogram *FGHJ* on the coordinate plane.

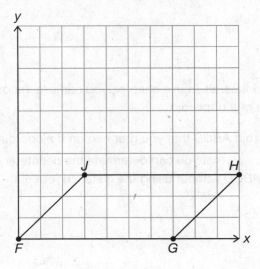

Recall that the formula for the area of a parallelogram is $A = bh$, where b represents the base and h represents the height. As you know, a parallelogram has both pairs of opposite sides parallel. But what happens if you divide the parallelogram into two congruent geometric figures?

a. Divide parallelogram *FGHJ* into two congruent geometric figures.

b. What do you notice about parallelogram *FGHJ* when it is divided into two congruent geometric figures?

14

c. Label the two vertices that make up the two congruent geometric figures.

d. Label the pair of bases that are congruent to each other.
Label one pair of bases b_1 and the other pair b_2.

e. Now write a formula for the area of the entire geometric figure. Make sure you use the bases you labeled and do not forget the height.

f. Now write the formula for the area for *half* of the entire figure.

2. What can you conclude about the area formula of a parallelogram and the area formula of a trapezoid? Why do you think this connection exists?

14

3. Plot each point on the coordinate plane shown:

- Q (−2, −2)
- R (5, −2)
- S (5, 2)
- T (1, 2)

Then, connect the points in alphabetical order.

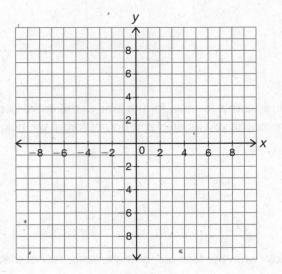

4. Determine the area of trapezoid *QRST*. Describe the strategy or strategies you used to determine your answer.

14

Now that you have determined the perimeters and areas of various quadrilaterals, you can use this knowledge to expand your ability to determine the perimeter and area of *regular polygons* and *composite figures*. A **regular polygon** is a polygon whose sides all have the same length and whose angles all have the same measure. A **composite figure** is a figure that is formed by combining different shapes.

1. Emma plots the following six points to create the polygon shown on the coordinate plane:

   $A(-6, 20)$, $B(-21, 12)$, $C(-21, -5)$, $D(-6, -13)$, $E(9, -5)$, and $F(9, 12)$.

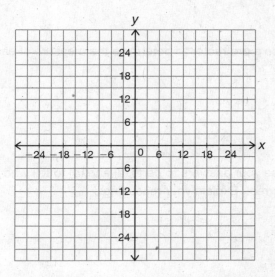

After analyzing the figure, she says that this polygon is a regular hexagon because all the sides are equal. Kevin disagrees and reminds her that she must measure the angles before she can say it is regular. Emma replies that if the side lengths are equal the angles must be equal. Who is correct?

14

a. Determine the length of each side of the hexagon.

b. Use a protractor to determine the measure of each angle.

Be very precise when measuring these angles!

c. Use your answers to parts (a) and (b) to tell who is correct. Explain your reasoning.

2. Determine the perimeter of hexagon *ABCDEF*.

3. Determine the area of hexagon *ABCDEF*. Describe how you determined the area and show your work.

© 2012 Carnegie Learning

14

4. A composite figure is graphed on the coordinate plane shown.

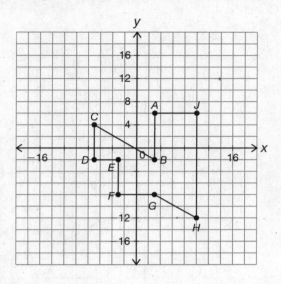

a. Draw line segments on the figure to divide it into familiar shapes.

b. What shape(s) did you divide the composite figure into?

c. Determine the perimeter of the composite figure. Round to the nearest tenth if necessary.

d. Determine the area of the composite figure. Round to the nearest tenth if necessary.

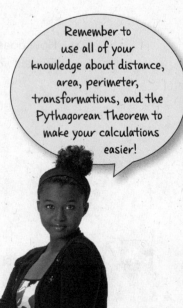

Remember to use all of your knowledge about distance, area, perimeter, transformations, and the Pythagorean Theorem to make your calculations easier!

5. Draw line segments on the composite figure to divide the figure differently from how you divided it in Question 4.

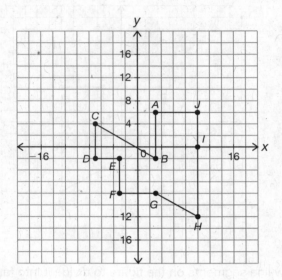

a. What shapes did you divide the composite figure into?

b. Determine the area of the composite figure. Round to the nearest tenth if necessary.

c. How does the area in Question 4 part (d) compare to the area in part (b)? Explain your reasoning.

Be prepared to share your solutions and methods.

Chapter 14 Summary

- bases of a trapezoid (14.4)
- legs of a trapezoid (14.4)
- regular polygon (14.4)
- composite figure (14.4)

14.1 Determining the Perimeter and Area of Rectangles and Squares on the Coordinate Plane

The perimeter or area of a rectangle can be calculated using the distance formula or by counting the units of the figure on the coordinate plane. When using the counting method, the units of the x-axis and y-axis must be considered to count accurately.

Example

Determine the perimeter and area of rectangle *JKLM*.

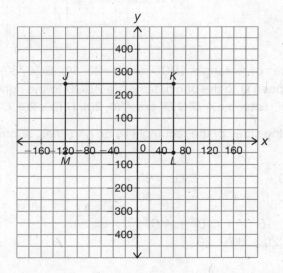

The coordinates for the vertices of rectangle *JKLM* are *J*(−120, 250), *K*(60, 250), *L*(60, −50), and *M*(−120, −50).

Because the sides of the rectangle lie on grid lines, subtraction can be used to determine the lengths.

$JK = 60 - (-120)$
$ = 180$

$KL = 250 - (-50)$
$ = 300$

$A = bh$
$ = 180(300)$
$ = 54{,}000$

$P = JK + KL + LM + JM$
$ = 180 + 300 + 180 + 300$
$ = 960$

The area of rectangle *JKLM* is 54,000 square units.

The perimeter of rectangle *JKLM* is 960 units.

14

14.1 Using Transformations to Determine the Perimeter and Area of Rectangles and Squares

If a rigid motion is performed on a geometric figure, not only are the pre-image and the image congruent, but both the perimeter and area of the pre-image and the image are equal. Knowing this makes solving problems with geometric figures more efficient.

Example

Determine the perimeter and area of rectangle *ABCD*.

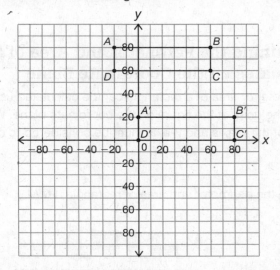

The vertices of rectangle *ABCD* are *A*(−20, 80), *B*(60, 80), *C*(60, 60), and *D*(−20, 60). To translate point *D* to the origin, translate *ABCD* to the right 20 units and down 60 units. The vertices of rectangle *A′B′C′D′* are *A′*(0, 20), *B′*(80, 20), *C′*(80, 0), and *D′*(0, 0).

Because the sides of the rectangle lie on grid lines, subtraction can be used to determine the lengths.

$A'D' = 20 - 0$ $C'D' = 80 - 0$
$\quad\;\; = 20$ $\quad\;\; = 80$

$P = A'B' + B'C' + C'D' + A'D'$
$\quad = 80 + 20 + 80 + 20$
$\quad = 200$

The perimeter of rectangle *A′B′C′D′* and, therefore, the perimeter of rectangle *ABCD*, is 200 units.

$A = bh$
$\quad = 20(80)$
$\quad = 1600$

The area of rectangle *A′B′C′D′* and, therefore, the area of rectangle *ABCD*, is 1600 square units.

Determining the Perimeter and Area of Triangles on the Coordinate Plane

The formula for the area of a triangle is half the area of a rectangle. Therefore, the area of a triangle can be found by taking half of the product of the base and the height. The height of a triangle must always be perpendicular to the base. On the coordinate plane, the slope of the height is the negative reciprocal of the slope of the base.

Example

Determine the perimeter and area of triangle *JDL*.

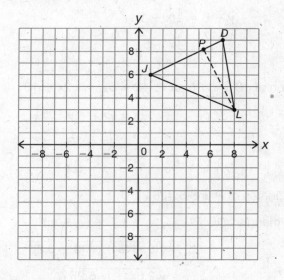

The vertices of triangle *JDL* are *J*(1, 6), *D*(7, 9), and *L*(8, 3).

$JD = \sqrt{(x_2 - x_1)^2 + (y_2 - y_1)^2}$ $DL = \sqrt{(x_2 - x_1)^2 + (y_2 - y_1)^2}$ $LJ = \sqrt{(x_2 - x_1)^2 + (y_2 - y_1)^2}$

$ = \sqrt{(7 - 1)^2 + (9 - 6)^2}$ $ = \sqrt{(8 - 7)^2 + (3 - 9)^2}$ $ = \sqrt{(1 - 8)^2 + (6 - 3)^2}$

$ = \sqrt{6^2 + 3^2}$ $ = \sqrt{1^2 + (-6)^2}$ $ = \sqrt{(-7)^2 + 3^2}$

$ = \sqrt{36 + 9}$ $ = \sqrt{1 + 36}$ $ = \sqrt{49 + 9}$

$ = \sqrt{45}$ $ = \sqrt{37}$ $ = \sqrt{58}$

$ = 3\sqrt{5}$

$P = JD + DL + LJ$
$ = 3\sqrt{5} + \sqrt{37} + \sqrt{58}$
$ \approx 20.4$

The perimeter of triangle *JDL* is approximately 20.4 units.

14

To determine the area of the triangle, first determine the height of triangle JDL.

Slope of JD: $m = \dfrac{y_2 - y_1}{x_2 - x_1}$

$\qquad\qquad = \dfrac{9 - 6}{7 - 1}$

$\qquad\qquad = \dfrac{3}{6}$

$\qquad\qquad = \dfrac{1}{2}$

Slope of PL: $m = -2$

Equation of JD: $(y - y_1) = m(x - x_1)$ $\qquad$ Equation of PL: $(y - y_1) = m(x - x_1)$

$\qquad\qquad y - 6 = \dfrac{1}{2}(x - 1)$ $\qquad\qquad\qquad\qquad y - 3 = -2(x - 8)$

$\qquad\qquad\qquad y = \dfrac{1}{2}x + 5\dfrac{1}{2}$ $\qquad\qquad\qquad\qquad\qquad y = -2x + 19$

Intersection of JD and PL, or P: $\dfrac{1}{2}x + 5\dfrac{1}{2} = -2x + 19$

$\qquad\qquad\qquad\qquad\qquad \dfrac{1}{2}x + 2x = 19 - 5\dfrac{1}{2} \qquad\qquad y = -2(5.4) + 19$

$\qquad\qquad\qquad\qquad\qquad\qquad 2\dfrac{1}{2}x = 13\dfrac{1}{2} \qquad\qquad\qquad y = 8.2$

$\qquad\qquad\qquad\qquad\qquad\qquad\qquad x = 5.4$

The coordinates of P are (5.4, 8.2).

Height of triangle JDL: $PL = \sqrt{(x_2 - x_1)^2 + (y_2 - y_1)^2}$

$\qquad\qquad\qquad\qquad\quad = \sqrt{(8 - 5.4)^2 + (3 - 8.2)^2}$

$\qquad\qquad\qquad\qquad\quad = \sqrt{(2.6)^2 + (-5.2)^2}$

$\qquad\qquad\qquad\qquad\quad = \sqrt{33.8}$

$\qquad\qquad\qquad\qquad\quad \approx 5.8$

Area of triangle JDL: $A = \dfrac{1}{2}bh$

$\qquad\qquad\qquad\qquad = \dfrac{1}{2}(JD)(PL)$

$\qquad\qquad\qquad\qquad = \dfrac{1}{2}(3\sqrt{5})(\sqrt{33.8})$

$\qquad\qquad\qquad\qquad = \dfrac{1}{2}(3\sqrt{169})$

$\qquad\qquad\qquad\qquad = 19.5$

The area of triangle JDL is 19.5 square units.

14

14.2 Doubling the Area of a Triangle

To double the area of a triangle, only the length of the base or the height of the triangle need to be doubled. If both the length of the base and the height are doubled, the area will quadruple.

Example

Double the area of triangle *ABC* by manipulating the height.

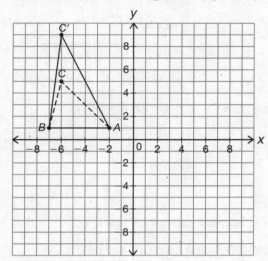

Area of *ABC*

$A = \frac{1}{2}bh$

$= \frac{1}{2}(5)(4)$

$= 10$

Area of *ABC'*

$A = \frac{1}{2}bh$

$= \frac{1}{2}(5)(8)$

$= 20$

By doubling the height, the area of triangle *ABC'* is double the area of triangle *ABC*.

14.3 Determining the Perimeter and Area of Parallelograms on the Coordinate Plane

The formula for calculating the area of a parallelogram is the same as the formula for calculating the area of a rectangle: $A = bh$. The height of a parallelogram is the length of a perpendicular line segment from the base to a vertex opposite the base.

Example

Determine the perimeter and area of parallelogram *WXYZ*.

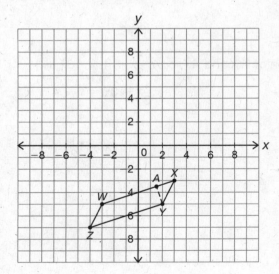

14

The vertices of parallelogram WXYZ are $W(-3, -5)$, $X(3, -3)$, $Y(2, -5)$, and $Z(-4, -7)$.

$$WX = \sqrt{(x_2 - x_1)^2 + (y_2 - y_1)^2}$$
$$= \sqrt{(3 - (-3))^2 + (-3 - (-5))^2}$$
$$= \sqrt{6^2 + 2^2}$$
$$= \sqrt{40}$$
$$= 2\sqrt{10}$$

$$YZ = \sqrt{(x_2 - x_1)^2 + (y_2 - y_1)^2}$$
$$= \sqrt{(-4 - 2)^2 + (-7 - (-5))^2}$$
$$= \sqrt{(-6)^2 + (-2)^2}$$
$$= \sqrt{40}$$
$$= 2\sqrt{10}$$

$$WZ = \sqrt{(x_2 - x_1)^2 + (y_2 - y_1)^2}$$
$$= \sqrt{(-4 - (-3))^2 + (-7 - (-5))^2}$$
$$= \sqrt{(-1)^2 + (-2)^2}$$
$$= \sqrt{5}$$

$$XY = \sqrt{(x_2 - x_1)^2 + (y_2 - y_1)^2}$$
$$= \sqrt{(2 - 3)^2 + (-5 - (-3))^2}$$
$$= \sqrt{(-1)^2 + (-2)^2}$$
$$= \sqrt{5}$$

$$P = WX + XY + YZ + WZ$$
$$= 2\sqrt{10} + \sqrt{5} + 2\sqrt{10} + \sqrt{5}$$
$$\approx 17.1$$

The perimeter of parallelogram WXYZ is approximately 17.1 units.

To determine the area of parallelogram WXYZ, first calculate the height, AY.

Slope of base WX: $m = \dfrac{y_2 - y_1}{x_2 - x_1}$

$$= \frac{-3 - (-5)}{3 - (-3)}$$
$$= \frac{2}{6}$$
$$= \frac{1}{3}$$

Slope of height AY: $m = -3$

Equation of base WX: $(y - y_1) = m(x - x_1)$

$$(y - (-3)) = \frac{1}{3}(x - 3)$$
$$y = \frac{1}{3}x - 4$$

Equation of height AY: $(y - y_1) = m(x - x_1)$

$$(y - (-5)) = -3(x - 2)$$
$$y = -3x + 1$$

Intersection of WX and AY, or A: $\dfrac{1}{3}x - 4 = -3x + 1$

$$\frac{1}{3}x + 3x = 1 + 4$$
$$\frac{10}{3}x = 5$$
$$x = 1\frac{1}{2}$$

$$y = -3x + 1$$
$$y = -3\left(1\frac{1}{2}\right) + 1$$
$$y = -3\frac{1}{2}$$

14

The coordinates of point A are $\left(1\frac{1}{2}, -3\frac{1}{2}\right)$.

$$AY = \sqrt{(x_2 - x_1)^2 + (y_2 - y_1)^2}$$

$$= \sqrt{\left(2 - 1\frac{1}{2}\right)^2 + \left(-5 - \left(-3\frac{1}{2}\right)\right)^2}$$

$$= \sqrt{\left(\frac{1}{2}\right)^2 + \left(-1\frac{1}{2}\right)^2}$$

$$= \sqrt{2.5}$$

Area of parallelogram $WXYZ$: $A = bh$

$$A = 2\sqrt{10}(\sqrt{2.5})$$

$$A = 10$$

The area of parallelogram $WXYZ$ is 10 square units.

14.3 Doubling the Area of a Parallelogram

To double the area of a parallelogram, only the length of the bases or the height of the parallelogram needs to be doubled. If both the length of the bases and the height are doubled, the area will quadruple.

Example

Double the area of parallelogram $PQRS$ by manipulating the length of the bases.

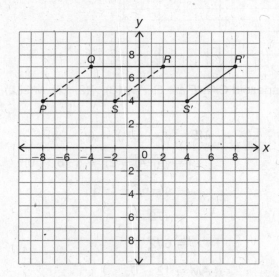

Area of $PQRS$

$A = bh$

$= (6)(3)$

$= 18$

Area of $PQR'S'$

$A = bh$

$= (12)(3)$

$= 36$

By doubling the length of the bases, the area of parallelogram $PQR'S'$ is double the area of parallelogram $PQRS$.

14

14.4 Determining the Perimeter and Area of Trapezoids on the Coordinate Plane

A trapezoid is a quadrilateral that has exactly one pair of parallel sides. The parallel sides are known as the bases of the trapezoid, and the non-parallel sides are called the legs of the trapezoid. The area of a trapezoid can be calculated by using the formula $A = \left(\dfrac{b_1 + b_2}{2}\right)h$, where b_1 and b_2 are the bases of the trapezoid and h is a perpendicular segment that connects the two bases.

Example

Determine the perimeter and area of trapezoid *GAME*.

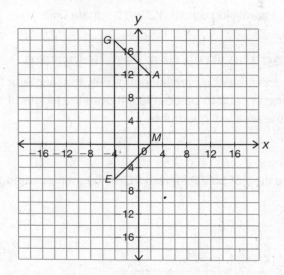

The coordinates of the vertices of trapezoid *GAME* are $G(-4, 18)$, $A(2, 12)$, $M(2, 0)$, and $E(-4, -6)$.

$GA = \sqrt{(x_2 - x_1)^2 + (y_2 - y_1)^2}$

$\quad = \sqrt{(2 - (-4))^2 + (12 - 18)^2}$

$\quad = \sqrt{6^2 + (-6)^2}$

$\quad = \sqrt{72}$

$\quad = 6\sqrt{2}$

$ME = \sqrt{(x_2 - x_1)^2 + (y_2 - y_1)^2}$

$\quad = \sqrt{((-4) - 2)^2 + ((-6) - 0)^2}$

$\quad = \sqrt{(-6)^2 + (-6)^2}$

$\quad = \sqrt{72}$

$\quad = 6\sqrt{2}$

$EG = 18 - (-6)$

$\quad = 24$

$AM = 12 - 0$

$\quad = 12$

$P = GA + AM + ME + EG$

$\quad = 6\sqrt{2} + 12 + 6\sqrt{2} + 24$

$\quad \approx 53.0$

The perimeter of trapezoid *GAME* is approximately 53.0 units.

© 2012 Carnegie Learning

The height of trapezoid *GAME* is 6 units.

$$A = \left(\frac{b_1 + b_2}{2}\right)h$$

$$= \left(\frac{24 + 12}{2}\right)(6)$$

$$= 108$$

The area of trapezoid *GAME* is 108 square units.

14.4 Determining the Perimeter and Area of Composite Figures on the Coordinate Plane

A composite figure is a figure that is formed by combining different shapes. The area of a composite figure can be calculated by drawing line segments on the figure to divide it into familiar shapes and determining the total area of those shapes.

Example

Determine the perimeter and area of the composite figure.

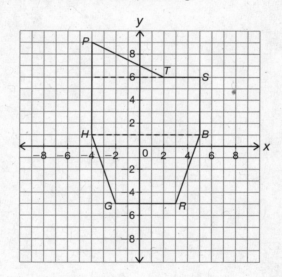

The coordinates of the vertices of this composite figure are $P(-4, 9)$, $T(2, 6)$, $S(5, 6)$, $B(5, 1)$, $R(3, -5)$, $G(-2, -5)$, and $H(-4, 1)$.

$TS = 3$, $SB = 5$, $RG = 5$, $HP = 8$

$$PT = \sqrt{(x_2 - x_1)^2 + (y_2 - y_1)^2} \quad BR = \sqrt{(x_2 - x_1)^2 + (y_2 - y_1)^2} \quad GH = \sqrt{(x_2 - x_1)^2 + (y_2 - y_1)^2}$$

$$= \sqrt{(2 - (-4))^2 + (6 - 9)^2} \qquad = \sqrt{(3 - 5)^2 + (-5 - 1)^2} \qquad = \sqrt{(-4 - (-2))^2 + (1 - (-5))^2}$$

$$= \sqrt{6^2 + (-3)^2} \qquad\qquad\quad = \sqrt{(-2)^2 + (-6)^2} \qquad\qquad = \sqrt{(-2)^2 + (6)^2}$$

$$= \sqrt{45} \qquad\qquad\qquad\quad = \sqrt{40} \qquad\qquad\qquad\quad = \sqrt{40}$$

$$= 3\sqrt{5} \qquad\qquad\qquad\quad = 2\sqrt{10} \qquad\qquad\qquad\quad = 2\sqrt{10}$$

$$P = PT + TS + SB + BR + RG + GH + HP$$

$$= 3\sqrt{5} + 3 + 5 + 2\sqrt{10} + 5 + 2\sqrt{10} + 8$$

$$\approx 40.4$$

14

The perimeter of the composite figure *PTSBRGH* is approximately 40.4 units.

The area of the figure is the sum of the triangle, rectangle, and trapezoid formed by the dotted lines.

Area of triangle:	Area of rectangle:	Area of trapezoid:
$A = \frac{1}{2}bh$	$A = bh$	$A = \left(\frac{b_1 + b_2}{2}\right)h$
$= \frac{1}{2}(6)(3)$	$= 9(5)$	$= \left(\frac{9 + 5}{2}\right)(6)$
$= 9$	$= 45$	$= 42$

The area of composite figure: $A = 9 + 45 + 42$
$$= 96$$

The area of the composite figure *PTSBRGH* is 96 square units.

Connecting Algebra and Geometry with Polygons

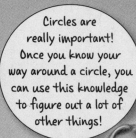

Circles are really important! Once you know your way around a circle, you can use this knowledge to figure out a lot of other things!

Name That Triangle!
Classifying Triangles on the Coordinate Plane

LEARNING GOALS

In this lesson, you will:

- Determine the coordinates of a third vertex of a triangle, given the coordinates of two vertices and a description of the triangle.
- Classify a triangle given the locations of its vertices on a coordinate plane.

Since you may soon be behind the steering wheel of a car, it is important to know the meaning of the many signs you will come across on the road. One of the most basic is the yield sign. This sign indicates that a driver must prepare to stop to give a driver on an adjacent road the right of way. The first yield sign was installed in the U.S. in 1950 in Tulsa, Oklahoma, and had been designed by a police officer of the town. Originally the sign was shaped like a keystone, but over time it was changed. Today it is an equilateral triangle and is used just about everywhere in the world. While some countries may use different colors or wording (some countries call it a "give way" sign) the signs are all the same in size and shape.

Why do you think road signs tend to be different, but basic shapes, such as rectangles, triangles, and circles? Would it matter if a stop sign was an irregular heptagon? Does the shape of a sign make it any easier or harder to recognize?

PROBLEM 1 Location, Location, Location!

1. Graph line segment AB using points $A(-6, 7)$ and $B(-6, 3)$.

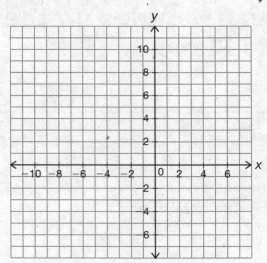

2. Recall that triangles can be classified by the measures of their angles as acute, right, or obtuse. Using line segment AB as one side of a triangle, determine the location for point C such that triangle ABC is:

   a. a right triangle.

If you are unsure about where this point would lie, think about the steps it took to construct different triangles. Draw additional lines or figures on your coordinate plane to help you.

   b. an acute triangle.

c. an obtuse triangle.

3. Recall that triangles can also be classified by the measures of their sides as equilateral, isosceles, and scalene. Using line segment *AB* as one side of a triangle, determine the location for point *C* such that triangle *ABC* is:

a. an equilateral triangle.

b. an isosceles triangle.

c. a scalene triangle.

1. Graph triangle *ABC* using points *A*(0, −4), *B*(0, −9), and *C*(−2, −5).

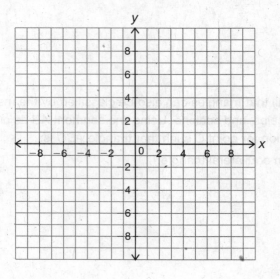

2. Classify triangle *ABC*.

    a. Determine if triangle *ABC* is scalene, isosceles, or equilateral. Explain your reasoning.

These classifications are all about the lengths of the sides. How can I determine the lengths of the sides of this triangle?

b. Determine if triangle *ABC* is a right triangle. Explain your reasoning. If it is not a right triangle, use a protractor to determine what type of triangle it is.

15

c. Zach does not like using the slope formula. Instead, he decides to use the Pythagorean Theorem to determine if triangle *ABC* is a right triangle since he already determined the lengths of the sides. His work is shown.

> **Zach**
>
> $$a^2 - b^2 = c^2$$
> $$(\sqrt{5})^2 + (\sqrt{20})^2 = 5^2$$
> $$5 + 20 = 25$$
> $$25 = 25$$

He determines that triangle *ABC* must be a right triangle because the sides satisfy the Pythagorean Theorem. Is Zach's reasoning correct? Explain why or why not.

15.1 Classifying Triangles on the Coordinate Plane ■ 859

© 2012 Carnegie Learning

3. Graph triangle *ABC* using points *A*(−2, 4), *B*(8, 4), and *C*(6, −2).

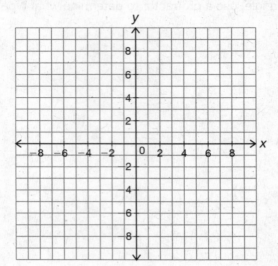

4. Classify triangle *ABC*.

   a. Determine if triangle *ABC* is a scalene, isosceles, or equilateral triangle. Explain your reasoning.

b. Determine if triangle *ABC* is a right triangle. Explain your reasoning. If it is not a right triangle, use a protractor to determine what type of triangle it is.

 Be prepared to share your solutions and methods.

Name That Quadrilateral!
Classifying Quadrilaterals on the Coordinate Plane

LEARNING GOALS

In this lesson, you will:

- Determine the coordinates of a fourth vertex, given the coordinates of three vertices of a quadrilateral and a description of the quadrilateral.
- Classify a quadrilateral given the locations of its vertices on a coordinate plane.

Have you ever mistaken a stranger for someone you know? While it may be embarrassing, this type of mistake is usually no big deal. However, some people struggle with a disorder known as facial blindness where their ability to recognize people's faces is impaired. Studies have found that this disorder usually occurs after a head trauma but it may also be genetic. Some people with this disorder can see the different parts of people faces—forehead, cheekbones, nose—however, their brains cannot put the pieces together to make the face. These people struggle to recognize their friends, parents, and even their children! While there is no cure for this disorder, many people are able to compensate by identifying a key feature of a person such as a haircut or moustache.

Think about a family member or good friend. Can you describe them? What type of features help you recognize this person from others who may look similar? Do you use some of the same features to describe other creatures or objects?

PROBLEM 1   **Where Can It Go?**

Recall that quadrilaterals can be described by the lengths of their sides and by the measures of their angles. The four quadrilaterals you will use in this lesson are parallelograms, squares, rectangles, and trapezoids.

1. Analyze the given points *A*, *B*, and *C*. You want to plot point *D* such that quadrilateral *ABCD* is a square.

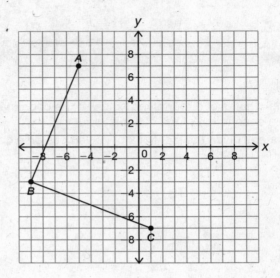

2. Even though point *D* is not in place, the fact that *ABCD* will be a square gives you the information needed to identify the location of point *D*.

   a. How does knowing that a square has two pairs of parallel sides help when determining the unknown point?

   b. How does knowing that a square has 4 right angles help when determining the unknown point?

3. Determine the location of point *D*. Plot and label point *D* on the coordinate plane.

I think this is similar to when we determined the height of a parallelogram on the coordinate plane.

4. Using the same locations for points *A*, *B*, and *C*, identify the location of point *D*, such that quadrilateral *ABCD* is a trapezoid.

   a. Identify information about a trapezoid that is helpful in determining the location of point *D*. Explain your reasoning.

   b. Describe the possible locations of point *D* such that quadrilateral *ABCD* is a trapezoid.

PROBLEM 2 Which One Are You Again?

1. Graph quadrilateral *ABCD* using points *A*(−5, 6), *B*(−8, 2), *C*(−5, −2), and *D*(−2, 2).

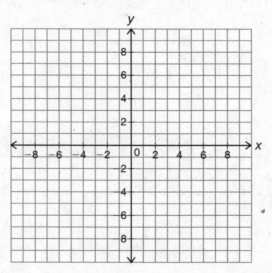

2. Determine if quadrilateral *ABCD* can best be described as a trapezoid, a rhombus, a rectangle, a square, or none of these.

   a. Determine the length of each side of quadrilateral *ABCD*.

What is the difference between a square and a rhombus again?

   b. Can you classify quadrilateral *ABCD* from its side lengths? If so, identify the type of figure. If not, explain why not.

15

c. Determine the slope of each line segment in the quadrilateral.

d. Describe the relationship between the slopes. Can you now identify the figure? If so, identify the type of figure. If not, explain why not.

3. Graph quadrilateral *ABCD* using points *A*(6, 2), *B*(4, −4), *C*(10, −6), and *D*(12, 0). Determine if this quadrilateral can best be described as a trapezoid, a rhombus, a rectangle, a square, or none of these. Explain your reasoning.

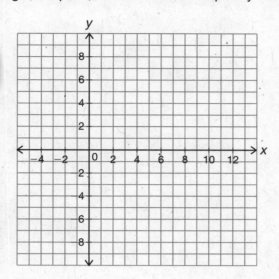

Try to eliminate different types of figures as you determine information about the figure.

 Be prepared to share your solutions and methods.

Is That Point on the Circle?
Determining Points on a Circle

LEARNING GOALS

In this lesson, you will:

- Determine if a point lies on a circle on the coordinate plane given the circle's center at the origin, the radius of the circle, and the coordinates of the point.
- Determine if a point lies on a circle on the coordinate plane given the circle's center not at the origin, the radius of the circle, and the coordinates of the point.
- Transform a circle about the coordinate plane and determine if a point lies on a circle's image given the pre-image's center, radius, and the coordinates of the point.

In the United States, most of the borders separating our states are straight lines or slightly irregular. This is because the borders were often decided by lines of longitude and latitude, meandering rivers, hulking mountain ranges, or other natural formations. However, there is an area on the Pennsylvania-Delaware border that is an arc. This arc, known as the Twelve-Mile Circle, has a radius of exactly 12 miles and is centered on the city of New Castle, Delaware's courthouse. This odd boundary was formed in 1682 when the Duke of York wrote out the original deed of Delaware. In this deed, the Duke claimed that all land within this twelve-mile circle that was not already a part of New Jersey or Maryland, including the Delaware River, would be a part of Delaware. Go take a look at a map of the United States and you will find the Twelve-Mile Circle separating Pennsylvania from Delaware.

PROBLEM 1 The Origin Is the Center

In this lesson, you will explore the connection between the Pythagorean Theorem and a circle which has a center at the origin.

1. Graph circle A so that the circle's center is at the origin, and contains a point P at (0, 5).

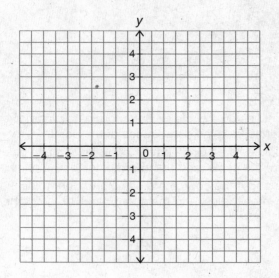

2. Analyze the circle you graphed in Question 1.

   a. Graph line segment AP. What is this line segment called in reference to circle A?

   b. A point, Q, is plotted on the y-axis so it sits on circle A. Describe the relationship between the length of line segment AQ and line segment AP. Explain your reasoning.

   c. How can you determine if circle A passes through a specific point that is not on either the x- or y-axis?

3. Plot point B on the coordinate plane at (4, 3). Do you think point B is on circle A? Explain your reasoning.

Points that do not lie exactly on gridlines may appear to be at certain locations, but you must use algebra to show their exact locations.

4. Analyze circle A and point B that you graphed.

   a. What information can you use from the graph to determine if point B is on circle A? Explain why you can use this information.

   b. Determine the length of segment AB using the Distance Formula. Show your work.

   c. Determine the length of segment AB using the Pythagorean Theorem. First, connect points A and B together to create the hypotenuse of a right triangle. Then, draw a perpendicular line segment from point B to the x-axis. Then use the dimensions to determine the length of segment AB.

d. What do you notice about the solutions using the Distance Formula and the Pythagorean Theorem?

5. What do you notice about the length of *AB* and the radius of circle *A*? How might you use this information to determine if point *B* is on circle *A*?

6. Does point *B* lie on circle *A*? Explain your reasoning.

Remember, the diameter of a circle is the distance across a circle through its center.

7. Circle *D* is centered at the origin and has a diameter of 16 units. Determine if point *H*, located at $(5, \sqrt{38})$, lies on circle *D*.

a. What is the radius of circle *D*? How do you know?

b. Do you know the exact value of $\sqrt{38}$? Explain why or why not.

c. Describe which method you will use to determine if point *H* lies on circle *D*. Explain why you will use this method.

© 2012 Carnegie Learning

d. Does point *H* lie on circle *D*? Show your work and explain how you determined your answer.

PROBLEM 2 — Oh No! The Center *Isn't* at the Origin?

A figure can be in any of the four quadrants of a coordinate plane—and sometimes they are in multiple quadrants. This is also true of circles.

1. Circle *K* has its center at (−2, −3), and contains point *N*(−4, −1.5). Determine if point *C* at (−2, −5.5) lies on circle *K*.

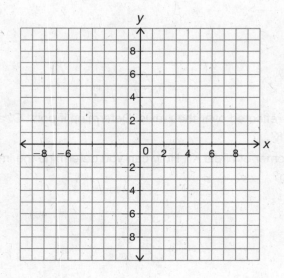

How does a center *not* at the origin affect which strategy you will use?

a. Describe what method(s) you will use to determine whether point C lies on circle K.

b. Determine whether point C lies on circle K. Describe how you determined your answer.

2. Suppose circle K is reflected over the x-axis. Determine if point C′ at (0.5, 5.25) lies on the image circle K′.

a. Determine the center of circle K′. How can you determine the image's center without graphing?

b. What is the radius of circle K′? How do you know?

c. Describe how you can determine if point C' lies on circle K'. Then determine if point C' does lie on circle K'.

 Be prepared to share your solutions and methods.

15

Name That Point on the Circle

Circles and Points on the Coordinate Plane

LEARNING GOALS

In this lesson, you will:

- Determine the coordinates of a point that lies on a circle given the location of the center point and the radius of the circle.
- Use the Pythagorean Theorem to determine the coordinates of a point.

While on the road you may have seen someone off to the side with a tripod and what looked like a camera. Unless you were at a scenic location, chances are that person wasn't taking a picture. This person may be a surveyor and if so he or she is taking measurements that are often used to make maps and determine boundaries. Surveyors must use their geometry and trigonometry skills regularly in order to determine the three-dimensional location of points and the distances and angles between them. Until very recently, the tools of a surveyor were relatively basic: a tape measure to measure distance, a level to measure height differences, and a theodolite, which is the instrument that sits on top of the tripod and measures angles. Today, surveyors are able to use GPS systems to gather most of these measurements much more quickly; however, the measurements are not always as accurate as measuring by hand, and as many people know, GPS is difficult to use in a densely wooded area or if there is a lot of cloud cover.

While working through this lesson keep the job of a surveyor in mind. While you will be working on a flat coordinate plane, the surveyor often has obstacles and obstructions in his or her way. How might the surveyor get around these obstacles when making measurements? How might these affect the accuracy of the measurements?

PROBLEM 1   **The Origin Is My Center**

In the previous lesson, you determined whether a given point was located on a circle. You worked with circles that were centered either on the origin or not. Now, given a circle, you will determine the locations of multiple points on the circle.

1. Circle *A* is centered at the origin and has a diameter of 20 units.

   a. Graph circle *A*.

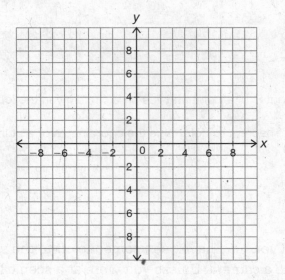

   b. Determine the coordinates of four points on the circle such that two points lie on the *x*-axis and two points lie on the *y*-axis. Explain how you determined your answers.

Can we determine the location of a point that would be on the circle but not on either axis?

To determine a point in a quadrant that lies on a circle, but not on an axis, follow the steps shown.

Step 1: Construct a line from the center to a point on the *x*-axis less than the radius. This will represent one side of a right triangle.

Step 2: Draw a vertical line connecting the end of this side to the circle. This represents the second side of a right triangle.

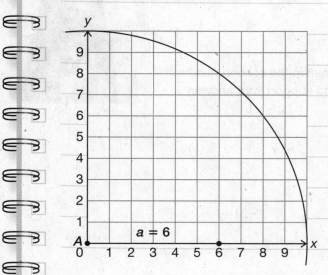

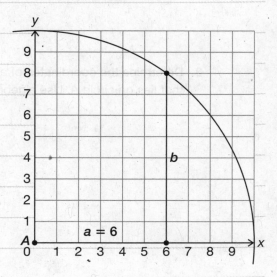

Step 3: Connect the intersection point of the vertical side of your triangle and the center of the circle. This represents the hypotenuse.

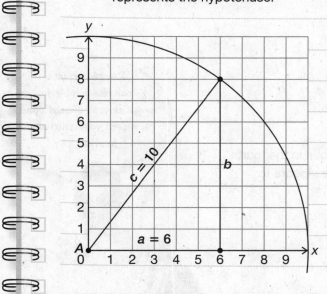

2. Use the Pythagorean Theorem to determine the coordinates of the point that lies on circle *A* in Quadrant I.

Keep in mind that you will have to interpret your answer based on which quadrant the point is located in.

3. Determine the coordinates of a point in the second quadrant that lies on circle *A*. Use algebra to support your answer.

4. Determine the coordinates of a point in the third quadrant that lies on circle *A*. Use algebra to support your answer.

Remember, you can use a table to organize your answers and represent your solutions in another way.

5. Determine the coordinates of a point in the fourth quadrant that lies on circle *A*. Use algebra to support your answer.

6. Use your answers from Questions 2 through 5 to complete the table.

Radius of circle A	x-intercepts	y-intercepts	Point in Quad I	Point in Quad II	Point in Quad III	Point in Quad IV

Determining points that lie on a circle can seem pretty simple when the points have whole number coordinates. However, more challenges arise when you are determining the coordinates of a point and only one of the coordinates is a whole number.

7. Circle *B* is centered at the origin and has a diameter of 8 units.

　a. Graph circle *B*.

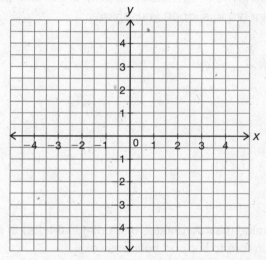

　b. Determine the coordinates of four points on the circle such that two points lie on the *x*-axis and two points lie on the *y*-axis.

　c. Determine the coordinates of a point in the first quadrant that lies on circle *B*. Use algebra to support your answer.

Determine the exact location of each point.

d. Determine the coordinates of a point in the second quadrant that lies on circle *B*. Use algebra to support your answer.

e. Determine the coordinates of a point in the third quadrant that lies on circle *B*. Use algebra to support your answer.

f. Determine the coordinates of a point in the fourth quadrant that lies on circle *B*. Use algebra to support your answer.

g. Use your answers from parts (c) through (f) to complete the table.

Radius of circle *B*	*x*-Intercepts	*y*-Intercepts	Point in Quad I	Point in Quad II	Point in Quad III	Point in Quad IV

PROBLEM 2 **The Circle Is Movin' Up!**

1. Circle *C* has a center at point (2, 5) with a radius of 3 units.

   a. Graph circle *C*.

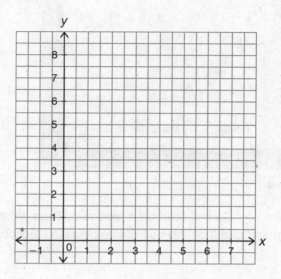

   b. Determine the coordinates of the points on the circle that lie directly above and directly below the center point of the circle. Explain how you determined these coordinates.

   c. Determine the coordinates of the points on the circle that lie directly to the left and directly to the right of the center point of the circle. Explain how you determined these coordinates.

2. Carlos determined the coordinates of an additional point that lies on circle C. His work is shown.

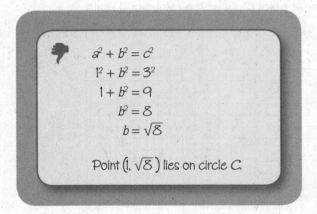

$$a^2 + b^2 = c^2$$
$$1^2 + b^2 = 3^2$$
$$1 + b^2 = 9$$
$$b^2 = 8$$
$$b = \sqrt{8}$$

Point $(1, \sqrt{8})$ lies on circle C.

Determine why Carlos' solution is incorrect. Then determine the correct coordinates of the point and plot it on the coordinate plane in Question 1.

Carlos's calculations bring up a new challenge. When determining the exact coordinates of a point that lies on a circle that is not centered on the origin, an additional step is required. In these situations, you must either add or subtract the vertical distance between the origin and the circle's center to the y-coordinate.

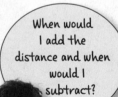

When would I add the distance and when would I subtract?

3. Use transformations to determine the coordinates of a different point that lies on circle C.

a. Explain how you can use reflection to locate a different point that lies on circle C.

b. Use reflection to determine the coordinates of a different point that lies on circle C.

4. Analyze the points of circle C.

a. Complete the table by using your answers from Questions 1 through 3.

Center	Radius	Points Above and Below Center	Points to the Left and Right of Center	Point on circle C (not on x- or y-axis)	Additional point on circle C (result of reflection)

b. What patterns do you notice in the table?

15

5. Circle *D* is centered at point $(-6, -5)$ with a radius of 2 units.

   a. Graph circle *D*.

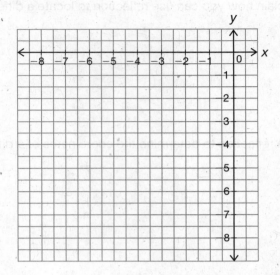

   b. Complete the table using circle *D*, that you graphed in Question 5 part (a).

Center	Radius	Points Above and Below the Center	Points to the Left and Right of Center	Point on circle *D* (not on *x*- or *y*-axis)	Additional point on circle *D* (result of transformation)

Be prepared to share your solutions and methods.

15.1 Determining the Third Vertex of a Triangle Given Two Points

A line segment formed by two points on the coordinate plane can represent one side of a triangle. The placement of the third point depends on the type of triangle being formed.

Example

The line segment AB has been graphed on the coordinate plane for the points $A(2, -3)$ and $B(2, 5)$. Determine the location of point C such that triangle ABC is an acute triangle.

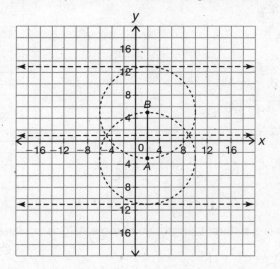

To create an acute triangle, point C can have an infinite number of locations as long as the location satisfies one of the following conditions:

- Point C could be located anywhere on circle A between the y-values of -3 and 5.

- Point C could be located anywhere on circle B between the y-values of -3 and 5.

15.1 **Describing a Triangle Given Three Points on a Coordinate Plane**

When given three points on the coordinate plane, the triangle formed can be described by the measures of its sides and angles. To determine if the triangle is scalene, isosceles, or equilateral, use the Distance Formula to determine the length of each side. To determine if the triangle is right, use the slope formula or the Pythagorean Theorem. If the triangle is not right, a protractor can be used to determine if it is obtuse or acute.

Example

Describe triangle ABC with points $A(-4, 3)$, $B(-4, -4)$, and $C(-1, -1)$.

$AB = 3 - (-4) = 7$

$BC = \sqrt{(-1 - (-4))^2 + (-1 - (-4))^2}$

$\quad = \sqrt{3^2 + 3^2}$

$\quad = \sqrt{9 + 9}$

$\quad = \sqrt{18}$

$AC = \sqrt{(-1 - (-4))^2 + (-1 - 3)^2}$

$\quad = \sqrt{3^2 + (-4)^2}$

$\quad = \sqrt{9 + 16}$

$\quad = \sqrt{25}$

$\quad = 5$

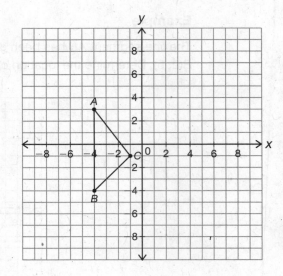

Each side is a different length, so triangle ABC is scalene.

$a^2 + b^2 = c^2$

$(\sqrt{18})^2 + 5^2 = 7^2$

$\quad 18 + 25 = 49$

$\quad\quad 43 \neq 49$

The side lengths do not satisfy the Pythagorean Theorem, so triangle ABC is not a right triangle. The triangle is acute because all of the angles are less than 90°.

15.2 Determining the Fourth Vertex of a Quadrilateral Given Three Points

When given three points on a coordinate plane, the location of the fourth point can affect the type of quadrilateral created. Slope and point-slope formulas can be used to determine the location of a fourth point.

Example

The points $A(3, 7)$, $B(-6, -2)$, and $C(-2, -6)$ are plotted. Determine the location for point D such that quadrilateral $ABCD$ is a rectangle.

Slope of line segments AB and CD:

$$m = \frac{y_2 - y_1}{x_2 - x_1}$$

$$= \frac{-2 - 7}{-6 - 3}$$

$$= \frac{-9}{-9}$$

$$= 1$$

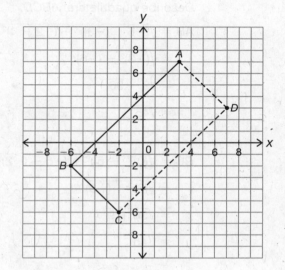

The slope of BC and AD must be the negative reciprocal of the slope of AB and CD. The slope of BC and AD is -1.

Equation of a line with a slope of -1 passing through point A:

$$(y - y_1) = m(x - x_1)$$

$$(y - 7) = -1(x - 3)$$

$$y - 7 = -x + 3$$

$$y = -x + 10$$

Equation of a line with a slope of 1 passing through point C:

$$(y - y_1) = m(x - x_1)$$

$$(y - (-6)) = 1(x - (-2))$$

$$y + 6 = x + 2$$

$$y = x - 4$$

Solution to the system of equations:

$$-x + 10 = x - 4 \qquad\qquad y = x - 4$$

$$-2x = -14 \qquad\qquad\quad = 7 - 4$$

$$x = 7 \qquad\qquad\qquad = 3$$

The coordinates of point D are $(7, 3)$.

Describing a Quadrilateral Given Four Points on a Coordinate Plane

A quadrilateral on the coordinate plane can be classified as a parallelogram, trapezoid, square, or rectangle. To identify the quadrilateral, use the distance formula to determine the length of each side. Then use the slope formula to determine the angles. If the slopes of two line segments are negative reciprocals, the line segments are perpendicular, and form a right angle. If the slopes of two line segments are equal, the line segments are parallel.

Example

Describe quadrilateral $ABCD$.

$$AB = \sqrt{(-6 - (-3))^2 + (-2 - 4)^2}$$
$$= \sqrt{(-3)^2 + (-6)^2}$$
$$= \sqrt{9 + 36}$$
$$= \sqrt{45}$$

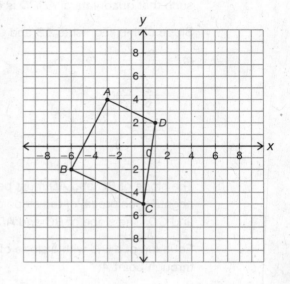

$$BC = \sqrt{(0 - (-6))^2 + (-5 - (-2))^2}$$
$$= \sqrt{(6)^2 + (-3)^2}$$
$$= \sqrt{36 + 9}$$
$$= \sqrt{45}$$

$$CD = \sqrt{(1 - 0)^2 + (2 - (-5))^2}$$
$$= \sqrt{(1)^2 + (7)^2}$$
$$= \sqrt{1 + 49}$$
$$= \sqrt{50}$$

Slope of line segment AB:

$$m = \frac{y_2 - y_1}{x_2 - x_1}$$
$$= \frac{-2 - 4}{-6 - (-3)}$$
$$= \frac{-6}{-3}$$
$$= 2$$

$$AD = \sqrt{(1 - (-3))^2 + (2 - 4)^2}$$
$$= \sqrt{(4)^2 + (-2)^2}$$
$$= \sqrt{16 + 4}$$
$$= \sqrt{20}$$

Slope of line segment BC:

$$m = \frac{y_2 - y_1}{x_2 - x_1}$$
$$= \frac{-5 - (-2)}{0 - (-6)}$$
$$= \frac{-3}{6}$$
$$= -\frac{1}{2}$$

Slope of line segment CD:

$$m = \frac{y_2 - y_1}{x_2 - x_1}$$

$$= \frac{2 - (-5)}{1 - 0}$$

$$= \frac{7}{1}$$

$$= 7$$

Slope of line segment AD:

$$m = \frac{y_2 - y_1}{x_2 - x_1}$$

$$= \frac{2 - 4}{1 - (-3)}$$

$$= \frac{-2}{4}$$

$$= -\frac{1}{2}$$

While line segments AB and BC are equal, line segments CD and AD are not. Line segments BC and AD are parallel because the line segments have the same slope. Line segment AB is perpendicular because its slope is the negative reciprocal of the slope of BC and AD. However, line segment CD is not parallel to line segment AB and is not perpendicular to line segments BC and AD. Quadrilateral $ABCD$ is a trapezoid.

15.3 Determining If a Given Point Is on a Circle When the Center Is at the Origin

When given a circle with the center at the origin and a given point on a circle the circle can be drawn and the radius determined. To determine if another point lies on the circle, the Pythagorean Theorem or the Distance Formula can be used. If the length of the line segment from the origin to the point is equal to the radius, then the point lies on the circle.

Example

Determine if point $R(-4, -3)$ lies on circle G.

$$GR = \sqrt{(-4 - 0)^2 + (-3 - 0)^2}$$

$$= \sqrt{(-4)^2 + (-3)^2}$$

$$= \sqrt{16 + 9}$$

$$= \sqrt{25}$$

$$= 5$$

$$a^2 + b^2 = c^2$$

$$4^2 + 3^2 = c^2$$

$$16 + 9 = c^2$$

$$25 = c^2$$

$$\sqrt{25} = c$$

$$5 = c$$

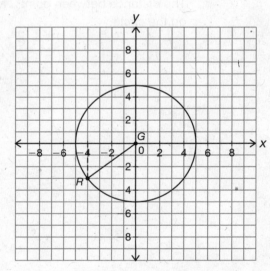

Circle G has a radius of 5 units. Point R lies on circle G because the distance between point G and point R is equal to the radius of circle G.

Determining If a Given Point Is on a Circle When the Center Is Not at the Origin

When given a circle with the center not at the origin and the location of a point on the circle, it can be determined if a third point lies on the circle. First determine the radius of the circle by using the Pythagorean Theorem. Then use the Distance Formula to determine the distance from the origin to the third point. If the distance is equal to the radius, the point lies on the circle.

Example

Circle H has its center at $(4, 5)$ and contains point $F(0, 2)$. Determine if point $J(8.75, 6.5)$ lies on the circle.

$$4^2 + 3^2 = c^2$$
$$16 + 9 = c^2$$
$$25 = c^2$$
$$5 = c$$

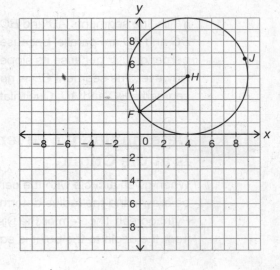

$$HJ = \sqrt{(8.75 - 4)^2 + (6.5 - 5)^2}$$
$$= \sqrt{(4.75)^2 + (1.5)^2}$$
$$= \sqrt{22.5625 + 2.25}$$
$$= \sqrt{24.8125}$$

$$HJ \approx 4.98$$

The distance between point J and the origin is not equal to the radius. Point J does not lie on the circle.

15.3 Determining If a Given Point Is on a Given Circle after a Transformation

The pre-image of a circle reflected over the x-axis can be used to determine the image's center. The x-coordinate of the center remains the same and the y-coordinate of the image's center is the opposite of the pre-image's center. The radius of the image will be the same as the pre-image because the image remains congruent to the pre-image. The Pythagorean Theorem or the Distance Formula can be used to determine if a point lies on the image.

Example

Circle Q has its center at (3, −6) and has a radius of 5 units. Circle Q is reflected over the x-axis to created Circle Q'. Determine if point T(6, 10) lies on circle Q'.

$Q' = (3, 6)$

$Q'T = \sqrt{(6 - 3)^2 + (10 - 6)^2}$

$ = \sqrt{3^2 + 4^2}$

$ = \sqrt{9 + 16}$

$ = \sqrt{25}$

$ = 5$

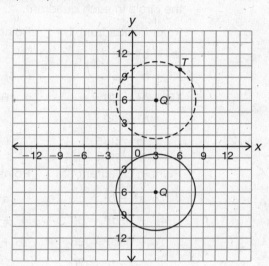

Point T(6, 10) lies on circle Q' because the distance of point T from point Q' is equal to the radius of circle Q, which is equal to the radius of its reflection.

Determining the Coordinates of Points on a Circle Given the Center and Radius

When given a circle with its center at the origin and the radius, points that lie on the circle in each quadrant can be determined using the Pythagorean Theorem. A line segment drawn from the center to any point on the x-axis that is less than the radius represents one side of a right triangle. A vertical line connecting the endpoint of this line segment to the circle represents the other side of a right triangle and is unknown. The distance from the center of the circle to the point on the circle, the radius, represents the hypotenuse.

Example

Circle A is centered at the origin and has a radius of 6 units. Determine a point that lies on the circle in each quadrant.

Point in Quadrant 1:

$$a^2 + b^2 = c^2$$
$$4^2 + b^2 = 6^2$$
$$16 + b^2 = 36$$
$$b^2 = 20$$
$$b = 2\sqrt{5}$$

Point in Quadrant 2:

$$a^2 + b^2 = c^2$$
$$(-4)^2 + b^2 = 6^2$$
$$16 + b^2 = 36$$
$$b^2 = 20$$
$$b = 2\sqrt{5}$$

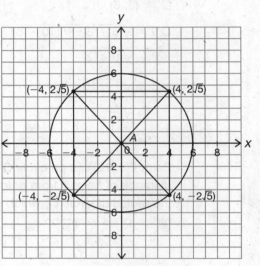

Point in Quadrant 3:

$$a^2 + b^2 = c^2$$
$$(-4)^2 + (-b)^2 = 6^2$$
$$16 + (-b)^2 = 36$$
$$-b^2 = 20$$
$$b = -2\sqrt{5}$$

Point in Quadrant 4:

$$a^2 + b^2 = c^2$$
$$4^2 + (-b)^2 = -6^2$$
$$16 + (-b)^2 = 36$$
$$-b^2 = 20$$
$$b = -2\sqrt{5}$$

Radius of circle A	x-Intercepts	y-Intercepts	Point in Quad 1	Point in Quad 2	Point in Quad 3	Point in Quad 4
4	(6, 0) (−6, 0)	(0, 6) (0, −6)	(4, 2√5)	(−4, 2√5)	(−4, −2√5)	(4, −2√5)

Determining Points on a Circle that Does Not Have Its Center at the Origin

The Pythagorean Theorem can also be used to determine points on a circle that is not centered on the origin. Because the center is not at the origin, the distance from the circle's center to the origin must be added or subtracted to the coordinate of the new point. The created triangle can then be reflected over the center of the circle to determine the location of a second point on the circle.

Example

Circle M is centered at the point of (3, 4) and has a radius of 2 units. Determine a point that lies on the circle.

Point on circle M:

$$a^2 + b^2 = c^2$$
$$1^2 + b^2 = 2^2$$
$$1 + b^2 = 4$$
$$b^2 = 3$$
$$b = \sqrt{3}$$

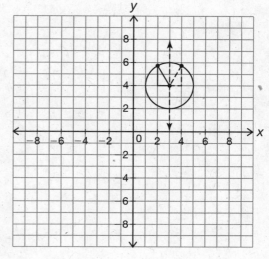

Add the number of units from the center to the origin to b: $4 + \sqrt{3}$.

A second point on the circle is determined by reflecting the triangle over $x = 3$.

Center	Radius	Points Above and Below Center	Points to the Left and Right of Center	Point on circle M (not on x- or y-axis)	Second point on circle M (result of reflection)
(3, 4)	2 units	(3, 2) (3, 6)	(1, 4) (5, 4)	(2, 4 + √3)	(4, 4 + √3)

Logic 16

Before taking the stand in a court trial, a witness promises to tell the truth; however, what does "truth" actually mean? In logic, the truth value of a statement might surprise you!

A Little Dash of Logic
Two Methods of Logical Reasoning

© 2012 Carnegie Learning

LEARNING GOALS

In this lesson, you will:

- Define inductive reasoning and deductive reasoning.
- Identify methods of reasoning.
- Compare and contrast methods of reasoning.
- Identify why a conclusion may be false.

KEY TERMS

- induction
- deduction

The Greek philosopher Aristotle greatly influenced our understanding of physics, linguistics, politics, and science. He also had a great influence on our understanding of logic. In fact, he is often credited with the earliest study of formal logic, and he wrote six works on logic which were compiled into a collection known as the *Organon*. These works were used for many years after his death. There were a number of philosophers who believed that these works of Aristotle were so complete that there was nothing else to discuss regarding logic. These beliefs lasted until the 19th century when philosophers and mathematicians began thinking of logic in more mathematical terms.

In one of Aristotle's other books, *Metaphysics*, he makes the following statement: "To say that that which is, is not or that which is not is, is a falsehood; and to say that that which is, is and that which is not is not, is true." What is Aristotle trying to say here, and do you agree? Can you prove or disprove this statement?

16

1. Emma considered these statements.

   • $4^2 = 4 \times 4$

   • nine cubed is equal to nine times nine times nine

   • 10 to the fourth power is equal to four factors of 10 multiplied together

   Emma concluded that raising a number to a power is the same as multiplying the number as many times as indicated by the exponent. How did Emma reach this conclusion?

2. Ricky read in a book that raising a number to a power is the same as multiplying that number as many times as indicated by the exponent. He had to determine seven to the fourth power using a calculator. So, he entered $7 \times 7 \times 7 \times 7$. How did Ricky reach this conclusion?

3. Compare the reasoning Emma used to the reasoning Ricky used.

4. Jennifer is a writing consultant. She is paid $900 for a ten-hour job and $1980 for a twenty-two-hour job.

   a. How much does Jennifer charge per hour?

   b. To answer Question 4, part (a), did you start with a general rule and make a conclusion, or did you start with specific information and create a general rule?

5. Your friend Aaron tutors elementary school students. He tells you that the job pays $8.25 per hour.

   a. How much does Aaron earn if he works 4 hours?

   b. To answer Question 5, part (a), did you start with a general rule and make a conclusion, or did you start with specific information and create a general rule?

PROBLEM 2   Is This English Class or Algebra?

The ability to use information to reason and make conclusions is very important in life and in mathematics. There are two common methods of reasoning. You can construct the name for each method of reasoning using your knowledge of prefixes, root words, and suffixes.

Remember, a prefix is at the beginning of a word and a suffix is at the end.

Look at the following information. Remember that a prefix is a beginning of a word, and a suffix is an ending of a word.

- *in*—a prefix that can mean *toward* or *up to*

- *de*—a prefix that can mean *down from*

- *duc*—a base or root word meaning *to lead* and often *to think*, from the Latin word *duco*

- *-tion*—a suffix that forms a noun meaning *the act of*

1. Form a word that means "the act of thinking down from."

2. Form a word that means "the act of thinking toward or up to."

Induction is reasoning that involves using specific examples to make a conclusion. Many times in life you must make generalizations about observations or patterns and apply these generalizations to new or unfamiliar situations. For example, you may notice that when you don't study for a test, your grade is lower than when you do study for a test. You apply what you learned from these observations to the next test you take.

These types of reasoning can also be known as inductive and deductive reasoning.

Deduction is reasoning that involves using a general rule to make a conclusion. For example, you may learn the rule for which direction to turn a screwdriver: "righty tighty, lefty loosey." If you want to unscrew a screw, you apply the rule and turn the screwdriver counterclockwise.

3. Refer back to Problem 1.

   a. Identify which Question(s) that used inductive reasoning.

   b. Identify which Question(s) that used deductive reasoning.

PROBLEM 3 Coming to Conclusions

A problem situation can provide you with a great deal of information which you can use to make conclusions. It is important to identify specific and general information in a problem situation in order to come to appropriate conclusions.

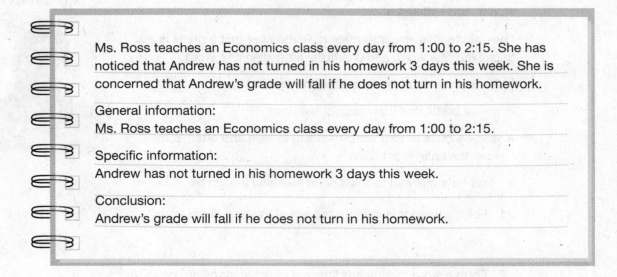

Ms. Ross teaches an Economics class every day from 1:00 to 2:15. She has noticed that Andrew has not turned in his homework 3 days this week. She is concerned that Andrew's grade will fall if he does not turn in his homework.

General information:
Ms. Ross teaches an Economics class every day from 1:00 to 2:15.

Specific information:
Andrew has not turned in his homework 3 days this week.

Conclusion:
Andrew's grade will fall if he does not turn in his homework.

1. Did Ms. Ross use induction or deduction to make this conclusion?
   Explain your answer.

2. Conner read a newspaper article that states that the use of tobacco greatly increases the risk of getting cancer. He then notices that his neighbor Matilda smokes. Connor is concerned that Matilda has a high risk of getting cancer.

   a. Which information is specific and which information would be considered general in this problem situation?

   b. What is the conclusion in this problem?

   c. Did Conner use inductive or deductive reasoning to make the conclusion?
      Explain your reasoning.

© 2012 Carnegie Learning

d. Is Conner's conclusion correct? Explain your reasoning.

3. Molly returned from a trip to England and tells you, "It rains every day in England!" She explains that it rained each of the five days she was there.

   a. Which information is specific and which information would be considered general in this problem situation?

   b. What is the conclusion in this problem?

   c. Did Molly use inductive or deductive reasoning to make the conclusion? Explain your answer.

   d. Is Molly's conclusion correct? Explain how you determine whether Molly is correct.

4. Dontrell takes detailed notes in history class and math class. His classmate Trang will miss biology class tomorrow to attend a field trip. Trang's biology teacher asks Trang if he knows someone in class who always takes detailed notes. Trang tells his biology teacher that Dontrell takes detailed notes. Trang's biology teacher suggests Trang borrow Dontrell's notes because the teacher concludes that Dontrell's notes will be detailed.

   a. What conclusion did Trang make? What information supports this conclusion?

b. What type of reasoning did Trang use? Explain your reasoning.

c. What conclusion did the biology teacher make? What information supports this conclusion?

d. What type of reasoning did the biology teacher use? Explain your reasoning.

e. Will Trang's conclusion always be true? Will the biology teacher's conclusion always be true? Explain your reasoning.

5. The first four numbers in a sequence are 4, 15, 26, and 37.

   a. What is the next number in the sequence? How did you calculate the next number?

   b. Describe how you used both induction and deduction, and what order you used these reasonings to make your conclusion.

6. Write a short note to a friend explaining induction and deduction. Include definitions of both terms and examples that are very easy to understand.

There are two reasons why a conclusion may be false. Either the assumed information is false, or the argument is not valid.

1. Derek tells his little brother that it will not rain for the next 30 days because he "knows everything." Why is this conclusion false?

2. Two lines are not parallel, so the lines must intersect. Why is this conclusion false?

3. Write an example of a conclusion that is false because the assumed information is false.

4. Write an example of a conclusion that is false because the argument is not valid.

Be prepared to share your solutions and methods.

© 2012 Carnegie Learning

What's Your Conclusion?
Understanding Conditional Statements, Arguments, and Truth Tables

LEARNING GOALS

In this lesson, you will:

- Define a conditional statement.
- Identify the hypothesis and conclusion of a conditional statement.
- Explore the truth value of conditional statements.
- Use a truth table.

KEY TERMS

- conditional statement
- propositional form
- propositional variables
- hypothesis
- conclusion
- truth value
- truth table
- converse
- inverse
- contrapositive
- logically equivalent
- biconditional statement

You have probably learned about "if-then" statements in language arts. You are now going to use "if-then" statements while studying logic. But did you also know that "if-then" statements are used in computer programming? These statements tell the computer program to perform different actions depending on whether the "if-then" statement is true or false. There can also be an "else" branch which gives the computer an alternative action to complete.

An example of this "if-then-else" programming code may be shown as follows.

```
If count = 0 Then
message = "There are no items."
Elseif count = 1 Then
message = "There is 1 item."
Elseif count = >1 Then
message = "There are" & count & "items."
```

Can you decipher this piece of computer programming language? What would be happening on the computer if it was reading this piece of code?

Read each pair of statements. Then write a valid conclusion.

1. **Statement:** Melanie's school guidance counselor tells her that if she applies for a scholarship, then she will have a chance to receive it.

   Statement: Melanie applies for a scholarship.

   Conclusion:

What will happen if Melanie does not apply for a scholarship?

2. **Statement:** If it rains, then the baseball game will be cancelled.

   Statement: It rains.

   Conclusion:

3. **Statement:** If Suzanne misses the application deadline for the Vocational Training School, then she will not be admitted.

   Statement: Suzanne missed the application deadline.

   Conclusion:

4. **Statement:** Marvin will know whether he enjoys waltz lessons if he attends his first waltz lesson.

   Statement: Marvin attended his first waltz lesson.

   Conclusion:

5. **Statement:** If having the most experience as a nuclear engineer had been the main requirement, then Olga would have gotten the job.

   Statement: Olga did not get the job.

   Conclusion:

Read each statement and conclusion. Then write the additional statement required to reach the conclusion.

6. Statement: If no evidence is found linking a suspect to the scene of a crime, then the suspect will be found innocent.

Statement: _____

Conclusion: Therefore, the suspect was found innocent.

7. Statement: If the community service program chooses the litter removal project, then Mayor Elder will have the carnival in the North Shore neighborhood.

Statement: _____

Conclusion: Therefore, the community service program did not choose the litter removal project.

8. Statement: If tulips are to survive, then they need sunlight.

Statement: _____

Conclusion: Therefore, the tulips did not survive.

9. Statement: The Secret Service will be at the dinner if the President shows up.

Statement: _____

Conclusion: Therefore, the President did not show up at the dinner.

10. Statement: _____

Statement: You have your umbrella.

Conclusion: Therefore, it must be raining.

11. Statement: _____

Statement: You ate a good breakfast.

Conclusion: Therefore, you were not hungry before lunch.

 12. Statement: _____

Statement: You did your math homework.

Conclusion: Therefore, your teacher was happy.

A **conditional statement** is a statement that can be written in the form "If p, then q." The form of this conditional statement is called the **propositional form**. The propositional form can also be written using symbols as $p \rightarrow q$ and is read as "p implies q." The variables p and q are **propositional variables**. The **hypothesis** of a conditional statement is the variable p, and the **conclusion** of a conditional statement is the variable q.

The **truth value** of a conditional statement is whether the statement is true or false. If a conditional statement *could* be true, then the truth value of the statement is considered true. The truth value of a conditional statement is either true or false, but not both.

16

PROBLEM 2 If This, Then That

Consider the conditional statement:

If the measure of an angle is 32°, then the angle is acute.

Use the conditional statement to answer each question.

1. What is the hypothesis p?

2. What is the conclusion q?

3. When p is true and q is true, the truth value of a conditional statement is true.

   a. What does the phrase "p is true" mean in terms of the given conditional statement?

   b. What does the phrase "q is true" mean in terms of the given conditional statement?

   c. Explain why the truth value of the given conditional statement is true.

4. When *p* is true and *q* is false, the truth value of a conditional statement is false.

   a. What does the phrase "*p* is true" mean in terms of the given conditional statement?

   b. What does the phrase "*q* is false" mean in terms of the given conditional statement?

   c. Explain why the truth value of the given conditional statement is false.

5. When *p* is false and *q* is true, the truth value of a conditional statement is true.

   a. What does the phrase "*p* is false" mean in terms of the given conditional statement?

   b. What does the phrase "*q* is true" mean in terms of the given conditional statement?

   c. Explain why the truth value of the given conditional statement is true.

6. When *p* is false and *q* is false, the truth value of a conditional statement is true.

    a. What does the phrase "*p* is false" mean in terms of the given conditional statement?

    b. What does the phrase "*q* is false" mean in terms of the given conditional statement?

    c. Explain why the truth value of the given conditional statement is true.

A **truth table** is a table that summarizes all possible truth values for a conditional statement $p \rightarrow q$. The first two columns of a truth table represent all possible truth values for the propositional variables *p* and *q*. The last column represents the truth value of the conditional statement $p \rightarrow q$.

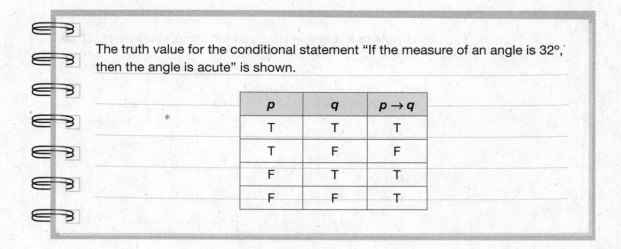

The truth value for the conditional statement "If the measure of an angle is 32°, then the angle is acute" is shown.

p	*q*	$p \rightarrow q$
T	T	T
T	F	F
F	T	T
F	F	T

7. Consider the conditional statement "If $m\overline{AB} = 6$ inches and $m\overline{BC} = 6$ inches, then $\overline{AB} \cong \overline{BC}$."

  a. What is the hypothesis p?

  b. What is the conclusion q?

  c. When both p and q are true, what does that mean? What is the truth value of the conditional statement when both p and q are true?

  d. When p is true and q is false, what does that mean? What is the truth value of the conditional statement when p is true and q is false?

  e. When p is false and q is true, what does that mean? What is the truth value of the conditional statement when p is false and q is true?

  f. When both p and q are false, what does that mean? What is the truth value of the conditional statement when both p and q are false?

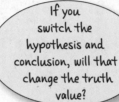 The **converse** of a conditional statement of the form "If p, then q" is the statement of the form "If q, then p." The converse is a new statement that results when the hypothesis and conclusion of the conditional statement are switched.

For each conditional statement written in propositional form, identify the hypothesis p and conclusion q. Then switch them to write the converse of the conditional statement.

 1. If a quadrilateral is a square, then the quadrilateral is a rectangle.

    a. Hypothesis, p:

If you switch the hypothesis and conclusion, will that change the truth value?

    b. Conclusion, q:

    c. What is the truth value of this conditional statement? Explain your reasoning.

    d. Converse:

    e. What is the truth value of this converse? Explain your reasoning.

2. If an integer is even, then the integer is divisible by two.

    a. Hypothesis, p:

    b. Conclusion, q:

    c. What is the truth value of this conditional statement? Explain your reasoning.

    d. Converse:

    e. What is the truth value of this converse? Explain your reasoning.

3. If a polygon has six sides, then the polygon is a pentagon.

    a. Hypothesis, *p*:

    b. Conclusion, *q*:

    c. What is the truth value of this conditional statement? Explain your reasoning.

    d. Converse:

    e. What is the truth value of this converse? Explain your reasoning.

4. If two lines intersect, then the lines are perpendicular.

    a. Hypothesis, *p*:

    b. Conclusion, *q*:

    c. What is the truth value of this conditional statement? Explain your reasoning.

    d. Converse:

    e. What is the truth value of this converse? Explain your reasoning.

 5. What do you notice about the truth value of a conditional statement and the truth value of its converse?

The **inverse** of a conditional statement of the propositional form "If p, then q" is the statement of the form "If not p, then not q." The inverse is a new statement that results when the hypothesis and conclusion of the conditional statement are negated.

Analyze each conditional statement and determine its truth value. Then identify the negation of the hypothesis and the conclusion. Finally write the inverse of the conditional statement.

1. If a quadrilateral is a square, then the quadrilateral is a rectangle.

    a. What is the truth value of this conditional statement? Explain your reasoning.

    b. Inverse:

    c. What is the truth value of the inverse? Explain your reasoning.

2. If an integer is even, then the integer is divisible by two.

    a. What is the truth value of this conditional statement? Explain your reasoning.

    b. Not p:

    c. Not q:

    d. Inverse:

    e. What is the truth value of the inverse? Explain your reasoning.

3. If a polygon has six sides, then the polygon is a pentagon.

a. What is the truth value of this conditional statement? Explain your reasoning.

b. Not *p*:

c. Not *q*:

d. Inverse:

e. What is the truth value of the inverse? Explain your reasoning.

4. If two lines intersect, then the lines are perpendicular.

a. What is the truth value of this conditional statement? Explain your reasoning.

b. Not *p*:

c. Not *q*:

d. Inverse:

e. What is the truth value of the inverse? Explain your reasoning.

5. What do you notice about the truth value of a conditional statement and the truth value of its inverse?

The **contrapositive** of a conditional statement of the propositional form "If p, then q" is the statement of the form "If not q, then not p." The contrapositive is a new statement that results when the hypothesis and conclusion of the conditional statement are negated and switched.

Analyze each conditional statement and determine its truth value. Then write the contrapositive of the conditional statement and the truth value of the contrapositive statement.

How do you think the truth value of the contrapositive will compare to the truth value of its conditional statement?

1. If a quadrilateral is a square, then the quadrilateral is a rectangle.

   a. What is the truth value of this conditional statement? Explain your reasoning.

   b. Contrapositive:

   c. What is the truth value of this contrapositive? Explain your reasoning.

2. If an integer is even, then the integer is divisible by two.

   a. What is the truth value of this conditional statement? Explain your reasoning.

   b. Contrapositive:

   c. What is the truth value of this contrapositive? Explain your reasoning.

3. If a polygon has six sides, then the polygon is a pentagon.

   a. What is the truth value of this conditional statement? Explain your reasoning.

   b. Contrapositive:

   c. What is the truth value of this contrapositive? Explain your reasoning.

4. If two lines intersect, then the lines are perpendicular.

   a. What is the truth value of this conditional statement? Explain your reasoning.

   b. Contrapositive:

   c. What is the truth value of this contrapositive? Explain your reasoning.

5. What do you notice about the truth value of a conditional statement and the truth value of its contrapositive?

1. For each statement, tell whether you agree or disagree. If you disagree, provide a counterexample.

   a. If a conditional statement is true, then its converse is true.

   b. If a conditional statement is true, then its inverse is true.

   c. If a conditional statement is true, then its contrapositive is true.

Two propositional forms are **logically equivalent** if they have the same truth values for corresponding values of the propositional variables.

2. Look at the four conditional statements used in Problems 2 through 4. Which conditional statement contained the most examples of logically equivalent relationships?

The negation of a statement p is logically equivalent to the statement "It is not true that p." The negation of a statement p is represented as "not p" or $\sim p$.

3. If the truth value of p is "true," what is the truth value of $\sim p$?

4. If the truth value of p is "false," what is the truth value of $\sim p$?

© 2012 Carnegie Learning

5. Complete the following truth table.

p	~p	q	~q	Conditional	
				$p \rightarrow q$	$\sim q \rightarrow \sim p$
T		T			
T		F			
F		T			
F		F			

6. What do you notice about the last two columns?

7. The truth table proves that a conditional statement is logically equivalent to what other propositional form?

PROBLEM 7 Biconditional Statements

When a conditional statement and its converse are both true, they can be combined and written as a single statement using "if and only if." This new statement is called a **biconditional statement**.

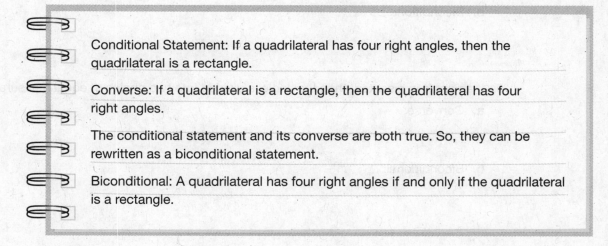

Conditional Statement: If a quadrilateral has four right angles, then the quadrilateral is a rectangle.

Converse: If a quadrilateral is a rectangle, then the quadrilateral has four right angles.

The conditional statement and its converse are both true. So, they can be rewritten as a biconditional statement.

Biconditional: A quadrilateral has four right angles if and only if the quadrilateral is a rectangle.

For each conditional statement, write the converse. If possible, write a true biconditional statement. If it is not possible, explain why.

1. If a triangle has at least two congruent sides, then the triangle is isosceles.

   a. Converse:

   b. Biconditional:

2. If two lines are parallel, then the two lines do not intersect.

   a. Converse:

   b. Biconditional:

3. If two circles have equal length radii, then the two circles are congruent.

   a. Converse:

   b. Biconditional:

4. If a quadrilateral is a square, then the quadrilateral is a rectangle.

   a. Converse:

   b. Biconditional:

5. If an angle is bisected, then the angle is divided into two angles of equal measure.

   a. Converse:

   b. Biconditional:

Be prepared to share your solutions and methods.

Proofs Aren't Just for Geometry

Introduction to Direct and Indirect Proof with the Properties of Numbers

LEARNING GOALS

In this lesson, you will:

- Use the commutative, associative, identity, and inverse properties for addition and multiplication.
- Use the distributive property.
- Use direct proof to prove a theorem.
- Use indirect proof to prove a theorem.

KEY TERM

- proof by contradiction

Throughout the day your teachers, friends, and other students are probably supplying you with a lot of new information. When they give you this new information, do you believe it or do you ask them to prove it? Hopefully, unless it is something you know to be a fact, you ask them to prove it. The word proof comes from the Latin word *probare* which means "to test." It used to be that people of authority were to be believed without having to provide proof. Luckily today this is not the case. You are able to ask for proof when given information, and this is especially important when dealing with math and science as there are many new ideas and theories being presented all the time.

Do you think all the information you learn throughout the day is true? How could you prove or disprove the information? Why is it important to ask for proof instead of just believing everything you hear without question?

PROBLEM 1 Direct Proofs and Number Laws

1. Some conditional statements can be proven using a direct proof. Read the conditional statement and each step of the direct proof. For each step, explain what changed from the previous step.

Conditional Statement: If $a + bc = c(b + a) + a$, then $a = 0$ or $c = 0$.

Steps	What Changed?
$a + bc = cb + ca + a$	_____
$a + bc = bc + ca + a$	_____
$a + bc = ca + a + bc$	_____
$a + bc - bc = ca + a + bc - bc$	_____
$a = ca + a$	_____
$a - a = ca + a - a$	_____
$0 = ca$	_____
$a = 0$ or $c = 0$	_____

2. Complete the table to summarize the real number properties, $\forall\, a, b \in \mathbb{R}$.

Name of Property	Symbolic Representation of Property Under Addition	Symbolic Representation of Property Under Multiplication
Commutative	$a + b = b + a$	
Associative		
Identity		
Inverse		$a \cdot \dfrac{1}{a} = 1 \ (a \neq 0)$
Distributive		

3. Refer to the direct proof from Question 1. Use the names of the properties from the table. If you cannot find a property that is a good fit, write a statement that summarizes the rule or property of real numbers.

Conditional Statement: If $a + bc = c(b + a) + a$, then $a = 0$ or $c = 0$.

Steps	Reasons
$a + bc = cb + ca + a$	
$a + bc = bc + ca + a$	
$a + bc = ca + a + bc$	
$a + bc - bc = ca + a + bc - bc$	
$a = ca + a$	
$a - a = ca + a - a$	
$0 = ca$	
$a = 0$ or $c = 0$	

16

Consider the associative properties $(a + b) + c = a + (b + c)$, and $a(bc) = (ab)c$.

The associative property can be stated in words shown.

> *When three terms are added, the first two terms can be grouped or the last two terms can be grouped.*
>
> *When three factors are multiplied, the first two factors can be grouped or the last two factors can be grouped.*

4. State the commutative property in words.

5. State the identity property in words.

6. State the inverse property in words.

7. State the distributive property in words.

PROBLEM 2   Indirect Proofs

In Problem 1, you used a direct proof to prove the theorem "If $a + bc = c(b + a) + a$, then $a = 0$ or $c = 0$." This theorem can also be proven using an indirect proof called **proof by contradiction**.

To prove a statement using proof by contradiction, assume that the conclusion is false. Then show that the hypothesis is false or state a contradiction. This is equivalent to showing that if the hypothesis is true, then the conclusion is also true.

In the theorem in Problem 1, the conclusion was $a = 0$ or $c = 0$. Now, begin by assuming that $a \neq 0$ and $c \neq 0$. So, let $a = 2$ and $c = 2$. Substitute these values into the equation and simplify.

A theorem is a statement that can be proven.

1. Complete the indirect proof. Use the names of the real number properties.

Steps	Reasons
$2 + 2b = 2(b + 2) + 2$	Assumption (negation of the conclusion)
$2 + 2b = 2b + 4 + 2$	
$2 + 2b = 4 + 2 + 2b$	
$0 = 4$	

2. Is this a contradiction? What does this tell you about the theorem?

3. Katie determines that the statement $\dfrac{ab + c}{a} = b + c$ is true for all real numbers a, b, and c. Is she correct? Show or explain your reasoning using proof by contradiction.

16

4. Prove or disprove the statement $\dfrac{ab + ac}{a} = b + c$.

5. Lamar proved that if $a = 0$, then $5 = 7$ using the steps shown. While he knows he is incorrect, he cannot identify his error.

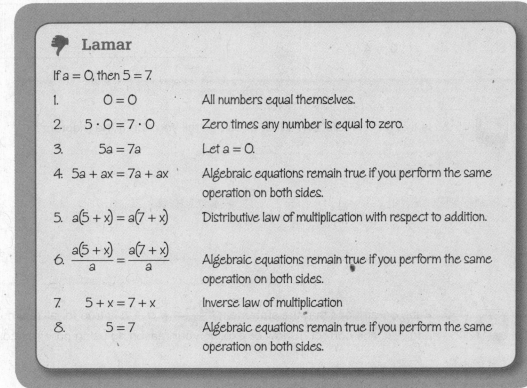

👎 **Lamar**

If $a = 0$, then $5 = 7$.

1.	$0 = 0$	All numbers equal themselves.
2.	$5 \cdot 0 = 7 \cdot 0$	Zero times any number is equal to zero.
3.	$5a = 7a$	Let $a = 0$.
4.	$5a + ax = 7a + ax$	Algebraic equations remain true if you perform the same operation on both sides.
5.	$a(5 + x) = a(7 + x)$	Distributive law of multiplication with respect to addition.
6.	$\dfrac{a(5 + x)}{a} = \dfrac{a(7 + x)}{a}$	Algebraic equations remain true if you perform the same operation on both sides.
7.	$5 + x = 7 + x$	Inverse law of multiplication
8.	$5 = 7$	Algebraic equations remain true if you perform the same operation on both sides.

Identify the error in Lamar's proof.

Be prepared to share your solutions and methods.

Your Oldest Likes Spinach?

Using Logic to Solve Problems, Part 1

LEARNING GOALS

In this lesson, you will:

- Solve problems using logic.
- Solve logic problems using grids.

"How often have I said to you that when you have eliminated the impossible, whatever remains, *however improbable*, must be the truth? We know that he did not come through the door, the window, or the chimney. We also know that he could not have been concealed in the room, as there is no concealment possible. When, then, did he come?"

This quote comes from a novel called *The Sign of the Four* by Sir Arthur Conan Doyle, and it features the famous detective Sherlock Holmes. Holmes and his companion Watson used logic to solve mysterious cases in which crimes were committed. Logical thinking is often used by detectives and police officers to solve crimes, but most of us also use logic every day. How do you use logical thinking in mathematics? How else might you use logical thinking?

PROBLEM 1 Can I Ask You a Few Questions?

A census taker was going from door to door in a neighborhood, gathering information on the number of people living at each address and their ages. He came to the door of a math teacher who answered the knock. The census taker and the math teacher had the following conversation.

Census Taker: Good morning, Miss! I am gathering information for the census. How many people are living at this address?

Math Teacher: I live here with my husband and three children.

Census Taker: Great! What are your children's ages?

Math Teacher: Well, since I teach math and I love creating mathematical riddles, I am going to ask you to figure out their ages. First, let me tell you that the product of their ages is 72.

Census Taker: That's fine, but I still need more information.

Math Teacher: Okay, the sum of their ages is the same as the street address number of my house.

Census Taker: Oh, I see!

At this point, the census taker looked at the number on the house and thought for a couple of minutes.

Census Taker: I see the house number, but unfortunately I still need more information.

Math Teacher: That's true. You do still need more information. Okay, my oldest child really likes spinach.

After thinking about this new information for a minute, the census taker recorded the children's ages. Then the census taker asked for the math teacher's age and her husband's age and recorded these as well. The census taker thanked the math teacher and went on his way.

1. How did the census taker figure out the children's ages from the information the math teacher provided?

2. What is the first clue the math teacher gave?

3. List all the possible ages for the children.

Do all of these possibilities make sense?

4. What is the second clue?

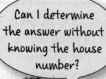

Can I determine the answer without knowing the house number?

5. Determine the sums of all the possible ages for the children.

6. After hearing the second clue, the census taker said he needed more information, and the math teacher agreed. Why was it true that the census taker still needed more information? What does this tell you about the possibilities?

7. What is the final clue?

8. How does this clue enable you to determine the children's ages?

9. What are the children's ages? Does your answer fit with the clues?

16

PROBLEM 2 Computer Games

Jose, Katie, and Sidney were playing computer games on different computers. One student used the laptop computer to play Sweepminer. Jose played a card game, while another student played pinball. Neither Jose nor Sidney used the netbook. Sidney did not use the desktop but played Sweepminer. If each student played one game on one type of computer, which student used which computer and what game did each student play?

This is an example of a type of problem called a logic puzzle. To solve a logic puzzle, a grid is often used to keep the information organized.

1. List each clue.

- One student playing Sweepminer used the laptop computer. _____

- _____

- _____

- _____

2. List the different categories and members of each category.

- Students: Jose, Katie, and Sidney _____

- _____

- _____

Since there are three categories with three possible members, you will use a 3 × 3 logic puzzle grid.

		Category 2			Category 3		
		Member 1	Member 2	Member 3	Member 1	Member 2	Member 3
Category 1	Member 1						
	Member 2						
	Member 3						
Category 3	Member 1						
	Member 2						
	Member 3						

Next, identify each category and list the members in each category.

> This grid shows the students in Category 1, the computers in Category 2, and the games in Category 3.

> Is this the only way to set up the grid or could I list the computers as Category 1, the games as Category 2, and the students as Category 3?

		Computers			Games		
		Laptop	Netbook	Desktop	Sweepminer	Card Game	Pinball
Students	Jose						
	Katie						
	Sidney						
Games	Sweepminer						
	Card Game						
	Pinball						

Once the grid is set up, use it to keep track of the clues by placing an X in a cell that is not true and an O in a cell that is true.

3. The first clue: One student playing Sweepminer used the laptop computer.

Locate the cell where the laptop column intersects with the Sweepminer row and place an O in the cell.

Was Sweepminer played on any other computers? Which cells should I place Xs in?

		Laptop	Netbook	Desktop	Sweepminer	Card Game	Pinball
Students	Jose						
	Katie						
	Sidney						
Games	Sweepminer						
	Card Game						
	Pinball						

Column groups: Computers (Laptop, Netbook, Desktop), Games (Sweepminer, Card Game, Pinball)

Were any other games played on the laptop? Can I place Xs in those cells?

4. The second clue: Jose played a card game, while another student played pinball.

Use this clue to place an X or O in the appropriate cells in the grid.

5. The third clue: Neither Jose nor Sidney used the netbook.

Use this clue to place an X or O in the appropriate cells in the grid.

6. The fourth clue: Sidney did not use the desktop, but played Sweepminer.

Use this clue to place an X or O in the appropriate cells in the grid.

Some extra information can be inferred from the clues.

7. Finish placing X's and O's in the cells to complete the grid. Then, complete each sentence.

   a. Sidney used the _____ and played _____ .
   (computer)   (game)

   b. Katie used the _____ and played _____ .
   (computer)   (game)

   c. Jose used the _____ and played _____ .
   (computer)   (game)

8. Explain how you were able to complete the grid.

PROBLEM 3   Favorite Sports

Matthew, Deanna, and Ashley are friends and they each go to three different middle schools: Washington, Jefferson, and Carver. Each friend likes a different sport: football, soccer, or basketball. Matthew likes football. Deanna does not attend Jefferson. The girl who attends Jefferson likes basketball. The friend who attends Carver likes soccer. Who goes to which school and likes what sport?

1. List the categories and the members of each.

   Category 1:   Members:

   Category 2:   Members:

   Category 3:   Members:

2. List the clues.

3. Complete the grid.

		Washington	Jefferson	Carver	Football	Soccer	Basketball
	Matthew						
	Deanna						
	Ashley						
	Football						
	Soccer						
	Basketball						

4. Who goes to which school and likes what sport?

Be prepared to share your solutions and methods.

Shoes and Math Scores?

Using Logic to Solve Problems, Part 2

LEARNING GOALS

In this lesson, you will:

- Solve problems using logic.
- Solve logic problems using grids.

You see four cards. Each card has a letter on one side and a number on the other side. The letters and numbers you see right now are D, K, 3, and 7.

D   K   3   7

Here is a rule: Every card that has a D on one side has a 3 on the other side. Which cards must you turn over to determine if the rule is true? This logical reasoning task is known as the Wason Selection Task. Research published in 2004 found that only about 30% of college students studying math came up with the correct answer. What is the correct answer?

PROBLEM 1 Shoes, Boots, and Sandals

 Kane, Toni, Darlene, and Brenda shop at The Athlete's Shoe. Each buys a different type of shoes. The Athlete's Shoe sells running shoes, cross-trainers, hiking boots, and sandals. The prices of the shoes are $35, $40, $45, and $50. Who bought which type of shoe, and how much did each person pay. Use the given clues.

- Kane did not buy sandals.

- Toni bought sandals.

- Darlene did not buy running shoes, sandals, or hiking boots.

- Brenda hates hiking.

- The sandals cost $40.

- The hiking boots are the most expensive.

- The running shoes do not cost $45.

1. Complete the grid.

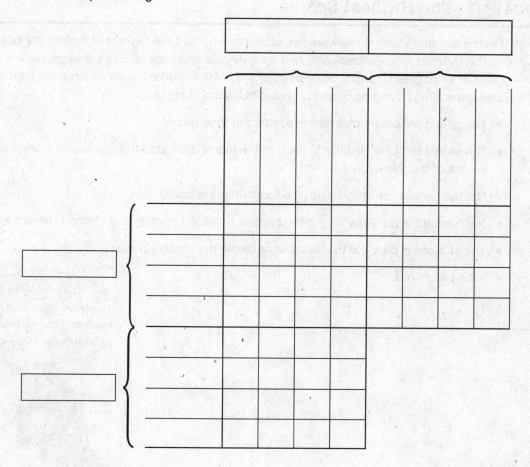

 2. Who bought which shoes, and how much did each person pay?

PROBLEM 2 The Highest Scores

On the last math test, there were five students who had the highest scores: three boys, Herbert, Albert, and Antonio, and two girls, Angela and Leticia. Each student wore a different color of shirt: green, brown, blue, pink, or red. Which student wore which color, and what was the score ranking he or she received? Use the clues given.

- The girls wore colors that had five letters in their name.

- The student in blue had the highest of the five scores, and the student in green had the lowest of the five scores.

- Neither Leticia nor Antonio got the fourth-highest score.

- Neither Leticia nor Antonio got the highest or lowest scores, and Herbert did not wear pink.

- The student in pink got the score right below the person in blue.

- Albert wore red.

The information doesn't give me the students' scores. How can I label these on my grid?

1. Complete the grid.

2. Which student wore which color, and what was the score ranking he or she received?

PROBLEM 3   Favorite Hobbies and Foods

Abbey, Lois, Mindy, Toni, and Xerxes are all friends who like to do their own thing. Their ages are 60, 50, 40, 23, and 20. Each friend likes one of the following hobbies: watching television, playing computer games, reading, playing board games, and writing poetry. Each friend also has a favorite food from the following list: fish, salad, chicken, spinach, and apples. What is each person's age, hobby, and favorite food? Use the clues given.

- Toni does not know how to operate a computer.
- Abbey loves salad.
- The oldest person loves to watch television.
- The name of the 20-year-old does not start with the letter M or X.
- Lois likes chicken.
- The youngest person likes to read.
- Xerxes is 10 years older than Toni.
- The person who is 40 years old likes to play computer games.
- The person who likes to watch TV likes to eat fish.
- Toni likes spinach.
- Toni does not write poetry.
- Abbey is younger than Lois.
- Lois does not like to play board games.
- Lois is not older than 29.
- Mindy loves apples.
- Mindy is twenty years older than Abbey.

> This problem has more categories. How will that affect your grid?

1. Complete the grid.

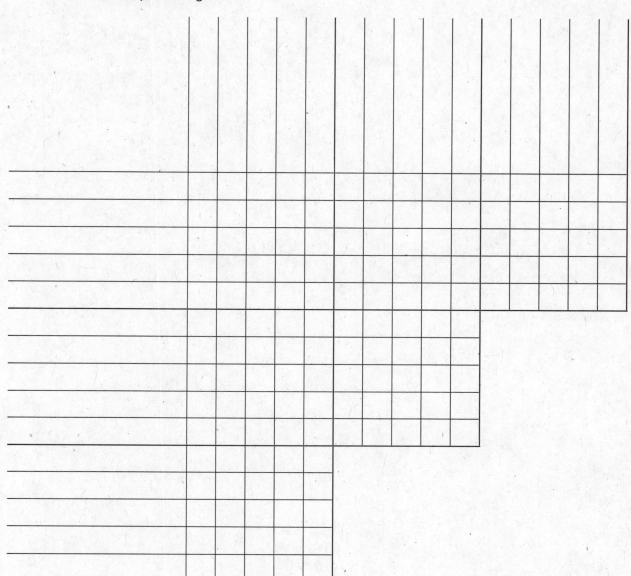

2. What is each person's age, hobby, and favorite food?

 Be prepared to share your solutions and methods.

Chapter 16 Summary

16

16.1 Identifying and Comparing Induction and Deduction

Induction uses specific examples to make a conclusion. Induction, also known as inductive reasoning is used when observing data, recognizing patterns, making generalizations about the observations or patterns, and reapplying those generalizations to unfamiliar situations. Deduction, also known as deductive reasoning, uses a general rule or premise to make a conclusion. It is the process of showing that certain statements follow logically from some proven facts or accepted rules.

Example

Kyra sees coins at the bottom of a fountain. She concludes that if she throws a coin into the fountain, it too will sink. Tyler understands the physical laws of gravity and mass and decides a coin he throws into the fountain will sink.

The specific information is the coins Kyra and Tyler observed at the bottom of the fountain.
The general information is the physical laws of gravity and mass.
Kyra's conclusion that her coin will sink when thrown into the fountain is induction.
Tyler's conclusion that his coin will sink when thrown into the fountain is deduction.

16.1 Identifying False Conclusions

It is important that all conclusions be tracked back to given truths. There are two reasons why a conclusion may be false. Either the assumed information is false or the argument is not valid.

Example

Erin noticed that every time she missed the bus, it rained. So, she concludes that next time she misses the bus it will rain.

Erin's conclusion is false because missing the bus is not related to what makes it rain.

16.2 Writing a Conditional Statement

A conditional statement is a statement that can be written in the form "If p, then q." The portion of the statement represented by p is the hypothesis. The portion of the statement represented by q is the conclusion.

Example

If <u>I plant an acorn</u>, then an <u>oak tree will grow</u>.

A solid line is drawn under the hypothesis, and a dotted line is drawn under the conclusion.

Statement: If I plant an acorn, then an oak tree will grow.

Statement: No oak tree grew.

Conclusion: Therefore, I did not plant an acorn.

16.2 Using a Truth Table to Explore the Truth Value of a Conditional Statement

The truth value of a conditional statement is whether the statement is true or false. If a conditional statement could be true, then its truth value is considered "true." The first two columns of a truth table represent the possible truth values for p (the hypothesis) and q (the conclusion). The last column represents the truth value of the conditional statement ($p \rightarrow q$). Notice that the truth value of a conditional statement is either "true" or "false," but not both.

Example

Consider the conditional statement, "If I eat too much, then I will get a stomach ache."

p	q	$p \rightarrow q$
T	T	T
T	F	F
F	T	T
F	F	T

When p is true, I ate too much. When q is true, I will get a stomach ache. It is true that when I eat too much, I will get a stomach ache. So, the truth value of the conditional statement is true.

When p is true, I ate too much. When q is false, I will not get a stomach ache. It is false that when I eat too much, I will not get a stomach ache. So, the truth value of the conditional statement is false.

When p is false, I did not eat too much. When q is true, I will get a stomach ache. It could be true that when I did not eat too much, I will get a stomach ache for a different reason. So, the truth value of the conditional statement in this case is true.

When p is false, I did not eat too much. When q is false, I will not get a stomach ache. It could be true that when I did not eat too much, I will not get a stomach ache. So, the truth value of the conditional statement in this case is true.

16.2 Writing the Converse of a Conditional Statement

The converse of a conditional statement of the form "If p, then q" is the statement of the form "If q, then p." The converse is a new statement that results when the hypothesis and conclusion of the conditional statement are switched. If a conditional statement is true, the converse may or may not be true.

Example

The converse of the conditional statement is shown.

Conditional Statement: "If a person is tall, then that person is a good basketball player."

Converse: If a person is a good basketball player, then that person is tall.

Both the conditional statement and the converse are false.

16.2 Writing the Inverse of a Conditional Statement

The inverse of a conditional statement of the form "If p, then q" is the statement of the form "If not p, then not q." The inverse is a new statement that results when the hypothesis and conclusion of the conditional statement are negated.

Example

The inverse of the conditional statement is shown.

Conditional Statement: "If Karen drives to school, then she will be on time."

Inverse: If Karen does not drive to school, then she will not be on time.

16.2 Writing the Contrapositive of a Conditional Statement

The contrapositive of a conditional statement of the form "If p, then q" is the statement of the form "If not q, then not p." The contrapositive is a new statement that results when the hypothesis and conclusion of the conditional statement are negated and switched.

Example

The contrapositive of the conditional statement is shown.

Conditional Statement: "If the sun is up, then it is daytime."

Contrapositive: If it is not daytime, then the sun is not up.

16.2 Writing a Biconditional Statement

When a conditional statement and its converse are both true, they can be combined and written as a single statement using "if and only if." This new statement is called a biconditional statement.

Example

The biconditional statement of the conditional statement is shown.

Conditional Statement: "If a figure is an equilateral triangle, then that figure has three sides of equal length."

Converse: If a figure has three sides of equal length, then that figure is an equilateral triangle. Biconditional Statement: A figure is an equilateral triangle if and only if that figure has three sides of equal length.

16.3 Using a Direct Proof

Some conditional statements can be proven using a direct proof by listing the logical steps and reasoning to get from the hypothesis to the conclusion.

Example

Conditional statement: If $a(b + c) + b(a + c) = c(b + a)$, then $a = 0$ or $b = 0$.

Steps	Reasons
$ab + ac + ba + bc = cb + ca$	Distributive Property
$ab + ac + ab + bc = bc + ac$	Commutative Property of Multiplication
$2ab + ac + bc = bc + ac$	Combine like terms.
$2ab + ac + bc = ac + bc$	Commutative Property of Addition
$2ab + ac + bc - bc = ac + bc - bc$	Algebraic equations are still true if you perform the same operation on both sides of an equation.
$2ab + ac = ac$	Inverse Property of Addition
$2ab + ac - ac = ac - ac$	Algebraic equations are still true if you perform the same operation on both sides of an equation.
$2ab = 0$	Inverse Property of Addition
$a = 0$ or $b = 0$	If a product is equal to zero, at least one factor in the product is equal to zero.

16.3 Using an Indirect Proof

Some conditional statements can be proven using an indirect proof. An indirect proof is also called proof by contradiction. To prove a statement using proof by contradiction, assume that the conclusion is false and then show that the hypothesis is false or state a contradiction. This is equivalent to showing that if the hypothesis is true, then the conclusion is also true.

Example

Conditional statement: If $a(b + c) + b(a + c) = c(b + a)$, then $a = 0$ or $b = 0$.

$1(2 + c) + 2(1 + c) = c(2 + 1)$	Assume $a = 1$ and $b = 2$. (negation of conclusion)
$2 + c + 2 + 2c = 2c + c$	Distributive Property
$4 + 3c = 3c$	Combine like terms.
$4 + 3c - 3c = 3c - 3c$	Algebraic equations are still true if you perform the same operation on both sides of an equation.
$4 = 0$	Inverse Property of Addition

This is a contradiction because $4 \neq 0$. So, the conditional statement must be true.

16.4 Solving Problems Using Logic

Many problems are solved using logical thinking. Use the clues in the problem to list and eliminate possible solutions. Often problems will need to be worked out backwards or out of order.

Example

Sharon was thinking of a number. To help Rico guess the number, she gave him these clues. The number is less than 20 and a multiple of 6. He still couldn't be sure of the number, so she told him that the sum of the digits of the correct number is the square of the sum of the digits of another possible number.

The numbers that are less than 20 and a multiple of 6 are 6, 12, and 18. Because the final clue talks about the sum of the digits, the number must have more than 1 digit, so 6 is not the number. The sum of the digits in 12 is 3, and the sum of the digits in 18 is 9. The number 9 is the square of 3, so 18 is Sharon's number.

16.5 Solving Logic Puzzles Using Grids

To solve a logic puzzle, a grid is often used to keep the information organized. First, list each clue. Next, list the different categories and members of each category. If there are three categories with three possible members, use a 3 by 3 logic puzzle grid.

Example

Victor and his friends Ty and Nathan are starting up a band. Each friend will play the drums, the keyboard, or the guitar. Each friend will also write the lyrics, write the music, or sing. Victor is the lead singer. The friend who writes the music also plays the keyboard. Nathan plays the drums.

		Jobs			Instruments		
		Writes lyrics	Writes music	Sings	Keyboard	Guitar	Drums
Friends	Victor	X	X	O	X	O	X
	Ty	X	O	X	O	X	X
	Nathan	O	X	X	X	X	O
Instruments	Keyboard	X	O	X			
	Guitar	X	X	O			
	Drums	O	X	X			

Victor sings and plays the guitar.

Ty writes music and plays the keyboard.

Nathan writes lyrics and plays the drums.

Calculator Instructions

Calculator Instructions

1.3 ## Graphing a Function

 You can use a graphing calculator to graph a function.

Step 1: Press **Y=**. Your cursor should be blinking on the line **\Y1=**. Enter the equation. To enter a variable like x, press the key with **X, T, Ø, n** once.

Step 2: Press **WINDOW** to set the bounds and intervals you want displayed.

Step 3: Press **GRAPH** to view the graph.

1.3 ## Graphing a Piecewise Function

 You can use a graphing calculator to graph piecewise functions.

Step 1: Press **Y=**. Enter the first section of the function within parentheses. Then press the division button.

Step 2: Press the (key twice and enter the first part of the compound inequality within parentheses.

Step 3: Enter the second part of the compound inequality within parentheses and then type two closing parentheses.

Press **GRAPH** here to see the first section of the piecewise function.

Step 4: Enter the remaining sections of the piecewise functions as Y_2 and Y_3.

Completing a Table of Values

 You can use a graphing calculator to complete a table of values for a given function.

Step 1: Press **Y=**

Step 2: Enter the function. Press **ENTER**.

Step 3: Press **2ND TBLSET** (above **WINDOW**).

TblStart is the starting data value for your table. Enter this value.

ΔTbl (read "delta table") is the increment. This value tells the table what intervals to count by for the independent quantity. If **ΔTbl = 1** then the values in your table would go up by 1s. If **ΔTbl = -1**, the values would go *down* by 1s. Enter the **ΔTbl**.

Step 4: Press **2ND TABLE** (above **GRAPH**). Use the up and down arrows to scroll through the data.

2.2 **Using the Value Feature**

 You can use the **value** feature on a graphing calculator to determine an exact data value on a graph.

Step 1: Press **Y=**. Enter your function.

Step 2: Press **WINDOW**. Set appropriate values for your function. Then press **GRAPH**.

Step 3: Press **2ND** and then **CALC**. Select **1:value**. Press **ENTER**. Then type the given independent value next to **X=** and press **ENTER**. The cursor moves to the given independent value and the corresponding dependent value is displayed at the bottom of the screen.

Calculator

© 2012 Carnegie Learning

You can use the **intersect** feature to determine an independent value when given a dependent value.

Step 1: Press **Y=**. Enter the two equations, one next to **Y₁=** and one next to **Y₂=**.

Step 2: Press **WINDOW**. Set appropriate bounds so you can see the intersection of the two equations. Then press **GRAPH**.

Step 3: Press **2ND CALC** and then select **5:intersect**. The cursor should appear somewhere on one of the graphs, and at the bottom of the screen you will see **First curve?** Press **ENTER**. The cursor should then move to somewhere on the other graph, and you will see **Second curve?** Press **ENTER**. You will see **Guess?** at the bottom of the screen. Move the cursor to where you think the intersection point is and Press **ENTER**. The intersection point will appear.

Calculator

Calculator

 You can use a graphing calculator to represent a data set.

Step 1: Press **STAT** and then press **ENTER** to select **1:Edit**. In the **L1** column, enter the independent quantity values by typing each value followed by **ENTER**.

Step 2: Use the right arrow key to move to the **L2** column. Enter the dependent quantity values.

Step 3: Press **2ND** and **STAT PLOT**. Press **4** to turn off any plots. Press **ENTER**. Then press **2ND** and **STAT PLOT** again. Press **ENTER** to access the information about Plot 1. The cursor should be on the word **On**. Press **ENTER** to turn on Plot 1.

Step 4: Use the arrow keys to move down to **Xlist**. Press **2ND L1** to set your L1 values as your x-values. Scroll to **Ylist** and Press **2ND L2** to set your L2 values as your y-values.

Step 5: Press **WINDOW** to set the bounds of your graph. Press **GRAPH** to create a graph of the data.

Step 6: Use the **TRACE** feature and the left and right arrow keys to move between the points on the plot.

You can use a graphing calculator to determine the linear regression equation of a data set.

Step 1: **Diagnostics** must be turned on so that all needed data is displayed. Press **2nd CATALOG** to display the catalog. Scroll to **DiagnosticOn** and press **ENTER**. Then press **ENTER** again. The calculator should display the word **Done**.

Step 2: Press **STAT** and use the right arrow key to show the **CALC** menu. Type **4** to choose **LinReg(ax+b)** and press **ENTER**.

Step 3: Make sure **L1** is listed next to **Xlist** and **L2** is listed next to **Ylist**. Scroll down to **Calculate** and press **ENTER**.

The calculator should show $y = ax + b$ as well as four values labeled **a**, **b**, **r²**, and **r**.

Step 4: Press **Y=**. Enter the linear regression equation next to **Y₁=**. Then press **GRAPH** to see the line of best fit.

The calculator will automatically copy the linear regression equation to Y1 if you enter LinReg($ax + b$) **Y1**. Repeat Step 2 to enter LinReg($ax + b$), then press **VARS** and use the right arrow keys to show **Y-VARS**. Press **FUNCTION** and select **Y1**. When you press **ENTER** the equation will appear in **Y1**.

Calculator

4.3 Generating Two Sequences

 You can use a graphing calculator to generate two sequences at the same time in order to determine a certain term in a sequence.

Step 1: Within a set of brackets, enter the first term number followed by a comma and then the first term value of the sequence. The **2ND** key is used to enter the brackets. Press **ENTER**.

Step 2: Provide direction to the calculator on how to generate each term of the sequence.

Press **2ND{2NDANS(1)** and then indicate how the term numbers will increase or decrease, and by how much by entering the plus or minus sign and the amount of increase or decrease.

Then press **,2ND ANS(2)** and enter the common difference of the term values. Then close the brackets by pressing **2ND}** and press **ENTER**.

The calculator will display the next term number and value.

Step 3: Press **ENTER** and the next term number and value will be displayed.

Step 4: Continue pressing **ENTER** until you reach the nth term number and value you want to determine.

7.2 Graphing a System of Linear Inequalities

 You can use a graphing calculator to graph a system of linear inequalities.

Step 1: Press **Y=** and enter the two inequalities as **Y₁** and **Y₂**.

Step 2: While still in the **Y=** window, access the inequality function by moving your cursor to the left until the \ flashes. Press **ENTER** to select the appropriate inequality symbol (◤ or ◥).

Step 3: Press **WINDOW** and set the bounds.

Step 4: Press **GRAPH**.

8.2 Constructing a Box-and-Whisker Plot

 You can use a graphing calculator to construct a box-and-whisker plot.

Step 1: Press **STAT** and then press **ENTER** to select **1:**Edit.

Step 2: Enter the data values of the data set in List 1.

Step 3: Press **2nd** and **STAT PLOT**, which is above the **Y=** button.

Step 4: Select **1:** and press **ENTER**. Then highlight **PLOT 1** and press **ENTER** to turn Plot 1 on. Then scroll down to **Type:** and select the box-and-whisker icon. ⊢▢⊣ Press **ENTER**.

Step 5: Make sure the **XList** is using the correct list. Then press **GRAPH**.

8.4 Determining Standard Deviation

 You can use a graphing calculator to determine the standard deviation of a data set.

Step 1: Press **STAT** and then **ENTER** to select **1:**Edit. Enter each data set into its own List.

Step 2: Press **STAT** then scroll to the right to highlight **CALC**. Press **ENTER** to select **1:**Var-Stats. Press **ENTER**.

Step 3: Your screen should display 1-Var Stats. Press **2ND** then the list you want the calculator to use for these calculations.

Step 4: Your calculator should display the same data values as when you determined the mean. However, this time use the value for σx.

Calculator

You can use a graphing calculator to show how the actual values of a data set differ from the values predicted by a linear regression.

Step 1: Enter the data values, press **STAT**, select **CALC**, and then select **4:LinReg(ax+b)**. Scroll down to **Store RegEQ:** Press **VARS**, select **Y-VARS** at the top, and then press **1** two times. Then select **Calculate**.

Step 2: Press **STAT** and then **1**. Then press the right arrow key until you get to **L6**. Press the up arrow key and then the right arrow key.

Step 3: If the list of residuals is not already displayed, press **2ND** and then **LIST**. Select **7↓RESID**. Press **ENTER**.

Step 4: Press **2ND**, **STAT PLOT**, **1** to turn on the plot and choose the type of display for the graph. Press **ZOOM** and then **9** to show the data and the line of best fit.

You can also use a graphing calculator to graph a residual plot.

Step 5: Press **STAT** and then **1**. Copy the data from the residuals list to **L6**. You can round the data values if you wish.

Step 6: Press **2ND**, **STAT PLOT**, and then **1**. Make sure L1 is entered next to **Xlist** and L6 is entered next to **Ylist**.

Step 7: Press **STAT**, select **CALC**, and then select **2:2-Var Stats**. Make sure L1 is entered next to **Xlist** and L6 is entered next to **Ylist**. Select **Calculate** and then press **ZOOM**, **9** to see the residual plot.

11.3 Determining an Exponential Regression Equation

 You can use a graphing calculator to determine the exponential regression equation for a data set.

Step 1: Press **STAT** and select **1:Edit**. Enter the data set with the independent variable in **L1** and the dependent variable in **L2**.

Step 2: Press **STAT** and scroll to **CALC**. Then scroll down to **0:ExpReg**. Press **ENTER** twice.

The calculator will display the values of each variable in the form $y = a \cdot b^x$.

Step 3: The r-value displayed represents the correlation coefficient.

Calculator

Glossary

absolute maximum

A function has an absolute maximum if there is a point that has a y-coordinate that is greater than the y-coordinates of every other point on the graph.

Example

The ordered pair (4, 2) is the absolute maximum of the graph of the function $f(x) = -\frac{1}{2}x^2 + 4x - 6$.

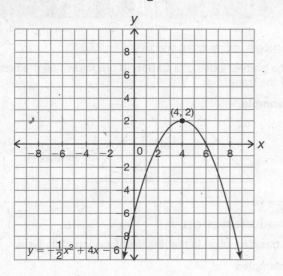

absolute minimum

A function has an absolute minimum if there is a point that has a y-coordinate that is less than the y-coordinates of every other point on the graph.

Example

The ordered pair (1, −4) is the absolute minimum of the graph of the function $y = \frac{2}{3}x^2 - \frac{4}{3}x - \frac{10}{3}$.

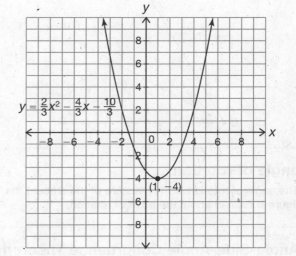

absolute value

The absolute value of a number is its distance from zero on the number line.

Examples

$|5| = 5$ because 5 is 5 units from 0 on the number line.
$|-3| = 3$ because −3 is 3 units from 0 on the number line.

angle

An angle is formed by two rays that share a common endpoint.

Glossary ■ **G-1**

Angle-Angle-Side Congruence Theorem

The Angle-Angle-Side Theorem states that if two angles and a non-included side of one triangle are congruent to the corresponding angles and the corresponding non-included side of a second triangle, then the triangles are congruent.

angle bisector

An angle bisector is a ray drawn through the vertex of an angle that divides the angle into two angles of equal measure, or two congruent angles.

Example

Ray *BY* is an angle bisector.

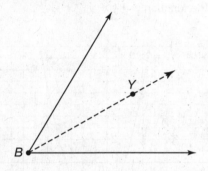

angle of rotation

The angle of rotation is the measure of the amount the figure is rotated about the point of rotation.

Angle-Side-Angle Congruence Theorem

The Angle-Side-Angle Congruence Theorem states that if two angles and the included side of one triangle are congruent to the corresponding two angles and the included side of another triangle, then the triangles are congruent.

arc

An arc is a part of a circle that is the curve between two points on the circle.

Example

Arc *CD* is an arc of circle *O*.

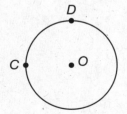

argument of a function

The argument of a function is the variable on which the function operates.

Example

In the function $f(x + 5) = 32$, the argument is $x + 5$.

arithmetic sequence

An arithmetic sequence is a sequence of numbers in which the difference between any two consecutive terms is a constant.

Example

The sequence 1, 3, 5, 7 is an arithmetic sequence with a common difference of 2.

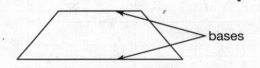

bases of a trapezoid

The parallel sides of a trapezoid are known as the bases of the trapezoid.

Example

bases

basic function

A basic function is the simplest function of its type.

Examples

The basic linear function is $f(x) = x$.
The basic exponential function is $g(x) = 2^x$.
The basic quadratic function is $h(x) = x^2$.

biconditional statement

When a conditional statement and its converse are both true, they can be combined and written as a single statement using "if and only if." This statement is called a biconditional statement.

bin

The width of a bar in a histogram represents an interval of data and is often referred to as a bin.

Glossary

box-and-whisker plot

A box-and-whisker plot displays a data distribution based on a five number summary.

Example

The box-and-whisker plots compare the test scores from two algebra classes.

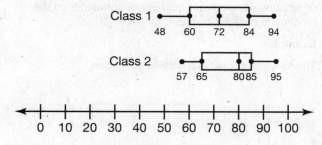

break-even point

The break-even point is the point where two functions are equal.

Example

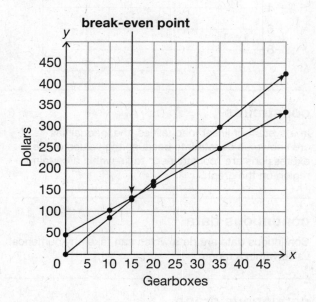

C

categorical data

Data that can be grouped into categories are called categorical data.

causation

Causation is when one event causes a second event.

common difference

The difference between any two consecutive terms in an arithmetic sequence is called the common difference. It is typically represented by the variable d.

Example

The sequence 1, 3, 5, 7 is an arithmetic sequence with a common difference of 2.

common ratio

The ratio between any two consecutive terms in a geometric sequence is called the common ratio. It is typically represented by the variable r.

Example

The sequence 2, 4, 8, 16 is a geometric sequence with a common ratio of 2.

common response

A common response is when a variable other than the ones measured cause the same result as the one observed in the experiment.

composite figure

A composite figure is a figure that is formed by combining different shapes.

compound inequality

A compound inequality is an inequality that is formed by the union, "or," or the intersection, "and," of two simple inequalities.

Example

The statement "$x > 5$ or $x < -5$" is a compound inequality.

compound interest

In a compound interest account, the interest earned at the end of each year is a percent of the account balance at the beginning of the year.

Example

Sonya opens a savings account with $100. She earns $4 in interest the first year. The compound interest y is found by using the equation $y = 100(1 + 0.04)^t$, where t is the time in years.

conclusion

The conclusion of a conditional statement is the variable q.

conditional statement

A conditional statement is a statement that can be written in the form "If p, then q." This form is also known as the propositional form.

confounding variable

A confounding variable is when there are other variables in an experiment that are unknown or unobserved.

congruent

Congruent means to have the same size, shape, and measure. The symbol $\cong$ indicates that two figures are congruent.

congruent angles

Congruent angles are angles that are equal in measure.

Example

Angles A and B are congruent angles.

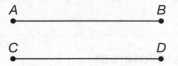

congruent line segments

Line segments that have the same length are called congruent line segments.

Example

Line segments AB and CD are congruent line segments.

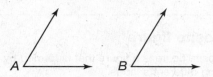

conjunction

A compound inequality in the form $a < x < b$, where a and b are any real numbers, is a conjunction.

Example

The compound inequality "$x \leq 1$ and $x > -3$" is a conjunction.

consistent systems

Systems that have one or many solutions are called consistent systems.

constant function

If the dependent variable of a function does not change or remains constant over the entire domain, then the function is called a constant function.

Example

The function shown is a constant function.

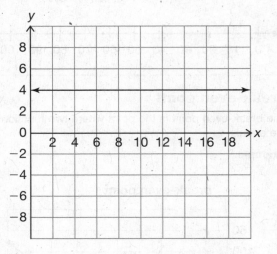

constraints

In a system of linear inequalities, the inequalities are known as constraints because the values of the expressions are "constrained" to lie within a certain region on the graph.

continuous data

Continuous data are data which can take any numerical value within a range.

continuous graph

A continuous graph is a graph of points that are connected by a line or smooth curve on the graph.

contrapositive

The contrapositive of a conditional statement of the propositional form "If p, then q" is the statement of the form "If not q, then not p."

converse

The converse of a conditional statement of the form "If p, then q" is the statement of the form "If q, then p."

coordinate notation

Coordinate notation is a notation that uses ordered pairs to describe a transformation on a coordinate plane.

Example

The coordinate notation $(x, y) \rightarrow (x + a, y)$, where a is a real number, indicates a horizontal translation.

correlation coefficient

The correlation coefficient indicates how closely the data points form a straight line.

Example

The correlation coefficient for these data is -0.9935. The value is negative because the equation has a negative slope. The value is close to -1 because the data are very close to forming a straight line.

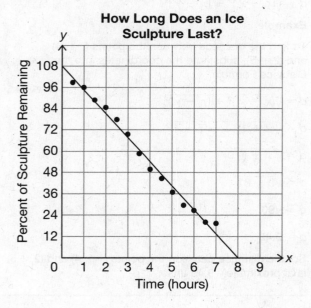

corresponding angles

Corresponding angles are angles that have the same relative positions in geometric figures.

Example

Angle B and Angle E are corresponding angles.

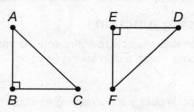

corresponding sides

Corresponding sides are sides that have the same relative positions in corresponding geometric figures.

Example

Side lengths AB and DE are corresponding sides in similar triangles ABC and DEC.

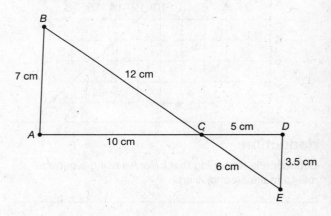

cube root

A number b is a cube root of a number a if $b^3 = a$.

Example

The cube root of 8 is 2.

Glossary

D

data distribution

A data distribution is the way in which data are spread out or clustered together.

decreasing function

If a function decreases across the entire domain, then the function is called a decreasing function.

Example

The function shown is a decreasing function.

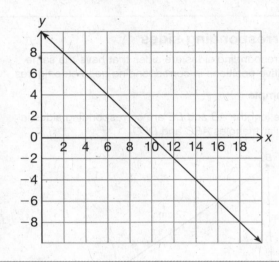

deduction

Deduction is reasoning that involves using a general rule to make a conclusion.

dependent quantity

When one quantity depends on another in a problem situation, it is said to be the dependent quantity.

Example

In the relationship between driving time and distance traveled, distance is the dependent quantity, because distance depends on the driving time.

discrete data

Discrete data are data that has only a finite number of values or data that can be "counted."

discrete graph

A discrete graph is a graph of isolated points.

disjunction

A compound inequality in the form $x < a$ or $x > b$, where a and b are any real numbers, is a disjunction.

Example

The compound inequality "$x < -2$ or $x > 1$" is a disjunction.

Distance Formula

The Distance Formula states that if (x_1, y_1) and (x_2, y_2) are two points on the coordinate plane, then the distance d between (x_1, y_1) and (x_2, y_2) is given by $d = \sqrt{[x_2 - x_1]^2 + [y_2 - y_1]^2}$.

Example

To find the distance between the points $(-1, 4)$ and $(2, -5)$, substitute the coordinates into the Distance Formula.

$$d = \sqrt{(x_2 - x_1)^2 + (y_2 - y_1)^2}$$

$$d = \sqrt{(2 + 1)^2 + (-5 - 4)^2}$$

$$d = \sqrt{3^2 + (-9)^2}$$

$$d = \sqrt{9 + 81}$$

$$d = \sqrt{90}$$

$$d \approx 9.49$$

So, the distance between the points $(-1, 4)$ and $(2, -5)$ is approximately 9.49 units.

domain

The domain is the set of input values in a relation.

Example

The domain of the function $y = 2x$ is the set of all real numbers.

Glossary

© 2012 Carnegie Learning

dot plot

A dot plot is a graph that shows how discrete data are graphed using a number line.

Example

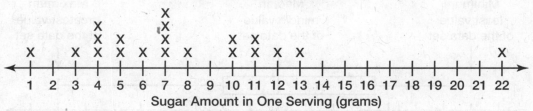

Sugar in Breakfast Cereals

Sugar Amount in One Serving (grams)

E

equivalent compound inequalities

An equivalent compound inequality is a compound inequality that is the equivalent of an absolute value inequality.

Examples

Absolute Value Inequality	Equivalent Compound Inequality
$|ax + b| < c$	$-c < ax + b < c$
$|ax + b| \leq c$	$-c \leq ax + b \leq c$
$|ax + b| > c$	$ax + b < -c$ or $ax + b > c$
$|ax + b| \geq c$	$ax + b \leq -c$ or $ax + b \geq c$

explicit formula

An explicit formula of a sequence is a formula for calculating the value of each term of a sequence using the term's position in the sequence.

Example

The sequence 1, 3, 5, 7, 9, . . . can be described by the rule $a_n = 2n - 1$ where n is the position of the term. The fourth term of the sequence a_4 is $2(4) - 1$, or 7.

exponential functions

The family of exponential functions includes functions of the form $f(x) = a \cdot b^x$, where a and b are real numbers, and b is greater than 0 but is not equal to 1.

Example

The function $f(x) = 2^x$ is an exponential function.

---

extrapolation

To make predictions for values of x that are outside of the data set is called extrapolation.

F

finite sequence

If a sequence terminates, it is called a finite sequence.

Example

The sequence 22, 26, 30 is a finite sequence.

first differences

First differences are the values determined by subtracting consecutive y-values in a table when the x-values are consecutive integers.

Example

Time (minutes)	Height (feet)	First Differences
0	0	
		$1800 - 0 = 1800$
1	1800	
		$3600 - 1800 = 1800$
2	3600	
		$5400 - 3600 = 1800$
3	5400	

$1 - 0 = 1$
$2 - 1 = 1$
$3 - 2 = 1$

Glossary

five number summary

The five number summary consists of the minimum value, the first quartile (Q1), the median, the third quartile (Q3), and the maximum value of a data set.

Example

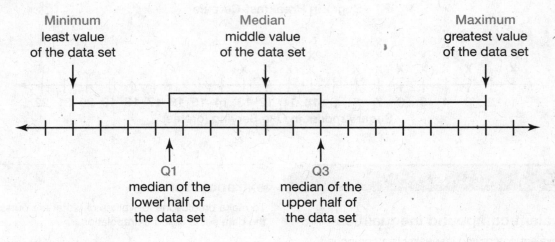

frequency

The height of each bar in a histogram indicates the frequency, which is the number of data values included in any given bin.

frequency distribution

A frequency distribution displays the frequencies for categorical data in a two-way table.

Example

Favorite Meals of Students

		Burgers	Chicken Nuggets	Pizza	Salad Bar
Grade Level	9th grade	4	1	3	5
	10th grade	3	7	3	4

frequency marginal distribution

A frequency marginal distribution displays the total of the frequencies of the rows or columns of a frequency distribution.

Favorite Meals of Students

		Burgers	Chicken Nuggets	Pizza	Salad Bar	Total
Grade Level	9th grade	4	1	3	5	13
	10th grade	3	7	3	4	17
	Total	7	8	6	9	30

function

A function is a relation between a given set of elements, such that for each element in the domain there exists exactly one element in the range.

Example

The equation $y = 2x$ is a function. Every value of x has exactly one corresponding y-value.

function family

A function family is a group of functions that share certain characteristics.

Examples

Linear functions and exponential functions are examples of function families.

function notation

Function notation is a way of representing functions algebraically.

Example

In the function $f(x) = 0.75x$, f is the name of the function, x represents the domain, and $f(x)$ represents the range.

G

geometric sequence

A geometric sequence is a sequence of numbers in which the ratio between any two consecutive terms is a constant.

Example

The sequence 2, 4, 8, 16 is a geometric sequence with a common ratio of 2.

H

half-plane

The graph of a linear inequality is a half-plane, or half of a coordinate plane.

Example

The shaded portion of the graph is a half-plane.

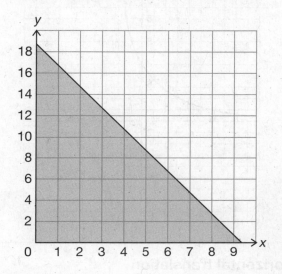

histogram

A histogram is a graphical way to display quantitative data using vertical bars.

Example

Hours Spent Playing Video Games on the Weekends

Glossary

horizontal asymptote

A horizontal asymptote is a horizontal line that a function gets closer and closer to, but never intersects.

Example

The graph shows a horizontal asymptote at $y = -1$.

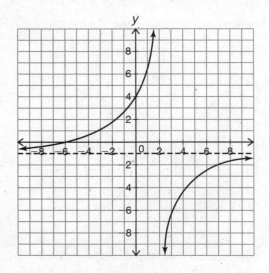

horizontal translation

A horizontal translation of a graph is a shift of the entire graph left or right. A horizontal translation affects the x-coordinate of each point on the graph.

Examples

The graphs of $t(x + 3)$ and $t(x - 1)$ are horizontal translations of the graph of $t(x)$.

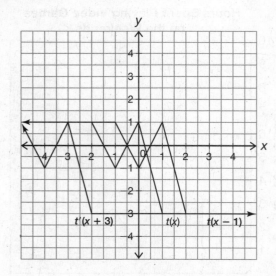

hypothesis

The hypothesis of a conditional statement is the variable p.

image

The new figure created from a transformation is called the image.

Example

The image of a rectangle under a translation is shown.

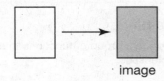

image

included angle

An included angle is the angle formed by two sides of a triangle.

included side

An included side is the side between two angles of a triangle.

inconsistent systems

Systems with no solution are called inconsistent systems.

increasing function

If a function increases across the entire domain, then the function is called an increasing function.

Example

The function shown is an increasing function.

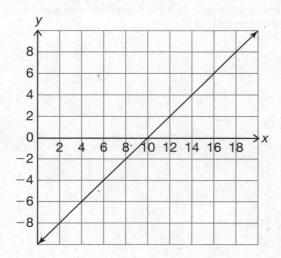

Glossary

independent quantity

The quantity that the dependent quantity depends upon is called the independent quantity.

Example

In the relationship between driving time and distance traveled, driving time is the independent quantity, because it does not depend on any other quantity

index

The index is the position of a term (its term number) in a sequence. Also, the value that sits outside the radical is called the index of the radical.

Examples

In the sequence 125, 143, 161 . . . the term 125 has an index of 1.

In the radical expression $\sqrt[4]{16}$, the number 4 is the index.

induction

Induction is reasoning that involves using specific examples to make a conclusion.

infinite sequence

If a sequence continues on forever, it is called an infinite sequence.

Example

The sequence 22, 26, 30, 34 . . . is an infinite sequence.

interpolation

Using a linear regression to make predictions within the data set is called interpolation.

interquartile range (IQR)

The interquartile range, IQR, measures how far the data are spread out from the median.

Example

In the data set 13, 17, 23, 24, 25, 29, 31, 45, 46, 53, 60, the median, 29, divides the data into two halves. The first quartile, 23, is the median of the lower half of the data. The third quartile, 46, is the median of the upper half of the data. The interquartile range is 46 − 23, or 23.

intersection point

If you have intersecting graphs, a solution is the ordered pair that satisfies both functions at the same time, or the intersection point of the graphs.

Example

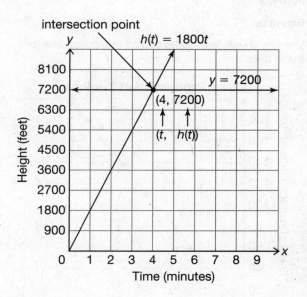

inverse

The inverse of a conditional statement of the proposition form "If p, then q" is the statement of the form "If not p, then not q."

J

---

joint frequency

Any frequency recorded within the body of a two-way frequency table is known as a joint frequency.

L

least squares regression line

A least squares regression line is the line of best fit that minimizes the squares of the distances of the points from the line.

Example

The line shown is a least squares regression line for these data.

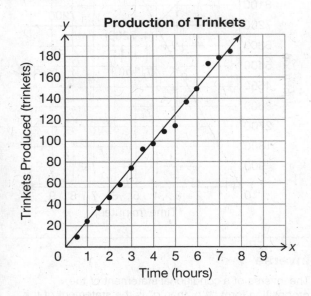

Production of Trinkets

legs of a trapezoid

The non-parallel sides of a trapezoid are known as the legs of the trapezoid.

Example

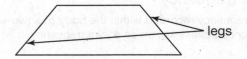

legs

linear absolute value equation

An equation in the form $|x + a| = c$ is a linear absolute value equation.

Example

The equation $|x - 1| = 6$ is a linear absolute value equation.

linear absolute value functions

The family of linear absolute value functions includes functions of the form $f(x) = a|x + b| + c$, where a, b, and c are real numbers, and a is not equal to 0.

Example

The function $f(x) = |x - 3| - 2$ is a linear absolute value function.

linear absolute value inequality

An inequality in the form $|x + a| < c$ is a linear absolute value inequality.

Example

The inequality $|w - 145.045| \leq 3.295$ is a linear absolute value inequality.

linear combinations method

The linear combinations method is a process used to solve a system of equations by adding two equations together, resulting in an equation with one variable.

Example

Solve the following system of equations by using the linear combinations method:

$$\begin{cases} 6x - 5y = 3 \\ 2x + 2y = 12 \end{cases}$$

First, multiply the second equation by -3. Then, add the equations and solve for the remaining variable. Finally, substitute $y = 3$ into the first equation and solve for x. The solution of the system is $(3, 3)$.

linear functions

The family of linear functions includes functions of the form $f(x) = mx + b$, where m and b are real numbers.

Example

The function $f(x) = 3x + 2$ is a linear function.

Glossary

linear piecewise functions

Linear piecewise functions include functions that have equation changes for different parts, or pieces, of the domain.

Example

The function $f(x)$ is a linear piecewise function.

$$f(x) = \begin{cases} x + 5 & x \leq -2 \\ -2x + 1 & -2 < x \leq 2 \\ 2x - 9 & x > 2 \end{cases}$$

linear programming

Linear programming is a branch of mathematics that determines the maximum and minimum value of linear expressions on a region produced by a system of linear inequalities.

linear regression

A linear regression models the relationship between two variables in a data set by producing a line of best fit.

linear regression equation

The equation that describes the line of best fit is called the linear regression equation.

Example

The linear regression equation for these data is $y = 25x$.

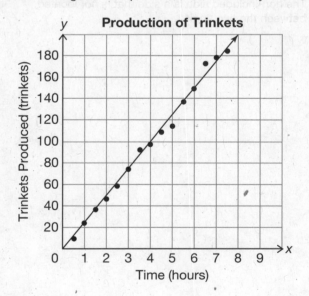

line of best fit

A line of best fit is the line that best approximates the linear relationship between two variables in a data set.

Example

The line shown is a line of best fit for these data.

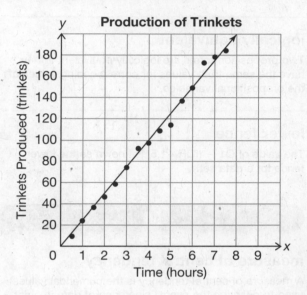

line of reflection

A line of reflection is the line that the graph is reflected about.

Example

The triangle on the left was reflected over the line $x = -3$ to create the triangle on the right.

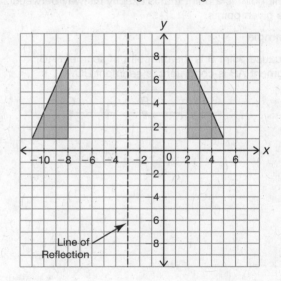

Glossary

literal equation

Literal equations are equations in which the variables represent specific measures.

Examples

The equations $I = Prt$ and $A = lw$ are literal equations.

logically equivalent

Two proposition forms are logically equivalent if they have the same truth values for corresponding values of the propositional variables.

lower fence

The value of $Q1 - (IQR \cdot 1.5)$ is known as the lower fence for a data set.

M

measure of central tendency

A measure of central tendency is the numerical values used to describe the overall clustering of data in a set.

Examples

The mean, median, and mode are the most common measures of central tendency.

midpoint

A midpoint is a point that is exactly halfway between two given points.

Example

Because point B is the midpoint of segment AC, segment AB is congruent to segment BC.

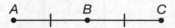

Midpoint Formula

The Midpoint Formula states that if (x_1, y_1) and (x_2, y_2) are two points on the coordinate plane, then the midpoint of the line segment that joins these two points is given by $\left(\dfrac{x_1 + x_2}{2}, \dfrac{y_1 + y_2}{2}\right)$.

Example

To find the midpoint between the points $(-1, 4)$ and $(2, -5)$, substitute the coordinates into the Midpoint Formula.

$$\left(\frac{x_1 + x_2}{2}, \frac{y_1 + y_2}{2}\right) = \left(\frac{-1 + 2}{2}, \frac{4 - 5}{2}\right)$$
$$= \left(\frac{1}{2}, \frac{-1}{2}\right)$$

So, the midpoint between the points $(-1, 4)$ and $(2, -5)$ is $\left(\dfrac{1}{2}, -\dfrac{1}{2}\right)$.

N

necessary condition

A correlation is a necessary condition for causation, meaning that for one variable to cause another, they must be correlated.

non-included side

The non-included side is a side that is *not* located between the two angles.

Glossary

normal distribution

A normal distribution is a collection of many data points that form a bell-shaped curve.

Example

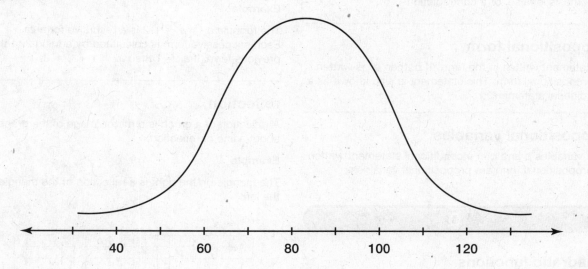

*n*th root

If *n* represents a positive number, then a number *b* is the *n*th root of *a* if $b^n = a$.

Example

The number 2 is the 4th root of 16, because $2^4 = 16$.

O

opposites

Two numbers that are an equal distance, but are in different directions, from zero on the number line are called opposites.

Example

The opposite of −3 is 3. Both numbers are 3 units from 0 on the number line.

outlier

An outlier is a data value that is significantly greater or lesser than other data values in a data set.

Example

In the data set 1, 1, 3, 3, 4, 4, 5, 1000, the outlier is 1000.

P

point of rotation

The fixed point about which a figure is rotated is called the point of rotation.

point-slope form

The point-slope form of the equation of the line that passes through (x_1, y_1) and has slope *m* is $y - y_1 = m(x - x_1)$.

postulate

A postulate is a mathematical statement that cannot be proved but is considered true.

pre-image

The original figure in a transformation is called the pre-image.

Example

The pre-image of a rectangle under a translation is shown.

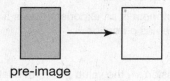

pre-image

Glossary

proof by contradiction

To prove a statement using proof by contradiction, assume that the conclusion is false. Then show that the hypothesis is false, or a contradiction.

propositional form

A statement written in the form "If p, then q" is written in propositional form. This statement is also known as a conditional statement.

propositional variables

The variables p and q in a conditional statement written in propositional form are propositional variables.

Q

quadratic functions

The family of quadratic functions includes functions of the form $f(x) = ax^2 + bx + c$, where a, b, and c are real numbers, and a is not equal to 0.

Examples

The equations $y = x^2 + 2x + 5$ and $y = -4x^2 - 7x + 1$ are quadratic functions.

R

radicand

The value that is inside a radical is called the radicand.

Example

In the radical expression $\sqrt{25}$, the number 25 is the radicand.

range

The range is the set of output values in a relation.

Example

The range of the function $y = x^2$ is the set of all numbers greater than or equal to zero.

rational exponent

A rational exponent is an exponent that is a rational number written as a fraction.

Example

In the expression $x^{\frac{2}{3}}$, the value $\frac{2}{3}$ is a rational exponent.

recursive formula

A recursive formula expresses each new term of a sequence based on the preceding term in the sequence.

Example

The formula $a_n = a_{n-1} + 2$ is a recursive formula. Each successive term is calculated by adding 2 to the previous term. If $a_1 = 1$ then $a_2 = 1 + 2 = 3$.

reflection

A reflection of a graph is a mirror image of the graph about a line of reflection.

Example

The triangle on the right is a reflection of the triangle on the left.

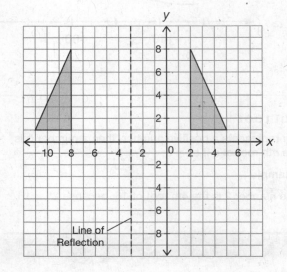

regular polygon

A regular polygon is a polygon whose sides all have the same length and whose angles all have the same measure.

relation

A relation is the mapping between a set of input values called the domain and a set of output values called the range.

Example

The set of points {(0, 1), (1, 8), (2, 5), (3, 7)} is a relation.

relative frequency conditional distribution

A relative frequency conditional distribution is the percent or ratio of occurrences of a category given the specific value of another category.

Grades of Mr. Lewis's Science Students

Science Classes		A	B	C	D	F	Total
	Biology	$\frac{6}{20} = 30\%$	$\frac{6}{20} = 30\%$	$\frac{5}{20} = 25\%$	$\frac{1}{20} = 5\%$	$\frac{2}{20} = 10\%$	$\frac{20}{20} = 100\%$
	Chemistry	$\frac{4}{30} \approx 13.3\%$	$\frac{8}{30} \approx 26.7\%$	$\frac{12}{30} = 40\%$	$\frac{4}{30} \approx 13.3\%$	$\frac{2}{30} \approx 6.7\%$	$\frac{30}{30} = 100\%$
	Physics	$\frac{2}{15} \approx 13.3\%$	$\frac{5}{15} \approx 33.3\%$	$\frac{6}{15} = 40\%$	$\frac{1}{15} \approx 6.7\%$	$\frac{1}{15} \approx 6.7\%$	$\frac{15}{15} = 100\%$

relative frequency distribution

Representing the relative frequencies for joint data displayed in a two-way table is called a relative frequency distribution. The relative frequency distribution provides the ratio of occurrences in each category to the total number of occurrences.

Activities Preferred During Hot Weather

	Sports	Movies	Reading	Walking
Students Age 18 Years Old and Under	$\frac{20}{280} \approx 7.1\%$	$\frac{30}{280} \approx 10.7\%$	$\frac{22}{280} \approx 7.9\%$	$\frac{8}{280} \approx 2.9\%$
Adults Age 19 Thru 50 Years Old	$\frac{10}{280} \approx 3.6\%$	$\frac{32}{280} \approx 11.4\%$	$\frac{25}{280} \approx 8.9\%$	$\frac{43}{280} \approx 15.4\%$
Adults Over 50 Years Old	$\frac{5}{280} \approx 1.8\%$	$\frac{20}{280} \approx 7.1\%$	$\frac{35}{280} \approx 12.5\%$	$\frac{30}{280} \approx 10.7\%$

relative frequency marginal distribution

Displaying the relative frequencies for the rows or columns in a two-way table is called a relative frequency marginal distribution. The relative frequency marginal distribution provides the ratio of total occurrences for each category to the total number of occurrences.

Activities Preferred During Hot Weather

	Sports	Movies	Reading	Walking	Total
Students Age 18 Years Old and Under	$\frac{20}{280} \approx 7.1\%$	$\frac{30}{280} \approx 10.7\%$	$\frac{22}{280} \approx 7.9\%$	$\frac{8}{280} \approx 2.9\%$	$\frac{80}{280} \approx 28.6\%$
Adults Age 19 Thru 50 Years Old	$\frac{10}{280} \approx 3.6\%$	$\frac{32}{280} \approx 11.4\%$	$\frac{25}{280} \approx 8.9\%$	$\frac{43}{280} \approx 15.4\%$	$\frac{110}{280} \approx 39.3\%$
Adults Over 50 Years Old	$\frac{5}{280} \approx 1.8\%$	$\frac{20}{280} \approx 7.1\%$	$\frac{35}{280} \approx 12.5\%$	$\frac{30}{280} \approx 10.7\%$	$\frac{90}{280} \approx 32.1\%$
Total	$\frac{35}{280} \approx 12.5\%$	$\frac{82}{280} \approx 29.3\%$	$\frac{82}{280} \approx 29.3\%$	$\frac{81}{280} \approx 28.9\%$	$\frac{280}{280} = 100\%$

residual

A residual is the distance between an observed data value and its predicted value using a regression equation.

residual plot

A residual plot is a scatter plot of the independent variable on the x-axis and the residuals on the y-axis.

Example

The graph at bottom shows a residual plot of the braking distance data.

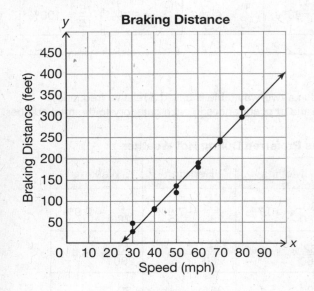

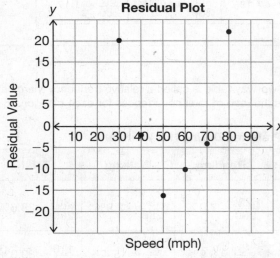

rigid motion

A rigid motion is a transformation of points in space.

rotation

A rotation is a rigid motion that turns a figure about a fixed point.

Example

The figure has been rotated 90° counterclockwise about the point (0, 0).

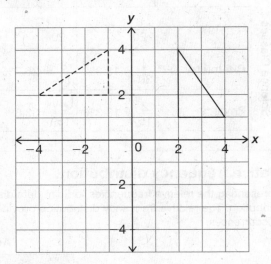

S

segment bisector

A segment bisector is a line, line segment, or ray that divides a line segment into two line segments of equal measure, or two congruent line segments.

Example

AB is a segment bisector of CD.

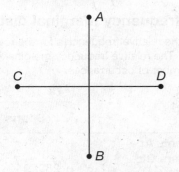

sequence

A sequence is a pattern involving an ordered arrangement of numbers, geometric figures, letters, or other objects.

Example

The numbers 1, 1, 2, 3, 5, 8, 13 form a sequence.

Glossary

Side-Angle-Side Congruence Theorem

The Side-Angle-Side Congruence Theorem states that if two sides and the included angle of one triangle are congruent to the corresponding sides and the included angle of the second triangle, then the triangles are congruent.

side-by-side stem-and-leaf plot

A side-by-side stem-and-leaf plot allows a comparison of two data sets. The two data sets share the same stem, but have leaves to the left and right of the stem.

Example

Difference in Departure Times (minutes)			
My Air Airlines		**Fly High Airlines**	
5 0	0	7 8	
9 5 1	1	4 5 6	
6 0 0	2	4 7 9	
4 3 3	3	0 2	
0	4	5 9	

$2|4 = 24$ minutes

Side-Side-Side Congruence Theorem

The Side-Side-Side Congruence Theorem states that if three sides of one triangle are congruent to the corresponding sides of another triangle, then the triangles are congruent.

significant digits

Significant digits are digits that carry meaning contributing to a number's precision.

simple interest

In a simple interest account, the interest earned at the end of each year is a percent of the original deposited amount (also known as the original principal).

Example

Tonya deposits $200 in a 3-year certificate of deposit that earns 4% interest. The amount of interest that Tonya earns can be found using the simple interest formula.

$I = (200)(0.04)(3)$
$I = 24$
Tonya earns $24 in interest.

skewed left distribution

In a skewed left distribution of data, the peak of the data is to the right side of the graph. There are only a few data points to the left side of the graph.

Example

These data show a skewed left distribution.

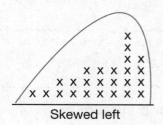

Skewed left

skewed right distribution

In a skewed right distribution of data, the peak of the data is to the left side of the graph. There are only a few data points to the right side of the graph.

Example

These data show a skewed right distribution.

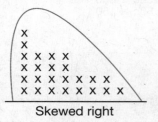

Skewed right

slope-intercept form

The slope-intercept form of a linear equation is $y = mx + b$ where b is the y-intercept and m is the slope.

Example

The linear equation $y = 2x + 1$ is written in slope-intercept form. The slope of the line is 2 and the y-intercept is 1.

solution

The solution of a linear equation is any value that makes the open sentence true.

Example

The solution of the equation $3x + 4 = 25$ is 7 because 7 makes the equation true: $3(7) + 4 = 25$, or $25 = 25$.

Glossary

solution of a compound inequality

The solution of a compound inequality is the part or parts of the solutions that satisfy both of the inequalities.

Example

The number line shows the solution of the compound inequality $x < -2$ or $x > 1$.

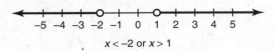

$x < -2$ or $x > 1$

solution of a system of linear inequalities

The solution of a system of linear inequalities is the intersection of the solutions to each inequality. Every point in the intersection region satisfies the solution.

Example

The solution of this system of linear inequalities is shown by the shaded region, which represents the intersection of the solutions to each inequality.

$$\begin{cases} 200a + 100c \leq 800 \\ 75(a - 1) + 50c \geq 150 \end{cases}$$

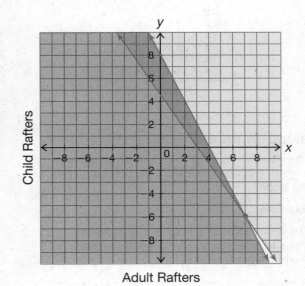

solve an inequality

To solve an inequality means to determine the values of the variable that make the inequality true.

Example

The inequality $x + 5 > 6$ can be solved by subtracting 5 from each side of the inequality. The solution is $x > 1$. Any number greater than 1 will make the inequality $x + 5 > 6$ true.

standard deviation

Standard deviation is a measure of how spread out the data are from the mean. The formula

$$\sigma = \sqrt{\dfrac{\sum\limits_{i=1}^{n}(X_i - \overline{X})^2}{n}}$$

can be used to determine the standard deviation of a data set.

standard form

The standard form of a linear equation is $Ax + By = C$ where A, B, and C are constants and A and B are not both zero.

Example

The linear equation $2x + 3y = 5$ is written in standard form.

statistic

Statistics are numerical characteristics of data.

stem-and-leaf plot

A stem-and-leaf plot is a graphical method used to represent ordered numerical data.

Example

The stem-and-leaf plot represents the data set 55, 62, 73, 75, 76, 79, 80, 83, 86, 87, 87, 88, 88, 89, 89, 89.

Stems	Leaves
1	
2	
3	
4	
5	5
6	2
7	3 5 6 9
8	0 3 6 7 7 8 8 9 9 9

$7 \mid 3 = 73$

Glossary

substitution method

The substitution method is a process of solving a system of equations by substituting a variable in one equation with an equivalent expression.

Example

Solve the following system of equations by using the substitution method:

$$\begin{cases} x - 3y = 4 \\ 2x + 5y = -14 \end{cases}$$

First, solve the first equation for x. Then, substitute in the second equation. Next, substitute $y = -2$ into the equation $x - 3y = 4$. The solution of the system is $(-2, -2)$.

sufficient condition

A correlation is not a sufficient condition for causation, meaning that a correlation between two variables is not enough to establish that one variables causes another.

symmetric distribution

In a symmetric distribution of data, the left and right halves of the graph are nearly mirror images of each other. There is often a "peak" in the middle of the graph.

Example

These data show a symmetric distribution.

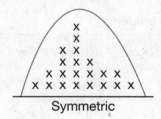

Symmetric

system of linear equations

When two or more equations define a relationship between quantities, they form a system of linear equations.

Example

The equations $y = 3x + 7$ and $y = -4x$ are a system of equations.

T

term of a sequence

A term of a sequence is an individual number, figure, or letter in the sequence.

Example

In the sequence 2, 4, 6, 8, 10, the first term is 2, the second term is 4, and the third term is 6.

theorem

A theorem is a statement that can be proven true using definitions, postulates, or other theorems.

transformation

A transformation is the mapping, or movement, of all the points of a figure in a plane according to a common operation.

Example

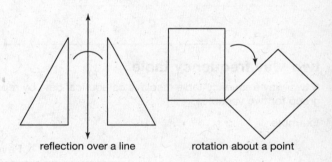

reflection over a line   rotation about a point

Glossary

translation

A translation is a rigid motion that "slides" each point of a figure the same distance and direction.

Example

The top trapezoid is a vertical translation of the bottom trapezoid by 5 units.

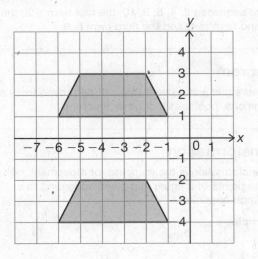

truth table

A truth table is a table that summarizes all possible truth values for a conditional statement $p \rightarrow q$.

truth value

The truth value of a conditional statement is whether the statement is true or false.

two-way frequency table

A two-way frequency table displays categorical data by representing the number of occurrences that fall into each group for two variables.

Example

Favorite Meals of Students

		Burgers	Chicken Nuggets	Pizza	Salad Bar
Grade Level	9th grade	////	/	///	++++
	10th grade	///	++++ //	///	////

U

upper fence

The value of Q3 + (IQR · 1.5) is known as the upper fence of a data set.

V

Vertical Line Test

The Vertical Line Test is a visual method used to determine whether a relation represented as a graph is a function.

Examples

The equation $y = 3x^2$ is a function, because the graph of the function passes the Vertical Line Test.

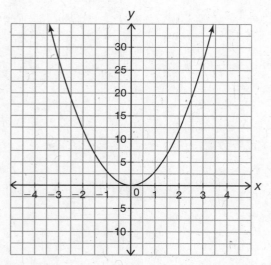

The equation $x^2 + y^2 = 9$ is not a function, because the graph of the function fails the Vertical Line Test.

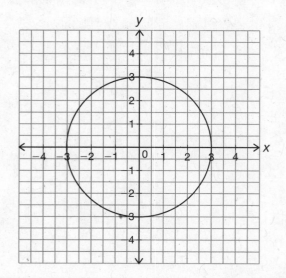

vertical translation

A vertical translation is a type of transformation that shifts the entire graph up or down. A vertical translation affects the y-coordinate of each point on the graph.

Example

The graphs of $z(x) + 3$ and $z(x) - 4$ are vertical translations of the graph of $z(x)$.

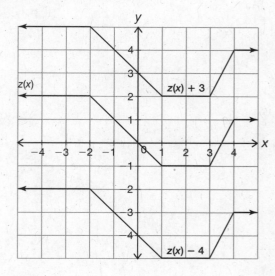

Glossary

Index

definition of, 113
disjunction, 117, 156
equivalent, 134
examples of, 114
"or" or "and" in, 113–114, 116, 118, 119, 120, 156, 157
solution of, 117–120
more than one, 115–117
on number line, 117–118, 156
table of, 112–113
writing, 156
Compound interest, 300–302, 355–356
formula for, 302, 306
rate of change for, 356
Conclusions, 564
of conditional statement, 912
false, 947
from logical reasoning, 904–911, 947
Conditional statements, 912–915
biconditional statements, 923, 950
contrapositive of, 920–921, 949
converse of, 916–917, 949
inverse of, 918–919, 949
proofs of, 925–930
direct, 926–928, 950
indirect, 928–930, 951
truth value of, 912, 914, 948
writing, 948
Confounding variable, 566
Congruence, 719–792
flipping for, 756–758
representing, 765–768
statements of, 748–750
understanding, 744–747
See also Congruent triangles
Congruent angles, 686, 744, 765
Congruent line segments, 662, 744, 765
Congruent triangles, 743–750
Angle-Angle-Side (AAS) Congruence Theorem of, 775–783, 791
constructions to support, 776–778
reflection to support, 778–781
Angle-Side-Angle (ASA) Congruence Theorem of, 769–774, 782–783, 790
corresponding angles of, 747
corresponding sides of, 746
properties of, 745
Side-Angle-Side (SAS) Congruence Theorem of, 759–768, 789
constructions to support, 760–761
rotation to support, 762–764
Side-Side-Side (SSS) Congruence Theorem of, 751–758, 788
Conjunctions, 117, 156
Consistent system of linear equations, 381
Constant functions, 38–39, 66
Constraints, 420, 448
Construction tools
AAS Congruence Theorem supported using, 776–778
bisecting a line segment using, 711
bisecting an angle using, 713
duplicating a line using, 664, 710
SAS Congruence Theorem supported using, 760–761

Continuous data, 463, 515
Continuous graph, 32, 64, 65
Contradiction, proof by, 928
Contrapositive of conditional statement, 920–921, 949
Converse of conditional statement, 916–917, 949
Coordinate notation, 315
horizontal translation using, 320, 360
reflections using, 329–330, 362
vertical translation using, 315, 358
Coordinate plane
inequalities represented on, 155
length and distance equivalence on, 657
points on, 9, 64
transformations of geometric figures on, 725–740
reflection, 734–740, 756–758, 787
rotation, 726–733, 786
translation, 725–726, 785
See also Geometric figures; Geometry
Coordinates of intersection point of two graphs, 369
Coordinate system, 251
Copying (duplicating)
angles, 684–685
line segments, 660–665, 710
Correlation, 533–540, 571
causation vs., 563–568, 575
definition of, 535
Correlation coefficient (r-value), 169, 204, 535, 542, 543, 574
analyzing correlation using, 571
determining and interpreting, 571
formula for, 536, 571
Corresponding angles, 747
Corresponding sides, 746
Cube root, 341, 363
Curves of best fit, 625–630, 646

D

Data
categorical, 581, 609
continuous, 463, 515
discrete, 457, 513
interval of, 515
raw, 613
representing, 584–586
Data distribution, 458–459
normal, 498, 519
skewed, 458, 459, 476, 513, 516
Data sets
exponential models from, 647
variables in vs. groups in, 581
Data sets for one variable, 453–520
analyzing and interpreting, 505–512
graphically representing, 455–468
box-and-whisker plots, 460, 473, 483, 514
data distribution, 458–459, 513, 516
dot plots, 457, 513
histograms, 463, 515

side-by-side stem-and-leaf plot, 508, 520
interquartile range (IQR), 481, 492, 503, 510, 517
measures of central tendency, 469–478
definition of, 470
mean, 470, 472, 476, 503, 510, 516
median, 470, 476, 503, 510, 516
outliers, 482–483, 492, 502, 517
standard deviation, 489–504, 510, 536
calculating and interpreting, 518
definition of, 492
formula for, 492–493, 518
graphing calculator to determine, 495
graph of, 497–498, 501, 519
Data sets for two categorical variables, 577–614
drawing conclusions from, 601–608, 613–614
See also Frequency distributions
Decimal, percent converted to, 296
Decreasing functions, 38–39, 66
Deduction, 903, 947
Degrees, 683
Dependency, 4–8
Dependent quantities, 4–8, 36, 63
identifying, 149
Diameter of circle, 874
Direct proof, 926–928, 950
Discrete data, 457, 513
Discrete graph, 32, 64, 65
Disjunctions, 117, 156
Distance Formula, 655, 709
classifying quadrilaterals using, 892–893
classifying triangles using, 890
points on a circle determined using, 893–895
Distance on coordinate plane, 657
Distributive Property, 801
to combine linear equations, 209
to write linear equations, 208
Division Property of Equality, 85
Domain of relation, 32
Dot plots, 457, 513
Duplicating (copying)
angles, 684–685
line segments, 660–665, 710

E

Equations
analyzing, 78–80
relationship between function notation and, 36, 66
for solving linear situations, comparing tables, and graphs to, 153
with two variables, 205, 206
See also Linear equations; Literal equations
Equilateral triangle, 705–706, 715
Equivalent compound inequalities, 134
Experiments, 564

Explicit formulas
    for arithmetic sequences, 238–239,
        277, 289
    in function notation, 277, 282
    for geometric sequences, 242,
        282, 289
Exponential functions, 40, 48, 56, 68,
        293–364
    base of, 291
    exponential growth, 348–351
    graphs of, 305–312, 357, 364
        asymptotes of, 309, 357
        reflections of, 327–331, 361–362
        transformations of, 316–321,
            358–362
    increasing and decreasing, 356
    interest
        compound, 300–302, 306,
            355–356
        rate of change for, 356
        simple, 296–299, 302, 355–356
    inverses, 353–354
    linear functions compared to,
        295–304
    modeling with, 631–638, 647
    multiple representations of, 310–312
    nth roots in radical form, 341, 363
    population problems, 356
        intersecting points to solve, 357
    radical expressions, 363
    radicals as powers and powers as
        radicals, 363
    rational exponents, 337–346, 363
        definition of, 343
    solving, 347–354, 364
        using properties of exponents and
            common bases, 352
    writing, 364
Exponential regression equation, 633
Exponents
    negative, 338–339, 363
    rational, 337–346
    solving exponential functions using
        properties of, 352
Expressions, writing, 149
Extrapolation, 526, 569–570

F

Families of functions, 40–52
    distinguishing between, 54–55,
        67–68, 69
    graphical behaviors of, 55–62, 70
Fibonacci sequence, 221
Finite sequences, 220, 287
First differences, 76
    to determine unit rate of change, 150
Five number summary, 460, 514
Formulas, literal equations in, 188,
        193–194
Frequency, 463, 515
    joint, 582
Frequency distributions, 579–614
    definition of, 582
    frequency marginal distribution,
        583, 610
    graphs of, 584–586, 610
    interpreting, 579–588

relative, 589–594
    creating and analyzing, 611
    definition of, 590, 611
    graphs of, 612
relative frequency conditional
        distribution, 595–600
    creating and analyzing, 613
    definition of, 598
relative frequency marginal
        distribution, 590, 611
two-way frequency table to analyze,
        581, 609
Function notation, 36, 66
    arithmetic sequence in, 298
    explicit formula in, 277, 282
    solutions to linear equations using, 150
Functions
    absolute minimum and absolute
        maximum of, 40–41, 67
    adding, 201
    argument of, 319
    basic, 314, 358, 359, 361
    constant, 38–39, 66
    decreasing, 38–39, 66
    definition of, 32
    families of, 40–52
        distinguishing between, 54–55,
            67–68, 69
        graphical behaviors of, 55–62, 70
    graphing calculator to graph, 37
    increasing, 38–39, 66
    naming, 376
    as relation, 65
    representing linear inequalities,
        103, 110
    sequences and, 275–286
    in two variables, 174–186, 205
    See also Exponential functions; Linear
        functions
Future values, predicting, 647

G

Geometric figures, 721–742
    perimeter and area of, 793–852
        composite figures, 833–842,
            851–852
        determining, 796
        parallelograms, 823–832, 847–849
        rectangles, 797, 843–844
        squares, 843–844
        trapezoids, 833–838, 850–851
        triangles, 805–822, 845–847
    transformations of, 725–740,
        795–804, 844
        points on a circle after, 895
        reflection, 734–740, 756–758,
            778–781, 787
        rotation, 726–733, 786
        translation, 725–726, 785
Geometric sequences, 231, 288
    common ratio of, 231, 288
        as base of exponential function, 291
    definition of, 231
    explicit formulas for, 242, 289
        in function notation, 282
    graphs of, 290
    recursive formulas for, 246, 289

Geometry, 649–718
    analytic, 651
    angles, 681–688
        bisecting, 686–688, 713
        congruent, 686, 744, 765
        copying (duplicating), 684–685
        corresponding, 747
        definition of, 682
        graph of, 682
        included, 760
        measurement of, 683, 693,
            856–857
        sides of, 682
        translation of, 682–683, 688, 712
    equilateral triangle, 705–706, 715
    isosceles triangle, 706–707, 716
    line segments, 651–666
        bisecting, 676–679, 711
        congruent, 662, 744, 765
        copying (duplicating), 660–665,
            710
        Distance Formula, 655, 709
        translation of, 657–665, 710
    midpoints, 667–680
        bisectors to find, 676–679, 711
        definition of, 672
        Midpoint Formula to find, 672,
            674–675, 711
    parallel lines, 689–694, 713
        constructing, 703–704
        slopes of, 713
    perpendicular lines, 693–698, 713
        constructing, 700–702, 715
        definition of, 693
        as shortest distance between a
            point and a line, 697–698, 714
        slopes of, 694, 713, 813
    rectangle, 708, 718, 823
        area and perimeter of, 796–797,
            843–844
        constructing, 708, 718
    square, 707, 717
        area and perimeter of, 843–844
        congruent sides of, 801
        constructing, 707, 717
Graphic organizers, 45
Graphing calculator
    box-and-whisker plot on, 473
    to complete a table, 95
    data set represented in, 165
    exponential regression equation
        on, 633
    function graphed on, 37
    graphs analyzed with, 96–98
    intersect feature of **CALC**, 97–98
    intersection feature, 357, 364
    linear regression on, 167, 203
    mean on, 472
    parentheses on, 99
    piecewise functions graphed on, 43
    to plot residuals, 558
    recursive formula on a, 248–249
    scientific notation on, 42
    standard deviation determined
        using, 495
    TABLE feature of, 95–96
    value feature, 96, 449

Graphs, 617
  analyzing and sorting, 17–34
  bar, 610, 612
  continuous, 32, 64, 65
  coordinates of intersection point of
      two, 369
  of data sets for one variable, 455–468
    box-and-whisker plots, 460, 473,
      483, 514
    data distribution, 458–459,
      513, 516
    dot plots, 457, 513
    histograms, 463, 515
    side-by-side stem-and-leaf plot,
      508, 520
  discrete, 32, 64, 65
  of exponential functions, 305–312,
      357, 364
    asymptotes of, 309, 357
    reflections of, 327–331, 361–362
    transformations of, 316–321,
      358–362
  of frequency distribution, 584–586,
      610
  of functions, 56–62
  intersection point of, 82, 105
  key for, 585, 610
  labeling axes of, 74, 632
  of linear absolute value function,
      133–134
  of linear absolute value inequalities,
      158–159
  of linear equations, 150, 178–180
  of linear functions, 78–80
  of linear inequalities, 104–105, 108,
      411–418, 447
    as half-plane, 414, 447
    representing solution set in,
      414–417, 447
  of linear regression equation, 168
  matching scenarios and, 9–14, 64
  modeling with, 621–624
  of nonlinear functions, 160
  of normal distribution, 501
  of quantities, 4–8
  of relative frequency distribution,
      612
  of sequences, 251–274, 290
  for solving linear situations,
      comparing tables, and equations
      to, 153
  of standard deviation, 497–498,
      501, 519
  of system of linear equations,
      403, 406
  of systems of linear inequalities,
      433, 449
    with more than two linear
      inequalities, 450
    using graphing calculator,
      426, 449
  technology to analyze, 96–98
  transformations of. See
    Transformations
  visual display of data in, 9, 64
Grids, logic puzzle, 934, 952

H

Half-plane, 414, 447
Height
  of parallelogram, 824, 847
  of triangle, 813
Histograms, 463, 515
Horizontal asymptote, 309
Horizontal reflections, 362
Horizontal translations, 319–321,
      359–360, 658
Hypothesis, 912

I

Image, 658, 799
Included angle, 760
Included side, 771
Inconsistent system of linear equations,
      381
Increasing functions, 38–39, 66
Independent quantities, 4–8, 36, 63, 75
  identifying, 149
Index
  of radical, 341, 363
  of term, 238
Indirect proof, 928–930, 951
  proof by contradiction, 928
Induction, 903, 947
Inequalities
  definition of, 413
  with a negative rate of change, 155
  representing on a coordinate plane,
      155
  representing on a number line, 154
  simple, 113
  solving, 154
  writing, 154
  See also Compound inequalities;
      Linear inequalities
Inequality symbols, 413, 414, 422
Infinite sequences, 220, 287
Infinity, negative, 42
Intercepts of equation with two
      variables, 205
Interest
  compound, 300–302, 306, 355–356
  rate of change for, 356
  simple, 296–299, 302, 355–356
Interpolation, 525, 569–570
Interquartile range (IQR), 481, 492, 503,
      510, 517
Intersection points, 82, 105
  coordinates of, 369
  linear equations solved using, 150
  linear functions solved using, 82–84
  nonlinear functions solved using, 160
  population problems solved using,
      357
Interval of data, 515
Inverse of conditional statement,
      918–919, 949
Inverses, 353–354
Isosceles triangle, 706–707, 716

J

Joint frequency, 582

K

Key for graphs, 585, 610

L

Labeling axes of graphs, 74, 632
Least squares regression, 523–532
  See also Linear regression
Least squares regression equation,
      570, 574
Least squares regression line, 528, 570
Legs of trapezoid, 835, 850
Length, on coordinate plane, 657
Linear absolute value equation. See
      Absolute value equations, linear
Linear absolute value functions. See
      Absolute value functions, linear
Linear absolute value inequalities. See
      Absolute value inequalities, linear
Linear combinations method of solving
      system of linear equations,
      383–390, 405, 406
Linear equations, 173–186
  combining, 195–202
    Distributive Property of
      Multiplication for, 209
  converting to solve for specific
      variable, 207
  Distributive Property of Multiplication
      to write, 208
  graphing solution for, 150, 178–180
  point-slope form of, 690
  in slope-intercept form, 183, 184,
      191, 207
  solution of, 82
    on a graph using an intersection
      point, 151
    using function notation, 150
  in standard form, 183–186, 207
  table values for, 185–186
  unit analysis of, 181–183
  See also Systems of linear equations
Linear expressions, maximum and
      minimum values of, 439–446, 451
Linear functions, 40, 47, 56, 68, 73–101,
      161–210, 627
  exponential functions compared to,
      295–304
  graph of, 78–80
  parts of, 152
  slope of, common difference as, 291
  solutions of
    algebraic, 78–80
    graphing, 78–80
    using intersection points, 82–84
  tables for, 74–77
    technology to complete, 95–96
  transformations of, 322–324
    reflections, 331–332, 361, 362
    translations, 322–324, 358–360
  units of measure associated with,
      74–79
  See also Linear regression equations
Linear inequalities, 101–110
  algebraic solution for, 106–107
  function representing, 103, 110

Index

graph of, 104–105, 108, 411–418
  as half-plane, 414, 447
  representing solution set in,
    414–417, 447
  reversing sign of, 107–109
  in two variables, 447
  See also Systems of linear
    inequalities
Linear piecewise functions, 42–43,
  51, 68
  modeling with, 617–624
    characteristics of, 645
Linear programming, 439–446, 451
  definition of, 440
Linear regression, 163–172
  analyzing, 170–171
  correlation coefficient of, 169, 204,
    535, 536, 542, 543, 571, 574
  definition of, 167, 203
  graph of, 168
    using graphing calculator,
      167, 203
  interpolation and extrapolation from,
    525, 569–570
  to make predictions, 164–166, 203
  to model data, 163–172, 203
Linear regression equations, 167
  graphing calculator to determine, 167
  graph of, 168
  interpreting, 569
Linear regression line, correlation and,
  535
Lines
  of best fit, 167, 203
  as figure, 658
  linear regression, 535
  parallel, 689–694, 713
    constructing, 703–704
    slopes of, 713
  perpendicular, 693–698, 713
    constructing, 700–702, 715
    definition of, 693
    as shortest distance between a
      point and a line, 697–698, 714
    slopes of, 694, 713, 813
  of reflection, 329, 361, 362, 734, 787
Line segments, 651–666
  bisecting, 676–679, 711
  congruent, 662, 744, 765
  copying (duplicating), 660–665, 710
  Distance Formula, 655, 709
  translation of, 657–665, 710
Literal equations, 187–194
  definition of, 188
  in formulas, 188, 193–194
  in slope-intercept form, 191–192
  in standard form, 191–192
Logic, 899–952
  conditional statements, 912–915
    biconditional statements, 923, 950
    contrapositive of, 920–921, 949
    converse of, 916–917, 949
    inverse of, 918–919, 949
    truth value of, 914, 948
    writing, 948
  logically equivalent propositional
    forms, 922

methods of logical reasoning,
  901–908
    conclusions from, 904–911, 947
    deduction, 903, 947
    induction, 903, 947
  problem solving using, 931–946, 951
    logic puzzle grids in, 934, 952
  proofs, 925–930
    direct, 926–928, 950
    indirect, 928–930, 951
  truth tables, 914, 948
Lower fence, 482

M

Mathematical modeling, 615–648
  choosing best regression equation
    for, 639–644, 648
  with curves of best fit, 625–630, 646
  exponential functions for, 631–638,
    647
  with graphs, 621–624
  linear piecewise functions, 617–624
    characteristics of, 645
  linear regression for, 163–172, 203
Maximum of functions, absolute,
  40–41, 67
Mean, 470, 472, 476, 503, 510, 516
Measures of central tendency. *See*
  Central tendency, measures of
Median, 470, 476, 503, 510, 516
Midpoint Formula, 672, 674–675
Midpoints, 667–680
  bisectors to find, 676–679, 711
  definition of, 672
  Midpoint Formula to find, 672,
    674–675, 711
Minimum of functions, absolute,
  40–41, 67
Modeling. See Mathematical modeling
Motion, rigid, 658, 710
  See also Transformations
Multiplication Property of Equality, 85

N

Necessary condition, 565, 575
Negation, 918, 922
Negative exponents, 338–339, 363
Negative infinity, 42
Negative numbers, adding, 229
Negative reciprocals, 694
Non-included side, 776
Nonlinear functions, graphically solving
  using intersection points, 160
Normal distribution, 498, 519
  graph of, 501
NOW NEXT formulas. See Recursive
  formulas
*n*th root, 341, 363
Number laws, 926–928
  See also Associative Property;
    Commutative Property;
    Distributive Property
Number line
  inequalities represented on, 154
  linear absolute value inequality on,
    159
  opposites on, 124, 125

solution of compound inequality on,
  117–118, 156

O

One-to-one correspondence, 759
Opposites, 124, 125
Ordered pairs, unit rate of change from,
  76
Origin, center of circle on, 872–875,
  880–884
Outliers, 482–483, 492, 502, 517

P

Parallel lines, 689–694, 713
  constructing, 703–704
  slopes of, 713
Parallelograms
  area of, 823–832, 847–849
    doubling, 849
    formula for, 824
  base of, 824
  definition of, 823
  height of, 824, 847
  perimeter of, 823–832, 847–849
Parentheses, on graphing calculator, 99
Patterns, recognizing and describing,
  213–222, 287
  See also Sequences
Percent, calculations with, 296
Perimeter, 793–852
  of composite figures, 833–842,
    851–852
  determining, 796
  of parallelograms, 823–832, 847–849
  of rectangle, 797, 843–844
  rectangle constructed given, 708
  square constructed given, 707
  of squares, 843–844
  transformations to determine,
    795–804, 844
  of trapezoids, 833–838, 850–851
  of triangles, 805–822, 845–847
Perpendicular lines, 693–698, 713
  constructing, 700–702, 715
  definition of, 693
  as shortest distance between a point
    and a line, 697–698, 714
  slopes of, 694, 713, 813
Piecewise functions, linear, 42–43,
  51, 68
  modeling with, 617–624
    characteristics of, 645
Points
  on a circle, 871–888
    center not on origin, 875–877,
      885–888, 894, 897
    center on origin, 872–875,
      880–884, 893
    Distance Formula to determine,
      893–895
    given center and radius, 896
    Pythagorean Theorem to
      determine, 893–897
    in a quadrant, 881
    after a transformation, 895
  collinear, 527
  on coordinate plane, 9, 64

reflection of, 734–735
of rotation, 726, 786
Point-slope form of linear equation, 690
Polygons, 853–898
regular, 839
rotation of, 731
*See also specific types of polygons,
e.g. Triangle(s)*
Population problems, 356
intersecting points to solve, 357
Postulate, definition of, 752
Powers, as radicals, 363
Pre-image, 658, 799
reflection of, 736
Probability, relative, 640
Proof, 925–930
direct, 926–928, 950
indirect, 928–930, 951
Propositional forms, 912
logically equivalent, 922
Propositional variables, 912
Protractor, 683
angle measurement with, 693
Pythagorean Theorem, 655
circle with center at origin and, 872
classifying triangles using, 890
points on a circle determined using,
893–897

Q

Quadratic functions, 42, 49, 56, 68, 646
Quadrilaterals
classifying, 863–870
using slope formula and Distance
Formula, 892–893
description of, given four points on a
coordinate plane, 892–893
fourth vertex of, given three points, 891
See also Parallelograms; Rectangles;
Squares; Trapezoids
Qualitative (categorical) data, 581, 609
Quantities, 1–16
dependent, 4–8, 36, 63, 149
graphs of, 4–8
independent, 4–8, 36, 63, 75, 149

R

Radical expressions, 363
Radicals
index of, 341, 363
as powers, 363
Radicand, 341
Range of relation, 32
Rate of change
negative, 155
for simple and compound interest, 356
unit, 76–77, 150
Rational exponents, 337–346, 363
definition of, 343
Raw data, 613
Rays, 682
Reciprocals, 694
negative, 694
Rectangles, 708, 718, 823
area and perimeter of, 796–797,
843–844
constructing, 708, 718

Recursive formulas
for arithmetic sequences, 245–246,
289
for geometric sequences, 246, 289
on graphing calculator, 248–249
Reflections, 327–336, 721
of exponential functions, 328–331,
361–362
of geometric figures, 734–740,
756–758, 787
to support AAS Congruence
Theorem, 778–781
horizontal, 362
of linear functions, 331–332, 361–362
line of, 329, 361, 362, 734, 787
of triangles, 787
vertical, 361–362
Regression equations, modeling with,
639–644, 648
See also Linear regression equations
Regular polygon, 839
Relations
definition of, 32
domain of, 32
function as, 65
range of, 32
Relationships
dependency in, 4–8
between equation and function
notation, 36
mistaken for causation, 566
points on coordinate plane modeling
or representing, 9, 64
See also Functions; Graphs; Linear
functions
Relative frequency conditional
distribution, 595–600
creating and analyzing, 613
definition of, 598
Relative frequency distribution,
589–594
creating and analyzing, 611
definition of, 590, 611
graphs of, 612
Relative frequency marginal distribution,
590, 611
Relative probability, 640
Residual plots, 541–562
creating, 541–552, 572
definition of, 545
graphing calculator to create, 558
interpreting, 546
shape of, 546, 573, 574
using, 553–562
Residuals, 543
Response, common, 566
Rhombus, 823
Rigid motion, 658, 710
See also Transformations
Rotation, 721, 726–733
angle of, 726, 786
point of, 726, 786
of polygons, 731
of trapezoids, 731–732
of triangles, 786
r-value. See Correlation coefficient
(*r*-value)

S

Scatter plot, 542, 574
real life data modeled using, 646
See also Residual plots
Scenarios, matching graphs to, 9–14, 64
Scientific notation, on graphing
calculator, 42
Segment bisector, 676
Sequences, 211–292
definition of, 214, 287
Fibonacci, 221
finite, 220, 287
general rules for expressing, 238
graphs of, 251–274
infinite, 220, 287
recognizing, 213–222
terms in, 214, 287
formulas to determine, 235–250
index of, 238
initial, 238
*n*th, 238
term number, 238, 239
See also Arithmetic sequences;
Geometric sequences
Sets, one-to-one correspondence of,
759
See also Data sets; Data sets for
one variable; Data sets for two
categorical variables
Side-Angle-Side (SAS) Congruence
Theorem, 759–768, 789
constructions to support, 760–761
rotation to support, 762–764
Side-by-side stem-and-leaf plot,
508, 520
Sides
of angles, 682
classifying triangles by, 857
corresponding, 746
included, 771
non-included, 776
Side-Side-Side (SSS) Congruence
Theorem, 751–758, 788
Significant digits, 167, 203
Simple inequalities, 113
Simple interest, 296–299, 355–356
formula for, 302
rate of change for, 356
Simplifying expressions with negative
exponents, 363
Skewed data distributions, 458, 459,
476, 513, 516
Slope-intercept form
of linear equation, 183, 184, 191, 207
of literal equation, 191–192
Slopes
classifying quadrilaterals using,
892–893
common difference as, 291
of parallel lines, 713
of perpendicular lines, 694, 713, 813
Solutions
of absolute value equations, 125,
127–129, 157
of compound inequalities, 117–120
exact *vs.* approximate, 762
of linear equation, 82, 150, 151

of linear functions, 78–80, 82–84
of linear inequalities, 106–107
of systems of linear equations, 403
of systems of linear inequalities, 421, 448, 449
Squares, 707, 717
area and perimeter of, 843–844
congruent sides of, 801
constructing, 707, 717
Stacked bar graph, 612
Standard deviation, 489–504, 510, 536
calculating and interpreting, 518
definition of, 492
formula for, 492–493, 518
graphing calculator to determine, 495
graph of, 497–498, 501, 519
Standard form
of linear equations, 183–186, 207
of literal equation, 191–192
of systems of linear equations, 377
Statistics, 470
Stem-and-leaf plot, 508, 520
side-by-side, 508, 520
Straightedge
bisecting an angle using, 687
copying (duplicating) an angle using, 684
segment bisector using, 677
Substitution method for solving systems of linear equations, 370, 404, 406
Subtraction Property of Equality, 85
Sufficient condition, 565, 575
Symmetric data distribution, 458, 459, 476, 513, 516
Systems of linear equations, 365–408
consistent, 381
definition of, 370, 403
graphing method of solving, 403, 406
inconsistent, 381
linear combinations method of solving, 383–390, 405, 406
to represent problem context, 406
solution of, 403
in standard form, 377
substitution method for solving, 370, 404, 406
transforming, 377–379
Systems of linear inequalities, 419–452
constraints in, 420, 448
graph of, 426, 433, 449
linear programming, 439–446, 451
definition of, 440
with more than two linear inequalities, 431–438, 450
graph of, 450
steps for solving, 437
solution of, 421, 448, 449
writing, 448

T

Tables
analyzing, 74–77
for compound inequalities, 112–113
independent and dependent quantities identified in, 149
for linear equations, 185–186
for linear functions, 74–77, 95–96
sequences as, 252–255
for solving linear situations, comparing equations, and graphs to, 153
technology to complete, 95–96
truth, 914, 948
two-way frequency, 581, 609
Terms in sequences, 214, 287
formulas to determine, 235–250
index of, 238
initial, 238
nth, 238
term number, 238, 239
Theorems
definition of, 752, 928
proofs of, 925–930
direct, 926–928, 950
indirect, 928–930, 951
Transformations, 313–326, 358–362, 721
of angles, 682–683, 688, 712
characteristics of graphs after, 333–336, 362
definition of, 315, 329, 658
of exponential functions, 316–321, 358–362
reflections, 327–331, 361–362
translations, 313–326
of geometric figures, 725–740
to determine perimeter and area, 795–804, 844
points on a circle after, 895
reflection, 734–740, 756–758, 778–781, 787
rotation, 726–733, 786
translation, 725–726, 785
horizontal translation, 319–321, 359–360
of linear functions, 313–336
reflections, 328–331, 361–362
translations, 313–326, 358–360
of line segments, 657–665, 710
by copying (duplicating), 660–665, 710
of systems of linear equations, 377–379
of triangles, 785
using coordinate notation, 315, 320, 329–330, 358, 360, 362
vertical translation, 314–318, 358–359

Translations. *See* Transformations
Trapezoids
area and perimeter of, 833–838, 850–851
bases of, 835, 850
definition of, 850
legs of, 835, 850
rotation of, 731–732
Triangles
area of, 805–822, 845–847
doubling, 847
formula for, 806, 845
base of, 813
classifying, 855–862
by angle measures, 856–857
Distance Formula for, 890
Pythagorean Theorem for, 890
by side measures, 857
description of, given three points on a coordinate plane, 890
equilateral, 705–706, 715
height of, 813
isosceles, 706–707, 716
perimeter of, 805–822, 845–847
reflection of, 787
rotation of, 786
third vertex of, given two points, 889
translation of, 785
See also Congruent triangles
Truth value of conditional statement, 912, 914, 948
Two-way frequency table, 581, 609

U

Unit analysis, 181–183
Unit rate of change, 150
Upper fence, 482

V

Variables
confounding, 566
in data set, 581
propositional, 912
See also Categorical variables, data sets for two
Vertical Line Test, 32, 65
Vertical transformations
reflections, 361–362
translations, 314–318, 358–359, 658, 710

X

x-intercept, of equation with two variables, 205

Y

y-intercept, of equation with two variables, 205

Index